Scala Data Anal
Cookbook

Navigate the world of data analysis, visualization, and machine learning with over 100 hands-on Scala recipes

Arun Manivannan

BIRMINGHAM - MUMBAI

Scala Data Analysis Cookbook

First published: October 2015

Production reference: 1261015

Published by Packt Publishing Ltd.
Livery Place
35 Livery Street
Birmingham B3 2PB, UK.

ISBN 978-1-78439-674-9

www.packtpub.com

Credits

Author

Arun Manivannan

Reviewers

Amir Hajian

Shams Mahmood Imam

Gerald Loeffler

Commissioning Editor

Nadeem N. Bagban

Acquisition Editor

Larissa Pinto

Content Development Editor

Rashmi Suvarna

Technical Editor

Tanmayee Patil

Copy Editors

Ameesha Green

Vikrant Phadke

Project Coordinator

Milton Dsouza

Proofreader

Safis Editing

Indexer

Rekha Nair

Production Coordinator

Manu Joseph

Cover Work

Manu Joseph

About the Author

Arun Manivannan has been an engineer in various multinational companies, tier-1 financial institutions, and start-ups, primarily focusing on developing distributed applications that manage and mine data. His languages of choice are Scala and Java, but he also meddles around with various others for kicks. He blogs at `http://rerun.me`.

Arun holds a master's degree in software engineering from the National University of Singapore.

He also holds degrees in commerce, computer applications, and HR management. His interests and education could probably be a good dataset for clustering.

I am deeply indebted to my dad, Manivannan, who taught me the value of persistence, hard work and determination in life, and my mom, Arockiamary, without whose prayers and boundless love I'd be nothing. I could never try to pay them back. No words can do justice to thank my loving wife, Daisy. Her humongous faith in me and her support and patience make me believe in lifelong miracles. She simply made me the man I am today.

I can't finish without thanking my 6-year old son, Jason, for hiding his disappointment in me as I sat in front of the keyboard all the time. In your smiles and hugs, I derive the purpose of my life.

I would like to specially thank Abhilash, Rajesh, and Mohan, who proved that hard times reveal true friends.

It would be a crime not to thank my VCRC friends for being a constant source of inspiration. I am proud to be a part of the bunch.

Also, I sincerely thank the truly awesome reviewers and editors at Packt Publishing. Without their guidance and feedback, this book would have never gotten its current shape. I sincerely apologize for all the typos and errors that could have crept in.

About the Reviewers

Amir Hajian is a data scientist at the Thomson Reuters Data Innovation Lab. He has a PhD in astrophysics, and prior to joining Thomson Reuters, he was a senior research associate at the Canadian Institute for Theoretical Astrophysics in Toronto and a research physicist at Princeton University. His main focus in recent years has been bringing data science into astrophysics by developing and applying new algorithms for astrophysical data analysis using statistics, machine learning, visualization, and big data technology. Amir's research has been frequently highlighted in the media. He has led multinational research team efforts into successful publications. He has published in more than 70 peer-reviewed articles with more than 4,000 citations, giving him an h-index of 34.

I would like to thank the Canadian Institute for Theoretical Astrophysics for providing the excellent computational facilities that I enjoyed during the review of this book.

Shams Mahmood Imam completed his PhD from the department of computer science at Rice University, working under Prof. Vivek Sarkar in the Habanero multicore software research project. His research interests mostly include parallel programming models and runtime systems, with the aim of making the writing of task-parallel programs on multicore machines easier for programmers. Shams is currently completing his thesis titled *Cooperative Execution of Parallel Tasks with Synchronization Constraints*. His work involves building a generic framework that efficiently supports all synchronization patterns (and not only those available in actors or the fork-join model) in task-parallel programs. It includes extensions such as Eureka programming for speculative computations in task-parallel models and selectors for coordination protocols in the actor model. Shams implemented a framework as part of the cooperative runtime for the Habanero-Java parallel programming library. His work has been published at leading conferences, such as OOPSLA, ECOOP, Euro-Par, PPPJ, and so on. Previously, he has been involved in projects such as Habanero-Scala, CnC-Scala, CnC-Matlab, and CnC-Python.

Gerald Loeffler is an MBA. He was trained as a biochemist and has worked in academia and the pharmaceutical industry, conducting research in parallel and distributed biophysical computer simulations and data science in bioinformatics. Then he switched to IT consulting and widened his interests to include general software development and architecture, focusing on JVM-centric enterprise applications, systems, and their integration ever since. Inspired by the practice of commercial software development projects in this context, Gerald has developed a keen interest in team collaboration, the software craftsmanship movement, sound software engineering, type safety, distributed software and system architectures, and the innovations introduced by technologies such as Java EE, Scala, Akka, and Spark. He is employed by MuleSoft as a principal solutions architect in their professional services team, working with EMEA clients on their integration needs and the challenges that spring from them.

Gerald lives with his wife and two cats in Vienna, Austria, where he enjoys music, theatre, and city life.

www.PacktPub.com

Support files, eBooks, discount offers, and more

For support files and downloads related to your book, please visit www.PacktPub.com.

Did you know that Packt offers eBook versions of every book published, with PDF and ePub files available? You can upgrade to the eBook version at www.PacktPub.com and as a print book customer, you are entitled to a discount on the eBook copy. Get in touch with us at service@packtpub.com for more details.

At www.PacktPub.com, you can also read a collection of free technical articles, sign up for a range of free newsletters and receive exclusive discounts and offers on Packt books and eBooks.

https://www2.packtpub.com/books/subscription/packtlib

Do you need instant solutions to your IT questions? PacktLib is Packt's online digital book library. Here, you can search, access, and read Packt's entire library of books.

Why Subscribe?

- ▶ Fully searchable across every book published by Packt
- ▶ Copy and paste, print, and bookmark content
- ▶ On demand and accessible via a web browser

Free Access for Packt account holders

If you have an account with Packt at www.PacktPub.com, you can use this to access PacktLib today and view 9 entirely free books. Simply use your login credentials for immediate access.

Table of Contents

Preface

JVM has become a clear winner in the race between different methods of scalable data analysis. The power of JVM, strong typing, simplicity of code, composability, and availability of highly abstracted distributed and machine learning frameworks make Scala a clear contender for the top position in large-scale data analysis. Thanks to its dynamic-looking, yet static type system, scientists and programmers coming from Python backgrounds feel at ease with Scala.

This book aims to provide easy-to-use recipes in Apache Spark, a massively scalable distributed computation framework, and Breeze, a linear algebra library on which Spark's machine learning toolkit is built. The book will also help you explore data using interactive visualizations in Apache Zeppelin.

Other than the handful of frameworks and libraries that we will see in this book, there's a host of other popular data analysis libraries and frameworks that are available for Scala. They are by no means lesser beasts, and they could actually fit our use cases well. Unfortunately, they aren't covered as part of this book.

Apache Flink

Apache Flink (`http://flink.apache.org/`), just like Spark, has first-class support for Scala and provides features that are strikingly similar to Spark. Real-time streaming (unlike Spark's mini-batch DStreams) is its distinctive feature. Flink also provides a machine learning and a graph processing library and runs standalone as well as on the YARN cluster.

Scalding

Scalding (`https://github.com/twitter/scalding`) needs no introduction—Scala's idiomatic approach to writing Hadoop MR jobs.

Saddle

Saddle (`https://saddle.github.io/`) is the "pandas" (`http://pandas.pydata.org/`) of Scala, with support for vectors, matrices, and DataFrames.

Spire

Spire (`https://github.com/non/spire`) has a powerful set of advanced numerical types that are not available in the default Scala library. It aims to be fast and precise in its numerical computations.

Akka

Akka (`http://akka.io`) is an actor-based concurrency framework that has actors as its foundation and unit of work. Actors are fault tolerant and distributed.

Accord

Accord (`https://github.com/wix/accord`) is simple, yet powerful, validation library in Scala.

What this book covers

Chapter 1, Getting Started with Breeze, serves as an introduction to the Breeze linear algebra library's API.

Chapter 2, Getting Started with Apache Spark DataFrames, introduces powerful, yet intuitive and relational-table-like, data abstraction.

Chapter 3, Loading and Preparing Data – DataFrame, showcases the loading of datasets into Spark DataFrames from a variety of sources, while also introducing the Parquet serialization format.

Chapter 4, Data Visualization, introduces Apache Zeppelin for interactive data visualization using Spark SQL and Spark UDF functions. We also briefly discuss Bokeh-Scala, which is a Scala port of Bokeh (a highly customizable visualization library).

Chapter 5, Learning from Data, focuses on machine learning using Spark MLlib.

Chapter 6, Scaling Up, walks through various deployment alternatives for Spark applications: standalone, YARN, and Mesos.

Chapter 7, Going Further, briefly introduces Spark Streaming and GraphX.

What you need for this book

The most important installation that your machine needs is the Java Development Kit (JDK 1.7), which can be downloaded from `http://www.oracle.com/technetwork/java/javase/downloads/jdk7-downloads-1880260.html`.

To run most of the recipes in this book, all you need is SBT. The installation instructions for your favorite operating system are available at `http://www.scala-sbt.org/release/tutorial/Setup.html`.

There are a few other libraries that we will be using throughout the book, all of which will be imported through SBT. If there is any installation required (for example, HDFS) to run a recipe, the installation URL or the steps themselves will be mentioned in the respective recipe.

Who this book is for

Engineers and scientists who are familiar with Scala and would like to exploit the Spark ecosystem for big data analysis will benefit most from this book.

Sections

In this book, you will find several headings that appear frequently (*Getting ready*, *How to do it...*, *How it works...*, *There's more...*, and *See also*).

To give clear instructions on how to complete a recipe, we use these sections as follows:

Getting ready

This section tells you what to expect in the recipe, and describes how to set up any software or any preliminary settings required for the recipe.

How to do it...

This section contains the steps required to follow the recipe.

How it works...

This section usually consists of a detailed explanation of what happened in the previous section.

There's more...

This section consists of additional information about the recipe in order to make the reader more knowledgeable about the recipe.

See also

This section provides helpful links to other useful information for the recipe.

Conventions

In this book, you will find a number of text styles that distinguish between different kinds of information. Here are some examples of these styles and an explanation of their meaning.

Code words in text, database table names, folder names, filenames, file extensions, pathnames, dummy URLs, user input, and Twitter handles are shown as follows: "We can include other contexts through the use of the `include` directive."

A block of code is set as follows:

```
organization := "com.packt"

name := "chapter1-breeze"

scalaVersion := "2.10.4"

libraryDependencies ++= Seq(
  "org.scalanlp" %% "breeze" % "0.11.2",
  //Optional - the 'why' is explained in the How it works
section
  "org.scalanlp" %% "breeze-natives" % "0.11.2"
)
```

Any command-line input or output is written as follows:

```
sudo apt-get install libatlas3-base libopenblas-base
sudo update-alternatives --config libblas.so.3
sudo update-alternatives --config liblapack.so.3
```

New terms and **important words** are shown in bold. Words that you see on the screen, for example, in menus or dialog boxes, appear in the text like this: "Now, if we wish to share this chart with someone or link it to an external website, we can do so by clicking on the gear icon in this paragraph and then clicking on **Link this paragraph**."

Warnings or important notes appear in a box like this.

Tips and tricks appear like this.

Reader feedback

Feedback from our readers is always welcome. Let us know what you think about this book—what you liked or disliked. Reader feedback is important for us as it helps us develop titles that you will really get the most out of.

To send us general feedback, simply e-mail feedback@packtpub.com, and mention the book's title in the subject of your message.

If there is a topic that you have expertise in and you are interested in either writing or contributing to a book, see our author guide at www.packtpub.com/authors.

Customer support

Now that you are the proud owner of a Packt book, we have a number of things to help you to get the most from your purchase.

Downloading the example code

You can download the example code files from your account at http://www.packtpub.com for all the Packt Publishing books you have purchased. If you purchased this book elsewhere, you can visit http://www.packtpub.com/support and register to have the files e-mailed directly to you.

Errata

Although we have taken every care to ensure the accuracy of our content, mistakes do happen. If you find a mistake in one of our books—maybe a mistake in the text or the code—we would be grateful if you could report this to us. By doing so, you can save other readers from frustration and help us improve subsequent versions of this book. If you find any errata, please report them by visiting http://www.packtpub.com/submit-errata, selecting your book, clicking on the **Errata Submission Form** link, and entering the details of your errata. Once your errata are verified, your submission will be accepted and the errata will be uploaded to our website or added to any list of existing errata under the Errata section of that title.

To view the previously submitted errata, go to https://www.packtpub.com/books/content/support and enter the name of the book in the search field. The required information will appear under the **Errata** section.

Piracy

Piracy of copyrighted material on the Internet is an ongoing problem across all media. At Packt, we take the protection of our copyright and licenses very seriously. If you come across any illegal copies of our works in any form on the Internet, please provide us with the location address or website name immediately so that we can pursue a remedy.

Please contact us at copyright@packtpub.com with a link to the suspected pirated material.

We appreciate your help in protecting our authors and our ability to bring you valuable content.

Questions

If you have a problem with any aspect of this book, you can contact us at questions@packtpub.com, and we will do our best to address the problem.

1
Getting Started with Breeze

In this chapter, we will cover the following recipes:

- ▸ Getting Breeze—the linear algebra library
- ▸ Working with vectors
- ▸ Working with matrices
- ▸ Vectors and matrices with randomly distributed values
- ▸ Reading and writing CSV files

Introduction

This chapter gives you a quick overview of one of the most popular data analysis libraries in Scala, how to get them, and their most frequently used functions and data structures.

We will be focusing on Breeze in this first chapter, which is one of the most popular and powerful linear algebra libraries. Spark MLlib, which we will be seeing in the subsequent chapters, builds on top of Breeze and Spark, and provides a powerful framework for scalable machine learning.

Getting Breeze – the linear algebra library

In simple terms, Breeze (http://www.scalanlp.org) is a Scala library that extends the Scala collection library to provide support for vectors and matrices in addition to providing a whole bunch of functions that support their manipulation. We could safely compare Breeze to NumPy (http://www.numpy.org/) in Python terms. Breeze forms the foundation of MLlib—the Machine Learning library in Spark, which we will explore in later chapters.

In this first recipe, we will see how to pull the Breeze libraries into our project using **Scala Build Tool** (**SBT**). We will also see a brief history of Breeze to better appreciate why it could be considered as the "go to" linear algebra library in Scala.

 For all our recipes, we will be using Scala 2.10.4 along with Java 1.7. I wrote the examples using the Scala IDE, but please feel free to use your favorite IDE.

How to do it...

Let's add the Breeze dependencies into our `build.sbt` so that we can start playing with them in the subsequent recipes. The Breeze dependencies are just two—the `breeze` (core) and the `breeze-native` dependencies.

1. Under a brand new folder (which will be our project root), create a new file called `build.sbt`.

2. Next, add the `breeze` libraries to the project dependencies:

```
organization := "com.packt"

name := "chapter1-breeze"

scalaVersion := "2.10.4"

libraryDependencies  ++= Seq(
  "org.scalanlp" %% "breeze" % "0.11.2",
  //Optional - the 'why' is explained in the How it works
section
  "org.scalanlp" %% "breeze-natives" % "0.11.2"
)
```

3. From that folder, issue a `sbt compile` command in order to fetch all your dependencies.

You could import the project into your Eclipse using `sbt eclipse` after installing the `sbteclipse` plugin `https://github.com/typesafehub/sbteclipse/`. For IntelliJ IDEA, you just need to import the project by pointing to the root folder where your `build.sbt` file is.

There's more...

Let's look into the details of what the `breeze` and `breeze-native` library dependencies we added bring to us.

The org.scalanlp.breeze dependency

Breeze has a long history in that it isn't written from scratch in Scala. Without the native dependency, Breeze leverages the power of `netlib-java` that has a Java-compiled version of the FORTRAN Reference implementation of BLAS/LAPACK. The `netlib-java` also provides gentle wrappers over the Java compiled library. What this means is that we could still work without the native dependency but the performance won't be great considering the best performance that we could leverage out of this FORTRAN-translated library is the performance of the FORTRAN reference implementation itself. However, for serious number crunching with the best performance, we should add the `breeze-natives` dependency too.

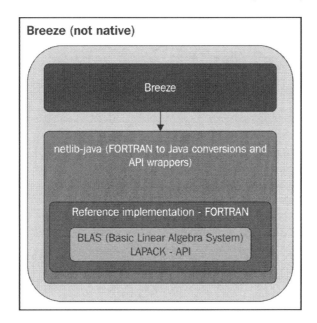

The org.scalanlp.breeze-natives package

With its native additive, Breeze looks for the machine-specific implementations of the BLAS/LAPACK libraries. The good news is that there are open source and (vendor provided) commercial implementations for most popular processors and GPUs. The most popular open source implementations include ATLAS (http://math-atlas.sourceforge.net) and OpenBLAS (http://www.openblas.net/).

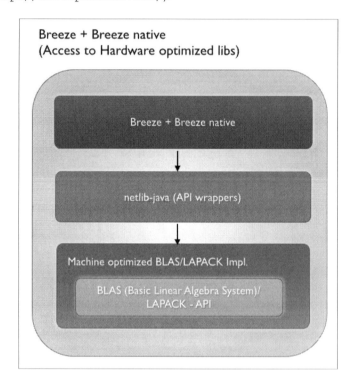

If you are running a Mac, you are in luck—Native BLAS libraries come out of the box on Macs. Installing NativeBLAS on Ubuntu / Debian involves just running the following commands:

```
sudo apt-get install libatlas3-base libopenblas-base
sudo update-alternatives --config libblas.so.3
sudo update-alternatives --config liblapack.so.3
```

Downloading the example code

You can download the example code files from your account at http://www.packtpub.com for all the Packt Publishing books you have purchased. If you purchased this book elsewhere, you can visit http://www.packtpub.com/support and register to have the files e-mailed directly to you.

```
File Edit View Search Terminal Help
arun@arun-VirtualBox:~$ sudo update-alternatives --config libblas.so.3
There are 2 choices for the alternative libblas.so.3 (providing /usr/lib/libblas.so.3).

  Selection    Path                                    Priority   Status
------------------------------------------------------------
* 0            /usr/lib/openblas-base/libblas.so.3      40        auto mode
  1            /usr/lib/atlas-base/atlas/libblas.so.3   35        manual mode
  2            /usr/lib/openblas-base/libblas.so.3      40        manual mode

Press enter to keep the current choice[*], or type selection number: 1
update-alternatives: using /usr/lib/atlas-base/atlas/libblas.so.3 to provide /usr/lib/libblas.so.3 (libblas.so.3) in manual mode
arun@arun-VirtualBox:~$ sudo update-alternatives --config liblapack.so.3
There is only one alternative in link group liblapack.so.3 (providing /usr/lib/liblapack.so.3): /usr/lib/atlas-base/atlas/liblapack.so.3
Nothing to configure.
arun@arun-VirtualBox:~$
```

For Windows, please refer to the installation instructions on `https://github.com/xianyi/OpenBLAS/wiki/Installation-Guide`.

Working with vectors

There are subtle yet powerful differences between Breeze vectors and Scala's own `scala.collection.Vector`. As we'll see in this recipe, Breeze vectors have a lot of functions that are linear algebra specific, and the more important thing to note here is that Breeze's vector is a Scala wrapper over `netlib-java` and most calls to the vector's API delegates the call to it.

Vectors are one of the core components in Breeze. They are containers of homogenous data. In this recipe, we'll first see how to create vectors and then move on to various data manipulation functions to modify those vectors.

In this recipe, we will look at various operations on vectors. This recipe has been organized in the form of the following sub-recipes:

- Creating vectors:
    - Creating a vector from values
    - Creating a zero vector
    - Creating a vector out of a function
    - Creating a vector of linearly spaced values
    - Creating a vector with values in a specific range
    - Creating an entire vector with a single value
    - Slicing a sub-vector from a bigger vector
    - Creating a Breeze vector from a Scala vector
- Vector arithmetic:
    - Scalar operations
    - Calculating the dot product of a vector
    - Creating a new vector by adding two vectors together

- ▸ Appending vectors and converting a vector of one type to another:
    - ❏ Concatenating two vectors
    - ❏ Converting a vector of int to a vector of double

- ▸ Computing basic statistics:
    - ❏ Mean and variance
    - ❏ Standard deviation
    - ❏ Find the largest value
    - ❏ Finding the sum, square root and log of all the values in the vector

Getting ready

In order to run the code, you could either use the Scala or use the Worksheet feature available in the Eclipse Scala plugin (or Scala IDE) or in IntelliJ IDEA. The reason these options are suggested is due to their quick turnaround time.

How to do it...

Let's look at each of the above sub-recipes in detail. For easier reference, the output of the respective command is shown as well. All the classes that are being used in this recipe are from the `breeze.linalg` package. So, an `"import breeze.linalg._"` statement at the top of your file would be perfect.

Creating vectors

Let's look at the various ways we could construct vectors. Most of these construction mechanisms are through the `apply` method of the vector. There are two different flavors of vector—`breeze.linalg.DenseVector` and `breeze.linalg.SparseVector`—the choice of the vector depends on the use case. The general rule of thumb is that if you have data that is at least 20 percent zeroes, you are better off choosing `SparseVector` but then the 20 percent is a variant too.

Constructing a vector from values

- ▸ **Creating a dense vector from values**: Creating a `DenseVector` from values is just a matter of passing the values to the `apply` method:

```
val dense=DenseVector(1,2,3,4,5)
println (dense) //DenseVector(1, 2, 3, 4, 5)
```

▶ **Creating a sparse vector from values**: Creating a `SparseVector` from values is also through passing the values to the `apply` method:

```
val sparse=SparseVector(0.0, 1.0, 0.0, 2.0, 0.0)

println (sparse) //SparseVector((0,0.0), (1,1.0), (2,0.0),
(3,2.0), (4,0.0))
```

Notice how the `SparseVector` stores values against the index.

Obviously, there are simpler ways to create a vector instead of just throwing all the data into its `apply` method.

Creating a zero vector

Calling the vector's `zeros` function would create a zero vector. While the numeric types would return a `0`, the object types would return `null` and the Boolean types would return `false`:

```
val denseZeros=DenseVector.zeros[Double](5)   //DenseVector(0.0,
0.0, 0.0, 0.0, 0.0)

val sparseZeros=SparseVector.zeros[Double](5)   //SparseVector()
```

Not surprisingly, the `SparseVector` does not allocate any memory for the contents of the vector. However, the creation of the `SparseVector` object itself is accounted for in the memory.

Creating a vector out of a function

The `tabulate` function in vector is an interesting and useful function. It accepts a size argument just like the `zeros` function but it also accepts a function that we could use to populate the values for the vector. The function could be anything ranging from a random number generator to a naïve index based generator, which we have implemented here. Notice how the return value of the function (`Int`) could be converted into a vector of `Double` by using the `type` parameter:

```
val
denseTabulate=DenseVector.tabulate[Double](5)(index=>index*index)
//DenseVector(0.0, 1.0, 4.0, 9.0, 16.0)
```

Creating a vector of linearly spaced values

The `linspace` function in `breeze.linalg` creates a new `Vector[Double]` of linearly spaced values between two arbitrary numbers. Not surprisingly, it accepts three arguments— the start, end, and the total number of values that we would like to generate. Please note that the start and the end values are inclusive while being generated:

```
val spaceVector=breeze.linalg.linspace(2, 10, 5)
//DenseVector(2.0, 4.0, 6.0, 8.0, 10.0)
```

Creating a vector with values in a specific range

The `range` function in a vector has two variants. The plain vanilla function accepts a start and end value (start inclusive):

```
val allNosTill10=DenseVector.range(0, 10)
//DenseVector(0, 1, 2, 3, 4, 5, 6, 7, 8, 9)
```

The other variant is an overloaded function that accepts a "step" value:

```
val evenNosTill20=DenseVector.range(0, 20, 2)
// DenseVector(0, 2, 4, 6, 8, 10, 12, 14, 16, 18)
```

Just like the `range` function, which has all the arguments as integers, there is also a `rangeD` function that takes the start, stop, and the step parameters as `Double`:

```
val rangeD=DenseVector.rangeD(0.5, 20, 2.5)
// DenseVector(0.5, 3.0, 5.5, 8.0, 10.5, 13.0, 15.5)
```

Creating an entire vector with a single value

Filling an entire vector with the same value is child's play. We just say HOW BIG is this vector going to be and then WHAT value. That's it.

```
val denseJust2s=DenseVector.fill(10, 2)
// DenseVector(2, 2, 2, 2, 2, 2 , 2, 2, 2, 2)
```

Slicing a sub-vector from a bigger vector

Choosing a part of the vector from a previous vector is just a matter of calling the slice method on the bigger vector. The parameters to be passed are the start index, end index, and an optional "step" parameter. The step parameter adds the step value for every iteration until it reaches the end index. Note that the end index is excluded in the sub-vector:

```
val allNosTill10=DenseVector.range(0, 10)
//DenseVector(0, 1, 2, 3, 4, 5, 6, 7, 8, 9)
val fourThroughSevenIndexVector= allNosTill10.slice(4, 7)
//DenseVector(4, 5, 6)
val twoThroughNineSkip2IndexVector= allNosTill10.slice(2, 9, 2)
//DenseVector(2, 4, 6)
```

Creating a Breeze Vector from a Scala Vector

A Breeze vector object's `apply` method could even accept a Scala Vector as a parameter and construct a vector out of it:

```
val
vectFromArray=DenseVector(collection.immutable.Vector(1,2,3,4))
// DenseVector(Vector(1, 2, 3, 4))
```

Vector arithmetic

Now let's look at the basic arithmetic that we could do on vectors with scalars and vectors.

Scalar operations

Operations with scalars work just as we would expect, propagating the value to each element in the vector.

Adding a scalar to each element of the vector is done using the + function (surprise!):

```
val inPlaceValueAddition=evenNosTill20 +2
//DenseVector(2, 4, 6, 8, 10, 12, 14, 16, 18, 20)
```

Similarly the other basic arithmetic operations—subtraction, multiplication, and division involves calling the respective functions named after the universally accepted symbols (-, *, and /):

```
//Scalar subtraction
val inPlaceValueSubtraction=evenNosTill20 -2
//DenseVector(-2, 0, 2, 4, 6, 8, 10, 12, 14, 16)

 //Scalar multiplication
val inPlaceValueMultiplication=evenNosTill20 *2
//DenseVector(0, 4, 8, 12, 16, 20, 24, 28, 32, 36)

//Scalar division
val inPlaceValueDivision=evenNosTill20 /2
//DenseVector(0, 1, 2, 3, 4, 5, 6, 7, 8, 9)
```

Calculating the dot product of two vectors

Each vector object has a function called `dot`, which accepts another vector of the same length as a parameter.

Let's fill in just 2s to a new vector of length 5:

```
val justFive2s=DenseVector.fill(5, 2)
  //DenseVector(2, 2, 2, 2, 2)
```

We'll create another vector from 0 to 5 with a step value of 1 (a fancy way of saying 0 through 4):

```
val zeroThrough4=DenseVector.range(0, 5, 1)
//DenseVector(0, 1, 2, 3, 4)
```

Here's the `dot` function:

```
val dotVector=zeroThrough4.dot(justFive2s)
//Int = 20
```

It is to be expected of the function to complain if we pass in a vector of a different length as a parameter to the dot product - Breeze throws an `IllegalArgumentException` if we do that. The full exception message is:

```
Java.lang.IllegalArgumentException: Vectors must be the same
length!
```

Creating a new vector by adding two vectors together

The + function is overloaded to accept a vector other than the scalar we saw previously. The operation does a corresponding element-by-element addition and creates a new vector:

```
val evenNosTill20=DenseVector.range(0, 20, 2)
//DenseVector(0, 2, 4, 6, 8, 10, 12, 14, 16, 18)

val denseJust2s=DenseVector.fill(10, 2)
//DenseVector(2, 2, 2, 2, 2, 2, 2, 2, 2, 2)

val additionVector=evenNosTill20 + denseJust2s
// DenseVector(2, 4, 6, 8, 10, 12, 14, 16, 18, 20)
```

There's an interesting behavior encapsulated in the addition though. Assuming you try to add two vectors of different lengths, if the first vector is smaller and the second vector larger, the resulting vector would be the size of the first vector and the rest of the elements in the second vector would be ignored!

```
val fiveLength=DenseVector(1,2,3,4,5)
//DenseVector(1, 2, 3, 4, 5)
val tenLength=DenseVector.fill(10, 20)
//DenseVector(20, 20, 20, 20, 20, 20, 20, 20, 20, 20)

fiveLength+tenLength
//DenseVector(21, 22, 23, 24, 25)
```

On the other hand, if the first vector is larger and the second vector smaller, it would result in an `ArrayIndexOutOfBoundsException`:

```
tenLength+fiveLength
// java.lang.ArrayIndexOutOfBoundsException: 5
```

Appending vectors and converting a vector of one type to another

Let's briefly see how to append two vectors and convert vectors of one numeric type to another.

Concatenating two vectors

There are two variants of concatenation. There is a `vertcat` function that just vertically concatenates an arbitrary number of vectors—the size of the vector just increases to the sum of the sizes of all the vectors combined:

```
val justFive2s=DenseVector.fill(5, 2)
  //DenseVector(2, 2, 2, 2, 2)

  val zeroThrough4=DenseVector.range(0, 5, 1)
  //DenseVector(0, 1, 2, 3, 4)


  val concatVector=DenseVector.vertcat(zeroThrough4, justFive2s)
  //DenseVector(0, 1, 2, 3, 4, 2, 2, 2, 2, 2)
```

No surprise here. There is also the `horzcat` method that places the second vector horizontally next to the first vector, thus forming a matrix.

```
val concatVector1=DenseVector.horzcat(zeroThrough4, justFive2s)
```

```
//breeze.linalg.DenseMatrix[Int]
```

```
0   2
1   2
2   2
3   2
4   2
```

> While dealing with vectors of different length, the `vertcat` function happily arranges the second vector at the bottom of the first vector. Not surprisingly, the `horzcat` function throws an exception:
>
> `java.lang.IllegalArgumentException`, meaning all vectors must be of the same size!

Converting a vector of Int to a vector of Double

The conversion of one type of vector into another is not automatic in Breeze. However, there is a simple way to achieve this:

```
val evenNosTill20Double=breeze.linalg.convert (evenNosTill20,
Double)
```

Computing basic statistics

Other than the creation and the arithmetic operations that we saw previously, there are some interesting summary statistics operations that are available in the library. Let's look at them now:

> Needs import of `breeze.linalg._` and `breeze.numerics._`. The operations in the Other operations section aim to simulate the NumPy's UFunc or universal functions.

Now, let's briefly look at how to calculate some basic summary statistics for a vector.

Mean and variance

Calculating the mean and variance of a vector could be achieved by calling the `meanAndVariance` universal function in the `breeze.stats` package. Note that this needs a vector of `Double`:

```
meanAndVariance (evenNosTill20Double)
//MeanAndVariance (9.0,36.666666666666664,10)
```

> As you may have guessed, converting an `Int` vector to a `Double` vector and calculating the mean and variance for that vector could be merged into a one-liner:
>
> ```
> meanAndVariance (convert (evenNosTill20, Double))
> ```

Standard deviation

Calling the `stddev` on a `Double` vector could give the standard deviation:

```
stddev (evenNosTill20Double)
//Double = 6.0553007081949835
```

Find the largest value in a vector

The `max` universal function inside the `breeze.linalg` package would help us find the maximum value in a vector:

```
val intMaxOfVectorVals=max (evenNosTill20)
//18
```

Finding the sum, square root and log of all the values in the vector

The same as with `max`, the `sum` universal function inside the `breeze.linalg` package calculates the `sum` of the vector:

```
val intSumOfVectorVals=sum (evenNosTill20)
//90
```

The functions `sqrt`, `log`, and various other universal functions in the `breeze.numerics` package calculate the square root and log values of all the individual elements inside the vector:

The Sqrt function

```
val sqrtOfVectorVals= sqrt (evenNosTill20)
// DenseVector(0.0, 1. 4142135623730951, 2.0, 2.449489742783178,

2.8284271247461903, 3.16227766016 83795, 3.4641016151377544,
3.7416573867739413, 4.0, 4.242640687119285)
```

The Log function

```
val log2VectorVals=log(evenNosTill20)
// DenseVector(-Infinity , 0.6931471805599453, 1.3862943611198906,
1.791759469228055, 2.079441541679 8357, 2.302585092994046,
2.4849066497880004, 2.6390573296152584, 2.77258872 2239781,
2.8903717578961645)
```

Working with matrices

As we discussed in the *Working with vectors* recipe, you could use the Eclipse or IntelliJ IDEA Scala worksheets for a faster turnaround time.

How to do it...

There are a variety of functions that we have in a matrix. In this recipe, we will look at some details around:

- ▶ Creating matrices:
    - ❏ Creating a matrix from values
    - ❏ Creating a zero matrix
    - ❏ Creating a matrix out of a function
    - ❏ Creating an identity matrix
    - ❏ Creating a matrix from random numbers
    - ❏ Creating from a Scala collection

- ▶ Matrix arithmetic:
    - ❑ Addition
    - ❑ Multiplication (also element-wise)
- ▶ Appending and conversion:
    - ❑ Concatenating a matrix vertically
    - ❑ Concatenating a matrix horizontally
    - ❑ Converting a matrix of Int to a matrix of Double
- ▶ Data manipulation operations:
    - ❑ Getting column vectors
    - ❑ Getting row vectors
    - ❑ Getting values inside the matrix
    - ❑ Getting the inverse and transpose of a matrix
- ▶ Computing basic statistics:
    - ❑ Mean and variance
    - ❑ Standard deviation
    - ❑ Finding the largest value
    - ❑ Finding the sum, square root and log of all the values in the matrix
    - ❑ Calculating the eigenvectors and eigenvalues of a matrix

Creating matrices

Let's first see how to create a matrix.

Creating a matrix from values

The simplest way to create a matrix is to pass in the values in a row-wise fashion into the `apply` function of the matrix object:

```
val simpleMatrix=DenseMatrix((1,2,3),(11,12,13),(21,22,23))
//Returns a DenseMatrix[Int]
 1   2   3
11  12  13
21  22  23
```

There's also a Sparse version of the matrix too—the **Compressed Sparse Column Matrix** (**CSCMatrix**):

```
val sparseMatrix=CSCMatrix((1,0,0),(11,0,0),(0,0,23))
//Returns a SparseMatrix[Int]
(0,0) 1
(1,0) 11
(2,2) 23
```

 Breeze's Sparse matrix is a **Dictionary of Keys** (**DOK**) representation with (row, column) mapped against the value.

Creating a zero matrix

Creating a zero matrix is just a matter of calling the matrix's `zeros` function. The first integer parameter indicates the rows and the second parameter indicates the columns:

```
val denseZeros=DenseMatrix.zeros[Double](5,4)
//Returns a DenseMatrix[Double]
0.0   0.0   0.0   0.0
0.0   0.0   0.0   0.0
0.0   0.0   0.0   0.0
0.0   0.0   0.0   0.0
0.0   0.0   0.0   0.0

val compressedSparseMatrix=CSCMatrix.zeros[Double](5,4)
//Returns a CSCMatrix[Double] = 5 x 4 CSCMatrix
```

 Notice how the `SparseMatrix` doesn't allocate any memory for the values in the zero value matrix.

Creating a matrix out of a function

The `tabulate` function in a matrix is very similar to the vector's version. It accepts a row and column size as a tuple (in the example `(5,4)`). It also accepts a function that we could use to populate the values for the matrix. In our example, we generated the values of the matrix by just multiplying the row and column index:

```
val denseTabulate=DenseMatrix.tabulate[Double](5,4)((firstIdx,secondIdx)=
>firstIdx*secondIdx)
```

```
Returns a DenseMatrix[Double] =
0.0   0.0   0.0   0.0
0.0   1.0   2.0   3.0
0.0   2.0   4.0   6.0
0.0   3.0   6.0   9.0
0.0   4.0   8.0   12.0
```

The `type` parameter is needed only if you would like to convert the type of the matrix from an `Int` to a `Double`. So, the following call without the parameter would just return an `Int` matrix:

```
val denseTabulate=DenseMatrix.tabulate(5,4)((firstIdx,secondIdx)=>firstId
x*secondIdx)
```

```
0   1   2   3
0   2   4   6
0   3   6   9
0   4   8   12
```

Creating an identity matrix

The `eye` function of the matrix would generate an identity square matrix with the given dimension (in the example's case, `3`):

```
val identityMatrix=DenseMatrix.eye[Int](3)
```

```
Returns a DenseMatrix[Int]
1   0   0
0   1   0
0   0   1
```

Creating a matrix from random numbers

The `rand` function in the matrix would generate a matrix of a given dimension (4 rows * 4 columns in our case) with random values between `0` and `1`. We'll have an in-depth look into random number generated vectors and matrices in a subsequent recipe.

```
val randomMatrix=DenseMatrix.rand(4, 4)
```

```
Returns DenseMatrix[Double]
0.09762565779429777    0.01089176285376725    0.2660579009292807
0.19428193961985674
0.9662568115400412     0.718377391997945      0.8230367668470933
0.3957540854393169
0.9080090988364429     0.7697780247035393     0.49887760321635066
0.26722019105654415
3.326843165250004E-4   0.447925644082819      0.8195838733418965
0.7682752255172411
```

Creating from a Scala collection

We could create a matrix out of a Scala array too. The constructor of the matrix accepts three arguments—the rows, the columns, and an array with values for the dimensions. Note that the data from the array is picked up to construct the matrix in the column first order:

```
val vectFromArray=new DenseMatrix(2,2,Array(2,3,4,5))
```

```
Returns DenseMatrix[Int]
```

```
2  4

3  5
```

If there are more values than the number of values required by the dimensions of the matrix, the rest of the values are ignored. Note how (6,7) is ignored in the array:

```
val vectFromArray=new DenseMatrix(2,2,Array(2,3,4,5,6,7))
```

```
DenseMatrix[Int]
```

```
2  4

3  5
```

However, if fewer values are present in the array than what is required by the dimensions of the matrix, then the constructor call would throw an `ArrayIndexOutOfBoundsException`:

```
val vectFromArrayIobe=new DenseMatrix(2,2,Array(2,3,4))
```

```
//throws java.lang.ArrayIndexOutOfBoundsException: 3
```

Matrix arithmetic

Now let's look at the basic arithmetic that we could do using matrices.

Let's consider a simple 3*3 `simpleMatrix` and a corresponding identity matrix:

```
val simpleMatrix=DenseMatrix((1,2,3),(11,12,13),(21,22,23))
//DenseMatrix[Int]
1    2    3
11   12   13
21   22   23


val identityMatrix=DenseMatrix.eye[Int](3)
//DenseMatrix[Int]
1   0   0
0   1   0
0   0   1
```

Addition

Adding two matrices will result in a matrix whose corresponding elements are summed up.

```
val additionMatrix=identityMatrix + simpleMatrix
// Returns DenseMatrix[Int]
2    2    3
11   13   13
21   22   24
```

Multiplication

Now, as you would expect, multiplying a matrix with its identity should give you the matrix itself:

```
val simpleTimesIdentity=simpleMatrix * identityMatrix
//Returns DenseMatrix[Int]
1    2    3
11   12   13
21   22   23
```

Breeze also has an alternative element-by-element operation that has the format of prefixing the operator with a colon, for example, `:+,:-`, `:*`, and so on. Check out what happens when we do an element-wise multiplication of the identity matrix and the simple matrix:

```
val elementWiseMulti=identityMatrix :* simpleMatrix

//DenseMatrix[Int]
1   0    0
0   12   0
0   0    23
```

Appending and conversion

Let's briefly see how to append two matrices and convert matrices of one numeric type to another.

Concatenating matrices – vertically

Similar to vectors, matrix has a `vertcat` function, which vertically concatenates an arbitrary number of matrices—the row size of the matrix just increases to the sum of the row sizes of all matrices combined:

```
val vertConcatMatrix=DenseMatrix.vertcat(identityMatrix, simpleMatrix)


//DenseMatrix[Int]
1    0    0
0    1    0
0    0    1
1    2    3
11   12   13
21   22   23
```

Attempting to concatenate a matrix of different columns would, as expected, throw an `IllegalArgumentException`:

```
    java.lang.IllegalArgumentException: requirement failed: Not all
    matrices have the same number of columns
```

Concatenating matrices – horizontally

Not surprisingly, the `horzcat` function concatenates the matrix horizontally—the column size of the matrix increases to the sum of the column sizes of all the matrices:

```
val horzConcatMatrix=DenseMatrix.horzcat(identityMatrix, simpleMatrix)

// DenseMatrix[Int]
1  0  0  1   2   3
```

```
0   1   0   11   12   13
0   0   1   21   22   23
```

Similar to the vertical concatenation, attempting to concatenate a matrix of a different row size would throw an `IllegalArgumentException`:

```
java.lang.IllegalArgumentException: requirement failed: Not all
matrices have the same number of rows
```

Converting a matrix of Int to a matrix of Double

The conversion of one type of matrix to another is not automatic in Breeze. However, there is a simple way to achieve this:

```
import breeze.linalg.convert
val simpleMatrixAsDouble=convert(simpleMatrix, Double)
// DenseMatrix[Double]  =
1.0    2.0    3.0
11.0   12.0   13.0
21.0   22.0   23.0
```

Data manipulation operations

Let's create a simple 2*2 matrix that will be used for the rest of this section:

```
val simpleMatrix=DenseMatrix((4.0,7.0),(3.0,-5.0))
//DenseMatrix[Double]  =
4.0   7.0
3.0   -5.0
```

Getting column vectors out of the matrix

The first column vector could be retrieved by passing in the column parameter as 0 and using `::` in order to say that we are interested in all the rows.

```
val firstVector=simpleMatrix(::,0)
//DenseVector(4.0, 3.0)
```

Getting the second column vector and so on is achieved by passing the correct zero-indexed column number:

```
val secondVector=simpleMatrix(::,1)
//DenseVector(7.0, -5.0)
```

Alternatively, you could explicitly pass in the columns to be extracted:

```
val firstVectorByCols=simpleMatrix(0 to 1,0)
//DenseVector(4.0, 3.0)
```

While explicitly stating the range (as in 0 to 1), we have to be careful not to exceed the matrix size. For example, the following attempt to select 3 columns (0 through 2) on a 2 * 2 matrix would throw an `ArrayIndexOutOfBoundsException`:

```
val errorTryingToSelect3ColumnsOn2By2Matrix=simpleMatrix(0,0 to 2)
//java.lang.ArrayIndexOutOfBoundsException
```

Getting row vectors out of the matrix

If we would like to get the row vector, all we need to do is play with the row and column parameters again. As expected, it would give a transpose of the column vector, which is simply a row vector.

Like the column vector, we could either explicitly state our columns or pass in a wildcard (::) to cover the entire range of columns:

```
val firstRowStatingCols=simpleMatrix(0,0 to 1)
//Transpose(DenseVector(4.0, 7.0))

val firstRowAllCols=simpleMatrix(0,::)
//Transpose(DenseVector(4.0, 7.0))
```

Getting the second row vector is achieved by passing the second row (1) and all the columns (::) in that vector:

```
val secondRow=simpleMatrix(1,::)
//Transpose(DenseVector(3.0, -5.0))
```

Getting values inside the matrix

Assuming we are just interested in the values within the matrix, pass in the exact row and the column number of the matrix. In order to get the first row and first column of the matrix, just pass in the row and the column number:

```
val firstRowFirstCol=simpleMatrix(0,0)
//Double = 4.0
```

Getting the inverse and transpose of a matrix

Getting the inverse and the transpose of a matrix is a little counter-intuitive in Breeze. Let's consider the same matrix that we dealt with earlier:

```
val simpleMatrix=DenseMatrix((4.0,7.0),(3.0,-5.0))
```

On the one hand, `transpose` is a function on the matrix object itself, like so:

```
val transpose=simpleMatrix.t

4.0   3.0
7.0   -5.0
```

inverse, on the other hand is a universal function under the `breeze.linalg` package:

```
val inverse=inv(simpleMatrix)
```

```
0.12195121951219512    0.17073170731707318
0.07317073170731708    -0.0975609756097561
```

Let's do a matrix product to its inverse and confirm whether it is an identity matrix:

```
simpleMatrix * inverse
```

```
1.0    0.0
-5.551115123125783E-17    1.0
```

As expected, the result is indeed an identity matrix with rounding errors when doing floating point arithmetic.

Computing basic statistics

Now, just like vectors, let's briefly look at how to calculate some basic summary statistics for a matrix.

This needs import of `breeze.linalg._`, `breeze.numerics._` and, `breeze.stats._`. The operations in the "Other operations" section aims to simulate the NumPy's UFunc or universal functions.

Mean and variance

Calculating the mean and variance of a matrix could be achieved by calling the `meanAndVariance` universal function in the `breeze.stats` package. Note that this needs a matrix of `Double`:

```
meanAndVariance(simpleMatrixAsDouble)
// MeanAndVariance(12.0,75.75,9)
```

Alternatively, converting an `Int` matrix to a `Double` matrix and calculating the mean and variance for that Matrix could be merged into a one-liner:

```
meanAndVariance(convert(simpleMatrix, Double))
```

Standard deviation

Calling the `stddev` on a `Double` vector could give the standard deviation:

```
stddev(simpleMatrixAsDouble)
//Double = 8.703447592764606
```

Next up, let's look at some basic aggregation operations:

```
val simpleMatrix=DenseMatrix((1,2,3),(11,12,13),(21,22,23))
```

Finding the largest value in a matrix

The (`apply` method of the) `max` object (a universal function) inside the `breeze.linalg` package will help us do that:

```
val intMaxOfMatrixVals=max (simpleMatrix)
//23
```

Finding the sum, square root and log of all the values in the matrix

The same as with `max`, the `sum` object inside the `breeze.linalg` package calculates the sum of all the matrix elements:

```
val intSumOfMatrixVals=sum (simpleMatrix)
//108
```

The functions `sqrt`, `log`, and various other objects (universal functions) in the `breeze.numerics` package calculate the square root and log values of all the individual values inside the matrix.

Sqrt

```
val sqrtOfMatrixVals= sqrt (simpleMatrix)

//DenseMatrix[Double] =
1.0                 1.4142135623730951   1.7320508075688772
3.3166247903554     3.4641016151377544   3.605551275463989
4.58257569495584    4.69041575982343     4.795831523312719
```

Log

```
val log2MatrixVals=log(simpleMatrix)

//DenseMatrix[Double]
0.0                 0.6931471805599453   1.0986122886681098
2.3978952727983707  2.4849066497880004   2.5649493574615367
3.044522437723423   3.091042453358316    3.1354942159291497
```

Calculating the eigenvectors and eigenvalues of a matrix

Calculating eigenvectors is straightforward in Breeze. Let's consider our `simpleMatrix` from the previous section:

```
val simpleMatrix=DenseMatrix((4.0,7.0),(3.0,-5.0))
```

Calling the `breeze.linalg.eig` universal function on a matrix returns a `breeze.linalg.eig.DenseEig` object that encapsulate eigenvectors and eigenvalues:

```
val denseEig=eig(simpleMatrix)
```

This line of code returns the following:

```
Eig(
DenseVector(5.922616289332565, -6.922616289332565),
DenseVector(0.0, 0.0)
,0.9642892971721949    -0.5395744865143975   0.26485118719604456
0.8419378679586305)
```

We could extract the eigenvectors and eigenvalues by calling the corresponding functions on the returned `Eig` reference:

```
val eigenVectors=denseEig.eigenvectors
//DenseMatrix[Double] =
0.9642892971721949    -0.5395744865143975
0.26485118719604456   0.8419378679586305
```

The two `eigenValues` corresponding to the two `eigenvectors` could be captured using the `eigenvalues` function on the `Eig` object:

```
val eigenValues=denseEig.eigenvalues
//DenseVector[Double] = DenseVector(5.922616289332565,
-6.922616289332565)
```

Let's validate the eigenvalues and the vectors:

1. Let's multiply the matrix with the first eigenvector:
    ```
    val matrixToEigVector=simpleMatrix*denseEig.eigenvectors (::,0)
    //DenseVector(5.7111154990610915, 1.568611955536362)
    ```

2. Then let's multiply the first eigenvalue with the first eigenvector. The resulting vector will be the same with a marginal error when doing floating point arithmetic:
    ```
    val vectorToEigValue=denseEig.eigenvectors(::,0) *
    denseEig.eigenvalues (0)
    //DenseVector(5.7111154990610915, 1.5686119555363618)
    ```

How it works...

The same as with vectors, the initialization of the Breeze matrices are achieved by way of the `apply` method or one of the various methods in the matrix's `Object` class. Various other operations are provided by way of polymorphic functions available in the `breeze.numeric`, `breeze.linalg` and `breeze.stats` packages.

Vectors and matrices with randomly distributed values

The `breeze.stats.distributions` package supplements the random number generator that is built into Scala. Scala's default generator just provides the ability to get the random values one by one using the "next" methods. Random number generators in Breeze provide the ability to build vectors and matrices out of these generators. In this recipe, we'll briefly see three of the most common distributions of random numbers.

In this recipe, we will cover at the following sub-recipes:

- ▶ *Creating vectors with uniformly distributed random values*
- ▶ *Creating vectors with normally distributed random values*
- ▶ *Creating vectors with random values that have a Poisson distribution*
- ▶ *Creating a matrix with uniformly random values*
- ▶ *Creating a matrix with normally distributed random values*
- ▶ *Creating a matrix with random values that has a Poisson distribution*

How it works...

Before we delve into how to create the vectors and matrices out of random numbers, let's create instances of the most common random number distribution. All these generators are under the `breeze.stats.distributions` package:

```
//Uniform distribution with low being 0 and high being 10
val uniformDist=Uniform(0,10)

//Gaussian distribution with mean being 5 and Standard deviation
being 1
val gaussianDist=Gaussian(5,1)

//Poission distribution with mean being 5
val poissonDist=Poisson(5)
```

We could actually directly sample from these generators. Given any distribution we created previously, we could sample either a single value or a sequence of values:

```
//Samples a single value
println (uniformDist.sample())
//eg. 9.151191360491392

//Returns a sample vector of size that is passed in as parameter
println (uniformDist.sample(2))
//eg. Vector(6.001980062275654, 6.210874664967401)
```

Creating vectors with uniformly distributed random values

With no generator parameter, the `DenseVector.rand` method accepts a parameter for the length of the vector to be returned. The result is a vector (of length `10`) with uniformly distributed values between `0` and `1`:

```
val uniformWithoutSize=DenseVector.rand(10)

println ("uniformWithoutSize \n"+ uniformWithoutSize)

//DenseVector(0.1235038023750481, 0.3120595941786264, 0.3575638744660876,
0.5640844223813524, 0.5336149399548831, 0.1338053814330793,
0.9099684427908603, 0.38690724148973166, 0.22561993631651522,
0.45120359622713657)
```

The `DenseVector.rand` method optionally accepts a distribution object and generates random values using that input distribution. The following line generates a vector of `10` uniformly distributed random values that are within the range `0` and `10`:

```
val uniformDist=Uniform(0,10)


val uniformVectInRange=DenseVector.rand(10, uniformDist)

println ("uniformVectInRange \n"+uniformVectInRange)

//DenseVector(1.5545833905907314, 6.172564377264846, 8.45578509265587,
7.683763574965107, 8.018688137742062, 4.5876187984930406,
3.274758584944064, 2.3873947264259954, 2.139988841403757,
8.314112884416943)
```

Creating vectors with normally distributed random values

In the place of the `uniformDist` generator, we could also pass the previously created Gaussian generator, which is configured to yield a distribution that has a mean of `5` and standard deviation of `1`:

```
val gaussianVector=DenseVector.rand(10, gaussianDist)

println ("gaussianVector \n"+gaussianVector)
```

```
//DenseVector(4.235655596913547, 5.535011377545014, 6.201428236839494,
6.046289604188366, 4.319709374229152,

4.2379652913447154, 2.957868021601233, 3.96371080427211,
4.351274306757224, 5.445022658876723)
```

Creating vectors with random values that have a Poisson distribution

Similarly, by passing the previously created Poisson random number generator, a vector of values that has a mean of 5 could be generated:

```
val poissonVector=DenseVector.rand(10, poissonDist)

println ("poissonVector \n"+poissonVector)

//DenseVector(5, 5, 7, 11, 7, 6, 6, 6, 6, 6)
```

We saw how easy it is to create a vector of random values. Now, let's proceed to create a matrix of random values. Similar to `DenseVector.rand` to generate vectors with random values, we'll use the `DenseMatrix.rand` function to generate a matrix of random values.

Creating a matrix with uniformly random values

The `DenseMatrix.rand` defaults to the uniform distribution and generates a matrix of random values given the row and the column parameter. However, if we would like to have a distribution within a range, then as in vectors, we could use the optional parameter:.

```
//Uniform distribution, Creates a 3 * 3 Matrix with random values from 0
to 1

val uniformMat=DenseMatrix.rand(3, 3)

println ("uniformMat \n"+uniformMat)


0.4492155777289115    0.9098840386699856    0.8203022252988292

0.0888975848853315    0.009677790736892788  0.6058885905934237

0.6201415814136939    0.7017492438727635    0.08404147915159443


//Creates a 3 * 3 Matrix with uniformly distributed random values with
low being 0 and high being 10

val uniformMatrixInRange=DenseMatrix.rand(3,3, uniformDist)

println ("uniformMatrixInRange \n"+uniformMatrixInRange)


7.592014659345548    8.164652560340933    6.966445294464401

8.35949395084735     3.442654641743763    3.6761640240938442

9.42626645215854     0.23658921372298636  7.327120138868571
```

Creating a matrix with normally distributed random values

Just as in vectors, in place of the `uniformDist` generator, we could also pass the previously created Gaussian generator to the `rand` function to generate a matrix of random values that has a mean of 5 and standard deviation of 1:

```
//Creates a 3 * 3 Matrix with normally distributed random values
with mean being 5 and Standard deviation being 1
val gaussianMatrix=DenseMatrix.rand(3, 3,gaussianDist)
println ("gaussianMatrix \n"+gaussianMatrix)
```

```
5.724540885605018    5.647051873430568    5.337906135107098
6.2228893721489875   4.799561665187845    5.12469779489833
5.136960834730864    5.176410360757703    5.262707072950913
```

Creating a matrix with random values that has a Poisson distribution

Similarly, by passing the previously created Poisson random number generator, a matrix of random values that has a mean of 5 could be generated:

```
//Creates a 3 * 3 Matrix with Poisson distribution with mean being 5
val poissonMatrix=DenseMatrix.rand(3, 3,poissonDist)
println ("poissonMatrix \n"+poissonMatrix)
4   11   3
6    6   5
6    4   2
```

Reading and writing CSV files

Reading and writing a CSV file in Breeze is really a breeze. We just have two functions in `breeze.linalg` package to play with. They are very intuitively named `csvread` and `csvwrite`.

In this recipe, you'll see how to:

1. Read a CSV file into a matrix

2. Save selected columns of a matrix into a new matrix

3. Write the newly created matrix into a CSV file

4. Extract a vector out of the matrix

5. Write the vector into a CSV

How it works...

There are just two functions that we need to remember in order to read and write data from and to CSV files. The signatures of the functions are pretty straightforward too:

```
csvread(file, separator, quote, escape, skipLines)
csvwrite(file, mat, separator, quote, escape, skipLines)
```

Let's look at the parameters by order of importance:

- `file`: `java.io.File`: Represents the file location.
- `separator`: Defaults to a comma so as to represent a CSV. Could be overridden when needed.
- `skipLines`: This is the number of lines to be skipped while reading the file. Generally, if there is a header, we pass a `skipLines=1`.
- `mat`: While writing, this is the matrix object that is being written.
- `quote`: This defaults to double quotes. It is a character that implies that the value inside is one single value.
- `escape`: This defaults to a backspace. It is a character used to escape special characters.

Let's see these in action. For the sake of clarity, I have skipped the quote and the escape parameter while calling the `csvread` and `csvwrite` functions. For this recipe, we will do three things:

- Read a CSV file as a matrix
- Extract a sub-matrix out of the read matrix
- Write the matrix

Read the CSV as a matrix:

1. Let's use the `csvread` function to read a CSV file into a 100*3 matrix. We'll also skip the header while reading and print 5 rows as a sample:

```
val usageMatrix=csvread(file=new File("WWWusage.csv"),
separator=',', skipLines=1)

//print first five rows

println ("Usage matrix \n"+ usageMatrix(0 to 5,::))

Output :

1.0    1.0    88.0

2.0    2.0    84.0

3.0    3.0    85.0

4.0    4.0    85.0

5.0    5.0    84.0

6.0    6.0    85.0
```

2. Extract a sub-matrix out of the read matrix:

    For the sake of generating a submatrix let's skip the first column and save the second and the third column into a new matrix. Let's call it `firstColumnSkipped`:

```
val firstColumnSkipped= usageMatrix(::, 1 to
usageMatrix.cols-1)


//Sample some data so as to ensure we are fine
```

```
println ("First Column skipped \n"+ firstColumnSkipped(0 to
5, ::))
```

Output :

1.0   88.0

2.0   84.0

3.0   85.0

4.0   85.0

5.0   84.0

6.0   85.0

3. Write the matrix:

    As a final step, let's write the `firstColumnSkipped` matrix to a new CSV file named `firstColumnSkipped.csv`:

    ```
    //Write this modified matrix to a file
    csvwrite(file=new File ("firstColumnSkipped.csv"),
    mat=firstColumnSkipped, separator=',')
    ```

    ```
    firstColumnSkipped.csv ⌧
        1.0,88.0
        2.0,84.0
        3.0,85.0
        4.0,85.0
        5.0,84.0
        6.0,85.0
        7.0,83.0
        8.0,85.0
        9.0,88.0
        10.0,89.0
        11.0,91.0
        12.0,99.0
        13.0,104.0
        14.0,112.0
    ```

2

Getting Started with Apache Spark DataFrames

In this chapter, we will cover the following recipes:

- ▶ Getting Apache Spark
- ▶ Creating a DataFrame from CSV
- ▶ Manipulating DataFrames
- ▶ Creating a DataFrame from Scala case classes

Introduction

Apache Spark is a cluster computing platform that claims to run about 10 times faster than Hadoop. In general terms, we could consider it as a means to run our complex logic over massive amounts of data at a blazingly fast speed. The other good thing about Spark is that the programs that we write are much smaller than the typical MapReduce classes that we write for Hadoop. So, not only do our programs run faster but it also takes less time to write them.

Spark has four major higher level tools built on top of the Spark Core: Spark Streaming, Spark MLlib (machine learning), Spark SQL (an SQL interface for accessing the data), and GraphX (for graph processing). The Spark Core is the heart of Spark. Spark provides higher level abstractions in Scala, Java, and Python for data representation, serialization, scheduling, metrics, and so on.

At the risk of stating the obvious, a DataFrame is one of the primary data structures used in data analysis. They are just like an RDBMS table that organizes all your attributes into columns and all your observations into rows. It's a great way to store and play with heterogeneous data. In this chapter, we'll talk about DataFrames in Spark.

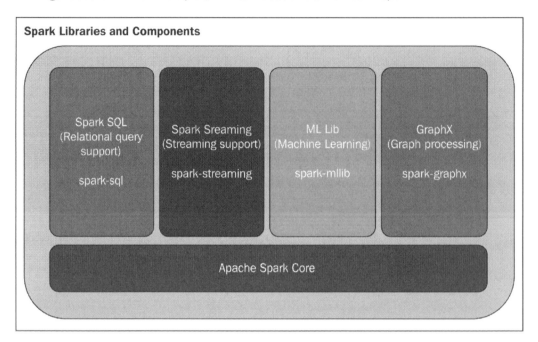

Getting Apache Spark

In this recipe, we'll take a look at how to bring Spark into our project (using **SBT**) and how Spark works internally.

 The code for this recipe can be found at `https://github.com/` `arunma/ScalaDataAnalysisCookbook/blob/master/` `chapter1-spark-csv/build.sbt.`

How to do it...

Let's now throw some Spark dependencies into our `build.sbt` file so that we can start playing with them in subsequent recipes. For now, we'll just focus on three of them: Spark Core, Spark SQL, and Spark MLlib. We'll take a look at a host of other Spark dependencies as we proceed further in this book:

1. Under a brand new folder (which will be your project root), create a new file called `build.sbt`.

2. Next, let's add the Spark libraries to the project dependencies.

3. Note that Spark 1.4.x requires Scala 2.10.x. This becomes the first section of our `build.sbt`:

```
organization := "com.packt"

name := "chapter1-spark-csv"

scalaVersion := "2.10.4"

val sparkVersion="1.4.1"

libraryDependencies ++= Seq(
  "org.apache.spark" %% "spark-core" % sparkVersion,
  "org.apache.spark" %% "spark-sql" % sparkVersion,
  "org.apache.spark" %% "spark-mllib" % sparkVersion
)
```

Creating a DataFrame from CSV

In this recipe, we'll look at how to create a new DataFrame from a delimiter-separated values file.

 The code for this recipe can be found at `https://github.com/ arunma/ScalaDataAnalysisCookbook/blob/master/ chapter1-spark-csv/src/main/scala/com/packt/ scaladata/spark/csv/DataFrameCSV.scala`.

How to do it...

This recipe involves four steps:

1. Add the `spark-csv` support to our project.

2. Create a Spark Config object that gives information on the environment that we are running Spark in.

3. Create a Spark context that serves as an entry point into Spark. Then, we proceed to create an `SQLContext` from the Spark context.

4. Load the CSV using the `SQLContext`.

5. CSV support isn't first-class in Spark, but it is available through an external library from Databricks. So, let's go ahead and add that to our `build.sbt`.

   After adding the `spark-csv` dependency, our complete `build.sbt` looks like this:

   ```
   organization := "com.packt"

   name := "chapter1-spark-csv"

   scalaVersion := "2.10.4"

   val sparkVersion="1.4.1"

   libraryDependencies ++= Seq(
      "org.apache.spark" %% "spark-core" % sparkVersion,
      "org.apache.spark" %% "spark-sql" % sparkVersion,
   "com.databricks" %% "spark-csv" % "1.0.3"
   )
   ```

6. `SparkConf` holds all of the information required to run this Spark "cluster." For this recipe, we are running locally, and we intend to use only two cores in the machine— `local[2]`. More details about this can be found in the *There's more...* section of this recipe:

   ```
   import org.apache.spark.SparkConf

   val conf = new
   SparkConf().setAppName("csvDataFrame").setMaster("local[2]")
   ```

 When we say that the master of this run is "local," we mean that we are running Spark on standalone mode. We'll see what "standalone" mode means in the *There's more...* section.

7. Initialize the Spark context with the Spark configuration. This is the core entry point for doing anything with Spark:

```
import org.apache.spark.SparkContext
val sc = new SparkContext(conf)
```

The easiest way to query data in Spark is by using SQL queries:

```
import org.apache.spark.sql.SQLContext
val sqlContext=new SQLContext(sc)
```

8. Now, let's load our pipe-separated file. The `students` is of type `org.apache.spark.sql.DataFrame`:

```
import com.databricks.spark.csv._
val students=sqlContext.csvFile(filePath="StudentData.csv",
useHeader=true, delimiter='|')
```

How it works...

The `csvFile` function of `sqlContext` accepts the full `filePath` of the file to be loaded. If the CSV has a header, then the `useHeader` flag will read the first row as column names. The delimiter flag defaults to a comma, but you can override the character as needed.

Instead of using the `csvFile` function, we could also use the `load` function available in `SQLContext`. The `load` function accepts the format of the file (in our case, it is CSV) and options as `Map`. We can specify the same parameters that we specified earlier using `Map`, like this:

```
val options=Map("header"->"true", "path"->"ModifiedStudent.csv")

val
newStudents=sqlContext.load("com.databricks.spark.csv",options)
```

There's more...

As we saw earlier, we now ran the Spark program in standalone mode. In standalone mode, the **Driver** program (the brain) and the **Worker** nodes all get crammed into a single JVM. In our example, we set `master` to `local[2]`, which means that we intend to run Spark in standalone mode and request it to use only two cores in the machine.

Spark can be run on three different modes:

- Standalone
- Standalone cluster, using its in-built cluster manager
- Using external cluster managers, such as Apache Mesos and YARN

In *Chapter 6*, *Scaling Up*, we have dedicated explanations and recipes for how to run Spark on inbuilt cluster modes on Mesos and YARN. In a clustered environment, Spark runs a Driver program along with a number of Worker nodes. As the name indicates, the Driver program houses the brain of the program, which is our main program. The Worker nodes have the data and perform various transformations on it.

Manipulating DataFrames

In the previous recipe, we saw how to create a DataFrame. The next natural step, after creating DataFrames, is to play with the data inside them. Other than the numerous functions that help us to do that, we also find other interesting functions that help us sample the data, print the schema of the data, and so on. We'll take a look at them one by one in this recipe.

 The code and the sample file for this recipe could be found at
https://github.com/arunma/ScalaDataAnalysisCookbook/
blob/master/chapter1-spark-csv/src/main/scala/com/
packt/scaladata/spark/csv/DataFrameCSV.scala.

How to do it...

Now, let's see how we can manipulate DataFrames using the following subrecipes:

▶ Printing the schema of the DataFrame

▶ Sampling data in the DataFrame

▶ Selecting specific columns in the DataFrame

▶ Filtering data by condition

▶ Sorting data in the frame

▶ Renaming columns

▶ Treating the DataFrame as a relational table to execute SQL queries

▶ Saving the DataFrame as a file

Printing the schema of the DataFrame

After creating the DataFrame from various sources, we would obviously want to quickly check its schema. The printSchema function lets us do just that. It prints our column names and the data types to the default output stream:

1. Let's load a sample DataFrame from the StudentData.csv file:

```
//Now, lets load our pipe-separated file
    //students is of type org.apache.spark.sql.DataFrame
```

```
     val
students=sqlContext.csvFile(filePath="StudentData.csv",
useHeader=true, delimiter='|')
```

2.   Let's print the schema of this DataFrame:

```
students.printSchema
```

Output

```
root
 |-- id: string (nullable = true)
 |-- studentName: string (nullable = true)
 |-- phone: string (nullable = true)
 |-- email: string (nullable = true)
```

Sampling the data in the DataFrame

The next logical thing that we would like to do is to check whether our data got loaded into the DataFrame correctly. There are a few ways of sampling the data in the newly created DataFrame:

►   Using the `show` method. This is the simplest way. There are two variants of the `show` method, as explained here:

   ❑   One with an integer parameter that specifies the number of rows to be sampled.

   ❑   The second is without the integer parameter. In it, the number of rows defaults to 20.

The distinct quality about the `show` method as compared to the other functions that sample data is that it displays the rows along with the headers and prints the output directly to the default output stream (console):

```
//Sample n records along with headers
  students.show (3)


  //Sample 20 records along with headers
  students.show ()


//Output of show(3)


  +--+-----------+--------------+--------------------+
  |id|studentName|         phone|               email|
```

```
+--+-----------+-------------+-------------------+
| 1|      Burke|1-300-746-8446|ullamcorper.velit...|
| 2|      Kamal|1-668-571-5046|pede.Suspendisse@...|
| 3|       Olga|1-956-311-1686|Aenean.eget.metus...|
+--+-----------+-------------+-------------------+
```

- Using the `head` method. This method also accepts an integer parameter representing the number of rows to be fetched. The `head` method returns an array of rows. To print these rows, we can pass the `println` method to the `foreach` function of the arrays:

```
//Sample the first 5 records
students.head(5).foreach(println)
```

If you are not a great fan of `head`, you can use the `take` function, which is common across all Scala sequences. The `take` method is just an alias of the `head` method and delegates all its calls to `head`:

```
//Alias of head
students.take(5).foreach(println)
```

```
//Output
[1,Burke,1-300-746-8446,ullamcorper.velit.in@ametnullaDonec.co.uk]
[2,Kamal,1-668-571-5046,pede.Suspendisse@interdumenim.edu]
[3,Olga,1-956-311-1686,Aenean.eget.metus@dictumcursusNunc.edu]
[4,Belle,1-246-894-6340,vitae.aliquet.nec@neque.co.uk]
[5,Trevor,1-300-527-4967,dapibus.id@acturpisegestas.net]
```

Selecting DataFrame columns

As you have seen, all DataFrame columns have names. The `select` function helps us pick and choose specific columns from a previously existing DataFrame and form a completely new one out of it:

- Selecting a single column: Let's say that you would like to select only the `email` column from a DataFrame. Since DataFrames are immutable, the selection returns a new DataFrame:

```
val emailDataFrame:DataFrame=students.select("email")
```

Now, we have a new DataFrame called `emailDataFrame`, which has only the e-mail as its contents. Let's sample and check whether that is true:

```
emailDataFrame.show(3)
```

```
//Output
+--------------------+
|               email|
+--------------------+
|ullamcorper.velit...|
|pede.Suspendisse@...|
|Aenean.eget.metus...|
+--------------------+
```

▶ Selecting more than one column: The `select` function actually accepts an arbitrary number of column names, which means that you can easily select more than one column from your source DataFrame:

```
val studentEmailDF=students.select("studentName", "email")
```

 The only requirement is that the string parameters that specify must be a valid column name. Otherwise, an `org.apache.spark.sql.AnalysisException` exception is thrown. The `printSchema` function serves as a quick reference for the column names.

Let's sample and check whether we have indeed selected the `studentName` and `email` columns in the new DataFrame:

```
studentEmailDF.show(3)
```

Output

```
+-----------+--------------------+
|studentName|               email|
+-----------+--------------------+
|      Burke|ullamcorper.velit...|
|      Kamal|pede.Suspendisse@...|
|       Olga|Aenean.eget.metus...|
+-----------+--------------------+
```

Filtering data by condition

Now that we have seen how to select columns from a DataFrame, let's see how to filter the rows of a DataFrame based on conditions. For row-based filtering, we can treat the DataFrame as a normal Scala collection and filter the data based on a condition. In all of these examples, I have added the `show` method at the end for clarity:

1. Filtering based on a column value:

   ```
   //Print the first 5 records that has student id more than 5
     students.filter("id > 5").show(7)
   ```

   Output

   ```
   +--+-----------+--------------+--------------------+
   |id|studentName|         phone|               email|
   +--+-----------+--------------+--------------------+
   | 6|     Laurel|1-691-379-9921|adipiscing@consec...|
   | 7|       Sara|1-608-140-1995|Donec.nibh@enimEt...|
   | 8|     Kaseem|1-881-586-2689|cursus.et.magna@e...|
   | 9|        Lev|1-916-367-5608|Vivamus.nisi@ipsu...|
   |10|       Maya|1-271-683-2698|accumsan.convalli...|
   |11|        Emi|1-467-270-1337|        est@nunc.com|
   |12|      Caleb|1-683-212-0896|Suspendisse@Quisq...|
   +--+-----------+--------------+--------------------+
   ```

   Notice that even though the `id` field is inferenced as a String type, it does the numerical comparison correctly. On the other hand, `students.filter("email > 'c'")` would give back all the e-mail IDs that start with a character greater than `'c'`.

2. Filtering based on an empty column value. The following filter selects all students without names:

   ```
   students.filter("studentName =''").show(7)
   ```

   Output

   ```
   +--+-----------+--------------+--------------------+
   |id|studentName|         phone|               email|
   +--+-----------+--------------+--------------------+
   |21|           |1-598-439-7549|consectetuer.adip...|
   |32|           |1-184-895-9602|accumsan.laoreet@...|
   ```

```
|45|                   |1-245-752-0481|Suspendisse.eleif...|
|83|                   |1-858-810-2204|sociis.natoque@eu...|
|94|                   |1-443-410-7878|Praesent.eu.nulla...|
+--+----------+--------------+--------------------+
```

3. Filtering based on more than one condition. This filter shows all records whose student names are empty or student name field has a NULL string value:

    ```
    students.filter("studentName ='' OR studentName = 'NULL'").show(7)
    ```

    Output

    ```
    +--+-----------+--------------+--------------------+
    |id|studentName|         phone|               email|
    +--+-----------+--------------+--------------------+
    |21|           |1-598-439-7549|consectetuer.adip...|
    |32|           |1-184-895-9602|accumsan.laoreet@...|
    |33|       NULL|1-105-503-0141|Donec@Inmipede.co.uk|
    |45|           |1-245-752-0481|Suspendisse.eleif...|
    |83|           |1-858-810-2204|sociis.natoque@eu...|
    |94|           |1-443-410-7878|Praesent.eu.nulla...|
    +--+-----------+--------------+--------------------+
    ```

    We are just limiting the output to seven records using the show(7) function.

4. Filtering based on SQL-like conditions.

    This filter gets the entries of all students whose names start with the letter 'M'.

    ```
    students.filter("SUBSTR(studentName,0,1) ='M'").show(7)
    ```

    Output

    ```
    +--+-----------+--------------+--------------------+
    |id|studentName|         phone|               email|
    +--+-----------+--------------+--------------------+
    |10|       Maya|1-271-683-2698|accumsan.convalli...|
    |19|    Malachi|1-608-637-2772|Proin.mi.Aliquam@...|
    |24|    Marsden|1-477-629-7528|Donec.dignissim.m...|
    |37|      Maggy|1-910-887-6777|facilisi.Sed.nequ...|
    |61|     Maxine|1-422-863-3041|aliquet.molestie....|
    |77|      Maggy|1-613-147-4380| pellentesque@mi.net|
    |97|    Maxwell|1-607-205-1273|metus.In@musAenea...|
    +--+-----------+--------------+--------------------+
    ```

Sorting data in the frame

Using the `sort` function, we can order the DataFrame by a particular column:

1. Ordering by a column in descending order:

   ```
   students.sort(students("studentName").desc).show(7)
   ```

   Output

   ```
   +--+-----------+--------------+--------------------+
   |id|studentName|         phone|               email|
   +--+-----------+--------------+--------------------+
   |50|      Yasir|1-282-511-4445|eget.odio.Aliquam...|
   |52|       Xena|1-527-990-8606|in.faucibus.orci@...|
   |86|     Xandra|1-677-708-5691|libero@arcuVestib...|
   |43|     Wynter|1-440-544-1851|amet.risus.Donec@...|
   |31|    Wallace|1-144-220-8159|   lorem.lorem@non.net|
   |66|      Vance|1-268-680-0857|pellentesque@netu...|
   |41|     Tyrone|1-907-383-5293|non.bibendum.sed@...|
   | 5|     Trevor|1-300-527-4967|dapibus.id@acturp...|
   |65|      Tiger|1-316-930-7880|nec@mollisnoncurs...|
   |15|      Tarik|1-398-171-2268|turpis@felisorci.com|
   +--+-----------+--------------+--------------------+
   ```

2. Ordering by more than one column (ascending):

   ```
   students.sort("studentName", "id").show(10)
   ```

   Output

   ```
   +--+-----------+--------------+--------------------+
   |id|studentName|         phone|               email|
   +--+-----------+--------------+--------------------+
   |21|           |1-598-439-7549|consectetuer.adip...|
   |32|           |1-184-895-9602|accumsan.laoreet@...|
   |45|           |1-245-752-0481|Suspendisse.eleif...|
   |83|           |1-858-810-2204|sociis.natoque@eu...|
   |94|           |1-443-410-7878|Praesent.eu.nulla...|
   |91|       Abel|1-530-527-7467|    urna@veliteu.edu|
   ```

```
|69|          Aiko|1-682-230-7013|turpis.vitae.puru...|
|47|          Alma|1-747-382-6775|     nec.enim@non.org|
|26|         Amela|1-526-909-2605| in@vitaesodales.edu|
|16|         Amena|1-878-250-3129|lorem.luctus.ut@s...|

+--+-----------+--------------+--------------------+
```

Alternatively, the `orderBy` alias of the `sort` function can be used to achieve this. Also, multiple column orders could be specified using the DataFrame's `apply` method:

```
students.sort(students("studentName").desc, students("id").asc).show(10)
```

Renaming columns

If we don't like the column names of the source DataFrame and wish to change them to something nice and meaningful, we can do that using the `as` function while selecting the columns.

In this example, we rename the `"studentName"` column to `"name"` and retain the `"email"` column's name as is:

```
val copyOfStudents=students.select(students("studentName").as("name"),
students("email"))
```

```
copyOfStudents.show()
```

Output

```
+--------+--------------------+
|    name|               email|
+--------+--------------------+
|   Burke|ullamcorper.velit...|
|   Kamal|pede.Suspendisse@...|
|    Olga|Aenean.eget.metus...|
|   Belle|vitae.aliquet.nec...|
|  Trevor|dapibus.id@acturp...|
|  Laurel|adipiscing@consec...|
|    Sara|Donec.nibh@enimEt...|
```

Treating the DataFrame as a relational table

The real power of DataFrames lies in the fact that we can treat it like a relational table and use SQL to query. This involves two simple steps:

1. Register the `students` DataFrame as a table with the name `"students"` (or any other name):

   ```
   students.registerTempTable("students")
   ```

2. Query it using regular SQL:

   ```
   val dfFilteredBySQL=sqlContext.sql("select * from students where
   studentName!='' order by email desc")
   ```

   ```
   dfFilteredBySQL.show(7)
   ```

id	studentName	phone	email
87	Selma	1-601-330-4409	vulputate.velit@p
96	Channing	1-984-118-7533	viverra.Donec.tem
4	Belle	1-246-894-6340	vitae.aliquet.nec
78	Finn	1-213-781-6969	vestibulum.massa@
53	Kasper	1-155-575-9346	velit.eget@pedeCu
63	Dylan	1-417-943-8961	vehicula.aliquet@
35	Cadman	1-443-642-5919	ut.lacus@adipisci

The lifetime of the temporary table is tied to the life of the `SQLContext` that was used to create the DataFrame.

Joining two DataFrames

Now that we have seen how to register a DataFrame as a table, let's see how to perform SQL-like join operations on DataFrames.

Inner join

An inner join is the default join and it just gives those results that are matching on both DataFrames when a condition is given:

```
val students1=sqlContext.csvFile(filePath="StudentPrep1.csv",
useHeader=true, delimiter='|')
```

```
val students2=sqlContext.csvFile(filePath="StudentPrep2.csv",
useHeader=true, delimiter='|')
```

```
val studentsJoin=students1.join(students2, students1("id")===students2("
id"))
```

```
studentsJoin.show(studentsJoin.count.toInt)
```

The output is as follows:

```
+--+------------+------------------+-----------------+--+-------------------+------------------+-----------------+
|id|studentName|            phone|            email|id|       studentName|            phone|            email|
+--+------------+------------------+-----------------+--+-------------------+------------------+-----------------+
| 1|       Burke|1-300-746-8446|ullamcorper.velit...| 1|BurkeDifferentName|1-300-746-8446|ullamcorper.velit...|
| 2|       Kamal|1-668-571-5046|pede.Suspendisse@...| 2|KamalDifferentName|1-668-571-5046|pede.Suspendisse@...|
| 3|        Olga|1-956-311-1686|Aenean.eget.metus...| 3|              Olga|1-956-311-1686|Aenean.eget.metus...|
| 4|       Belle|1-246-894-6340|vitae.aliquet.nec...| 4|BelleDifferentName|1-246-894-6340|vitae.aliquet.nec...|
| 5|      Trevor|1-300-527-4967|dapibus.id@acturp...| 5|            Trevor|1-300-527-4967|dapibusDifferentE...|
| 6|      Laurel|1-691-379-9921|adipiscing@consec...| 6|LaurelInvalidPhone|      000000000|adipiscing@consec...|
| 7|        Sara|1-608-140-1995|Donec.nibh@enimEt...| 7|              Sara|1-608-140-1995|Donec.nibh@enimEt...|
| 8|      Kaseem|1-881-586-2689|cursus.et.magna@e...| 8|            Kaseem|1-881-586-2689|cursus.et.magna@e...|
| 9|         Lev|1-916-367-5608|Vivamus.nisi@ipsu...| 9|               Lev|1-916-367-5608|Vivamus.nisi@ipsu...|
|10|        Maya|1-271-683-2698|accumsan.convalli...|10|              Maya|1-271-683-2698|accumsan.convalli...|
+--+------------+------------------+-----------------+--+-------------------+------------------+-----------------+
```

Right outer join

A right outer join shows all the additional unmatched rows that are available in the right-hand-side DataFrame. We can see from the following output that the entry with ID 999 from the right- hand-side DataFrame is now shown:

```
val studentsRightOuterJoin=students1.join(students2, students1("id")===st
udents2("id"), "right_outer")
```

```
studentsRightOuterJoin.show(studentsRightOuterJoin.count.toInt)
```

```
+----+------------+------------------+-----------------+---+-------------------+------------------+-----------------+
|  id|studentName|            phone|            email| id|       studentName|            phone|            email|
+----+------------+------------------+-----------------+---+-------------------+------------------+-----------------+
|   1|       Burke|1-300-746-8446|ullamcorper.velit...|  1|BurkeDifferentName|1-300-746-8446|ullamcorper.velit...|
|   2|       Kamal|1-668-571-5046|pede.Suspendisse@...|  2|KamalDifferentName|1-668-571-5046|pede.Suspendisse@...|
|   3|        Olga|1-956-311-1686|Aenean.eget.metus...|  3|              Olga|1-956-311-1686|Aenean.eget.metus...|
|   4|       Belle|1-246-894-6340|vitae.aliquet.nec...|  4|BelleDifferentName|1-246-894-6340|vitae.aliquet.nec...|
|   5|      Trevor|1-300-527-4967|dapibus.id@acturp...|  5|            Trevor|1-300-527-4967|dapibusDifferentE...|
|   6|      Laurel|1-691-379-9921|adipiscing@consec...|  6|LaurelInvalidPhone|      000000000|adipiscing@consec...|
|   7|        Sara|1-608-140-1995|Donec.nibh@enimEt...|  7|              Sara|1-608-140-1995|Donec.nibh@enimEt...|
|   8|      Kaseem|1-881-586-2689|cursus.et.magna@e...|  8|            Kaseem|1-881-586-2689|cursus.et.magna@e...|
|   9|         Lev|1-916-367-5608|Vivamus.nisi@ipsu...|  9|               Lev|1-916-367-5608|Vivamus.nisi@ipsu...|
|  10|        Maya|1-271-683-2698|accumsan.convalli...| 10|              Maya|1-271-683-2698|accumsan.convalli...|
|null|        null|              null|             null|999|LevUniqueToSecondRDD|1-916-367-5608|Vivamus.nisi@ipsu...|
+----+------------+------------------+-----------------+---+-------------------+------------------+-----------------+
```

Left outer join

Similar to a right outer join, a left outer join returns not only the matching rows, but also the additional unmatched rows of the left-hand-side DataFrame:

```
val studentsLeftOuterJoin=students1.join(students2, students1("id")===st
udents2("id"), "left_outer")
```

```
studentsLeftOuterJoin.show(studentsLeftOuterJoin.count.toInt)
```

Saving the DataFrame as a file

As the next step, let's save a DataFrame in a file store. The `load` function, which we used in an earlier recipe, has a similar-looking counterpart called `save`.

This involves two steps:

1. Create a map containing the various options that you would like the `save` method to use. In this case, we specify the filename and ask it to have a header:

    ```
    val options=Map("header"->"true", "path"->"ModifiedStudent.csv")
    ```

    To keep it interesting, let's choose column names from the source DataFrame. In this example, we pick the `studentName` and `email` columns and change the `studentName` column's name to just `name`.

    ```
    val copyOfStudents=students.select(students("studentName").
    as("name"), students("email"))
    ```

2. Finally, save this new DataFrame with the headers in a file named `ModifiedStudent.csv`:

    ```
    copyOfStudents.save("com.databricks.spark.csv", SaveMode.
    Overwrite, options)
    ```

The second argument is a little interesting. We can choose `Overwrite` (as we did here), `Append`, `Ignore`, or `ErrorIfExists`. `Overwrite`— as the name implies—overwrites the file if it already exists, `Ignore` ignores writing if the file exists, `ErrorIfExists` complains for pre-existence of the file, and `Append` continues writing from the last edit location. Throwing an error is the default behavior.

The output of the `save` method looks like this:

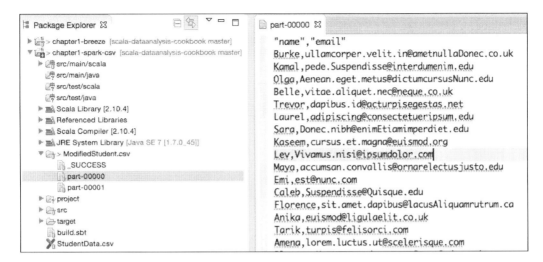

Creating a DataFrame from Scala case classes

In this recipe, we'll see how to create a new DataFrame from Scala case classes.

> The code for this recipe can be found at `https://github.com/arunma/ScalaDataAnalysisCookbook/blob/master/chapter1-spark-csv/src/main/scala/com/packt/scaladata/spark/csv/DataFrameFromCaseClasses.scala`.

How to do it...

1. We create a new entity called `Employee` with the `id` and `name` fields, like this:

```
case class Employee(id:Int, name:String)
```

Similar to the previous recipe, we create `SparkContext` and `SQLContext`.

```
val conf = new SparkConf().setAppName("colRowDataFrame").
setMaster("local[2]")


//Initialize Spark context with Spark configuration.  This is the
core entry point to do anything with Spark

val sc = new SparkContext(conf)
```

```
//The easiest way to query data in Spark is to use SQL queries.
val sqlContext=new SQLContext(sc)
```

2. We can source these employee objects from a variety of sources, such as an RDBMS data source, but for the sake of this example, we construct a list of employees, as follows:

```
val listOfEmployees =List(Employee(1,"Arun"), Employee(2,
"Jason"), Employee (3, "Abhi"))
```

3. The next step is to pass the `listOfEmployees` to the `createDataFrame` function of `SQLContext`. That's it! We now have a DataFrame. When we try to print the schema using the `printSchema` method of the DataFrame, we will see that the DataFrame has two columns, with names `id` and `name`, as defined in the `case` class:

```
//Pass in the Employees into the `createDataFrame` function.
val empFrame=sqlContext.createDataFrame(listOfEmployees)
empFrame.printSchema
```

Output:

```
root
 |-- id: integer (nullable = false)
 |-- name: string (nullable = true)
```

As you might have guessed, the schema of the DataFrame is inferenced from the case class using reflection.

4. We can get a different name for the DataFrame—other than the names specified in the `case` class—using the `withColumnRenamed` function, as shown here:

```
val empFrameWithRenamedColumns=sqlContext.createDataFrame(listOf
Employees).withColumnRenamed("id", "empId")


empFrameWithRenamedColumns.printSchema
```

Output:

```
root
 |-- empId: integer (nullable = false)
 |-- name: string (nullable = true)
```

5. Let's query the DataFrame using Spark's first-class SQL support. Before that, however, we'll have to register the DataFrame as a table. The `registerTempTable`, as we saw in the previous recipe, helps us achieve this. With the following command, we will have registered the DataFrame as a table by name `"employeeTable"`

```
"employeeTable"
```

```
empFrameWithRenamedColumns.registerTempTable("employeeTable")
```

6. Now, for the actual query. Let's arrange the DataFrame in descending order of names:

```
val sortedByNameEmployees=sqlContext.sql("select * from
employeeTable order by name desc")
```

```
sortedByNameEmployees.show()
```

Output:

```
+-----+-----+
|empId| name|
+-----+-----+
|    2|Jason|
|    1| Arun|
|    3| Abhi|
+-----+-----+
```

How it works...

The `createDataFrame` function accepts a sequence of `scala.Product`. Scala case classes extend from `Product`, and therefore it fits in the budget. That said, we can actually use a sequence of tuples to create a DataFrame, since tuples implement `Product` too:

```
val mobiles=sqlContext.createDataFrame(Seq((1,"Android"), (2, "iPhone")))
  mobiles.printSchema
  mobiles.show()
```

Output:

```
//Schema
root
|-- _1: integer (nullable = false)
|-- _2: string (nullable = true)
```

```
//Data
+--+-------+
|_1|    _2|
+--+-------+
| 1|Android|
| 2| iPhone|
+--+-------+
```

Of course, you can rename the column using `withColumnRenamed`.

3

Loading and Preparing Data – DataFrame

In this chapter, we will cover the following recipes:

- ▶ Loading more than 22 features into classes
- ▶ Loading JSON into DataFrames
- ▶ Storing data as Parquet files
- ▶ Using the Avro data model in Parquet
- ▶ Loading from RDBMS
- ▶ Preparing data in DataFrames

Introduction

In previous chapters, we saw how to import data from a CSV file to Breeze and Spark DataFrames. However, almost all the time, the source data that is to be analyzed is available in a variety of source formats. Spark, with its DataFrame API, provides a uniform API that can be used to represent any source (or multiple sources). In this chapter, we'll focus on the various input formats that we can load from in Spark. Towards the end of this chapter, we'll also briefly see some data preparation recipes.

Loading more than 22 features into classes

Case classes have an inherent limitation. They can hold only 22 attributes—Catch 22, if you will. While a reasonable percentage of datasets would fit in that budget, in many cases, the limitation of 22 features in a dataset is a huge turnoff. In this recipe, we'll take a sample `Student` dataset (`http://archive.ics.uci.edu/ml/datasets/Student+Performance`), which has 33 features, and we'll see how we can work around this.

 The 22-field limit is resolved in Scala version 2.11. However, Spark 1.4 uses Scala 2.10.

How to do it...

Case classes in Scala cannot go beyond encapsulating 22 fields because the companion classes that are generated (during compilation) for these case classes cannot find the matching `FunctionN` and `TupleN` classes. Let's take the example of the `Employee` case class that we created in *Chapter 2, Getting Started with Apache Spark DataFrames*:

```
case class Employee(id:Int, name:String)
```

When we look at its decompiled companion object, we notice that for the two constructor parameters of the case class, the companion class uses `Tuple2` and `AbstractFunction2` in its `unapply` method, the method that gets invoked when we pattern-match against a case class. The problem we face is that the Scala library has objects only until `Tuple22` and `Function22` (probably because outside the data analysis world, having an entity object with 10 fields is not a great idea). However, there is a simple yet powerful workaround, and we will be seeing it in this recipe.

```
Employee$.class

  package com.packt.scaladata.spark.csv;

*import scala.None.;

  public final class Employee$ extends AbstractFunction2<Object, String, Employee>
    implements Serializable
  {
    public static final  MODULE$;

    static
    {
      new ();
    }

    public final String toString()
    {
10     return "Employee"; }
10   public Employee apply(int id, String name) { return new Employee(id, name); }
10   public Option<Tuple2<Object, String>> unapply(Employee x$0) { return x$0 == null ? None..MODULE$ : new Some(new Tuple2(BoxesR
10   private Object readResolve() { return MODULE$; }
10   private Employee$() { MODULE$ = this; }

  }
```

We saw in *Chapter 2, Getting Started with Apache Spark DataFrames* (in the *Creating a DataFrame from CSV* recipe), that the requirement for creating a DataFrame using `SQLContext.createDataFrame` from a collection of classes is that the class must extend `scala.Product`. So, what we intend to do is write our own class that extends from `scala.Product`.

This recipe consists of four steps:

1. Creating `SQLContext` from `SparkContext` and `Config`.
2. Creating a `Student` class that extends `Product` and overrides the necessary functions.
3. Constructing an RDD of the `Student` classes from the sample dataset (`student-mat.csv`).
4. Creating a DataFrame from the RDD, followed by printing the schema and sampling the data.

> Refer to the *How it works...* section of this recipe for a basic introduction to RDD.
>
> The code for this recipe can be found at `https://github.com/arunma/ScalaDataAnalysisCookbook/tree/master/chapter3-data-loading`.

Let's now cover these steps in detail:

1. Creating `SQLContext`: As with our recipes from the previous chapter, we construct `SparkContext` from `SparkConfig` and then create an `SQLContext` from `SparkContext`:

```
val conf=new
SparkConf().setAppName("DataWith33Atts").setMaster("local[2]")
val sc=new SparkContext(conf)
val sqlContext=new SQLContext(sc)
```

2. Creating the `Student` class: Our next step is to create a simple Scala class that declares its constructor parameters, and make it extend `Product`.

   Making a class extend `Product` requires us to override two functions from `scala.Product` and one function from `scala.Equals` (which `scala.Product`, in turn, extends from). The implementation of each of these functions is pretty straightforward.

> Refer to the API docs of `Product` (`http://www.scala-lang.org/api/2.10.4/index.html#scala.Product`) and `Equals` (`http://www.scala-lang.org/api/2.10.4/index.html#scala.Equals`) for more details.

Firstly, let's make our `Student` class declare its fields and extend `Product`:

```
class Student (school:String,
      sex:String,
      age:Int,
      address:String,
      famsize:String,
      pstatus:String,
      medu:Int,
      fedu:Int,
      mjob:String,
      fjob:String,
      reason:String,
      guardian:String,
      traveltime:Int,
      studytime:Int,
      failures:Int,
      schoolsup:String,
      famsup:String,
      paid:String,
      activities:String,
      nursery:String,
      higher:String,
      internet:String,
      romantic:String,
      famrel:Int,
      freetime:Int,
      goout:Int,
      dalc:Int,
      walc:Int,
      health:Int,
      absences:Int,
      g1:Int,
      g2:Int,
      g3:Int) extends Product{
```

Next, let's implement these three functions after briefly looking at what they are expected to do:

- ❑ `productArity():Int`: This returns the size of the attributes. In our case, it's 33. So, our implementation looks like this:

  ```
  override def productArity: Int = 33
  ```

❏ `productElement(n:Int):Any`: Given an index, this returns the attribute. As protection, we also have a default case, which throws an `IndexOutOfBoundsException` exception:

```
@throws(classOf[IndexOutOfBoundsException])
  override def productElement(n: Int): Any = n match {
    case 0 => school
    case 1 => sex
    case 2 => age
    case 3 => address
    case 4 => famsize
    case 5 => pstatus
    case 6 => medu
    case 7 => fedu
    case 8 => mjob
    case 9 => fjob
    case 10 => reason
    case 11 => guardian
    case 12 => traveltime
    case 13 => studytime
    case 14 => failures
    case 15 => schoolsup
    case 16 => famsup
    case 17 -> paid
    case 18 => activities
    case 19 => nursery
    case 20 => higher
    case 21 => internet
    case 22 => romantic
    case 23 => famrel
    case 24 => freetime
    case 25 => goout
    case 26 => dalc
    case 27 => walc
    case 28 => health
    case 29 => absences
    case 30 => g1
    case 31 => g2
    case 32 => g3
    case _ => throw new
IndexOutOfBoundsException(n.toString())
  }
```

- ☐ `canEqual (that:Any):Boolean`: This is the last of the three functions, and it serves as a boundary condition when an equality check is being done against this class:

```
override def canEqual(that: Any): Boolean =
that.isInstanceOf[Student]
```

3. Constructing an RDD of students from the `student-mat.csv` file: Now that we have our `Student` class ready, let's convert the `"student-mat.csv"` input file into a DataFrame:

```
val rddOfStudents=convertCSVToStudents("student-mat.csv", sc)

def convertCSVToStudents(filePath: String, sc: SparkContext):
RDD[Student] = {
    val rddOfStudents: RDD[Student] = sc.textFile(filePath).
flatMap(eachLine => Student(eachLine))
    rddOfStudents
  }
```

As you can see, we have an `apply` method for `Student` that accepts a `String` and returns an `Option[Student]`. We use `flatMap` to filter out `None` thereby resulting in `RDD[Student]`.

Let's look at the `Student` companion object's `apply` function. It's a very simple function that takes a `String`, splits it based on semicolons into an array, and then passes the parameters to the `Student`'s constructor. The method returns `None` if there is an error:

```
object Student {

    def apply(str: String): Option[Student] = {
        val paramArray = str.split(";").map(param =>
param.replaceAll("\"", "")) //Few values have extra double
quotes around it
            Try(
              new Student(paramArray(0),
                paramArray(1),
                paramArray(2).toInt,
                paramArray(3),
                paramArray(4),
                paramArray(5),
                paramArray(6).toInt,
                paramArray(7).toInt,
                paramArray(8),
```

```
            paramArray(9),
            paramArray(10),
            paramArray(11),
            paramArray(12).toInt,
            paramArray(13).toInt,
            paramArray(14).toInt,
            paramArray(15),
            paramArray(16),
            paramArray(17),
            paramArray(18),
            paramArray(19),
            paramArray(20),
            paramArray(21),
            paramArray(22),
            paramArray(23).toInt,
            paramArray(24).toInt,
            paramArray(25).toInt,
            paramArray(26).toInt,
            paramArray(27).toInt,
            paramArray(28).toInt,
            paramArray(29).toInt,
            paramArray(30).toInt,
            paramArray(31).toInt,
            paramArray(32).toInt)) match {
            case Success(student) => Some(student)
            case Failure(throwable) => {
              println (throwable.getMessage())
              None
            }
          }
        }
      }
```

4. Creating a DataFrame, printing the schema, and sampling: Finally, we create
    a DataFrame from RDD[Student]. Converting an RDD[T] to a DataFrame
    of the same type is just a matter of calling the toDF() function. You are
    required to import sqlContext.implicits._. Optionally, you can use
    the createDataFrame method of sqlContext too.

  The toDF() function is overloaded so as to accept custom
column names while converting to a DataFrame.

We then print the schema using the DataFrame's `printSchema()` method and sample data for confirmation using the `show()` method:

```
import sqlContext.implicits._

//Create DataFrame
val studentDFrame = rddOfStudents.toDF()
  studentDFrame.printSchema()
  studentDFrame.show()
```

The following is the output of the preceding code:

```
root
 |-- school: string (nullable = true)
 |-- sex: string (nullable = true)
 |-- age: integer (nullable = false)
 |-- address: string (nullable = true)
 |-- famsize: string (nullable = true)
 |-- pstatus: string (nullable = true)
 |-- medu: integer (nullable = false)
 |-- fedu: integer (nullable = false)
 |-- mjob: string (nullable = true)
 |-- fjob: string (nullable = true)
 |-- reason: string (nullable = true)
 |-- guardian: string (nullable = true)
 |-- traveltime: integer (nullable = false)
 |-- studytime: integer (nullable = false)
 |-- failures: integer (nullable = false)
 |-- schoolsup: string (nullable = true)
 |-- famsup: string (nullable = true)
 |-- paid: string (nullable = true)
 |-- activities: string (nullable = true)
 |-- nursery: string (nullable = true)
 |-- higher: string (nullable = true)
 |-- internet: string (nullable = true)
 |-- romantic: string (nullable = true)
 |-- famrel: integer (nullable = false)
 |-- freetime: integer (nullable = false)
 |-- goout: integer (nullable = false)
 |-- dalc: integer (nullable = false)
 |-- walc: integer (nullable = false)
 |-- health: integer (nullable = false)
 |-- absences: integer (nullable = false)
```

```
|-- g1: integer (nullable = false)
|-- g2: integer (nullable = false)
|-- g3: integer (nullable = false)
```

```
[info] root
[info]  |-- school: string (nullable = true)
[info]  |-- sex: string (nullable = true)
[info]  |-- age: integer (nullable = false)
[info]  |-- address: string (nullable = true)
[info]  |-- famsize: string (nullable = true)
[info]  |-- pstatus: string (nullable = true)
[info]  |-- medu: integer (nullable = false)
[info]  |-- fedu: integer (nullable = false)
[info]  |-- mjob: string (nullable = true)
[info]  |-- fjob: string (nullable = true)
[info]  |-- reason: string (nullable = true)
[info]  |-- guardian: string (nullable = true)
[info]  |-- traveltime: integer (nullable = false)
[info]  |-- studytime: integer (nullable = false)
[info]  |-- failures: integer (nullable = false)
[info]  |-- schoolsup: string (nullable = true)
[info]  |-- famsup: string (nullable = true)
[info]  |-- paid: string (nullable = true)
[info]  |-- activities: string (nullable = true)
[info]  |-- nursery: string (nullable = true)
[info]  |-- higher: string (nullable = true)
[info]  |-- internet: string (nullable = true)
[info]  |-- romantic: string (nullable = true)
[info]  |-- famrel: integer (nullable = false)
[info]  |-- freetime: integer (nullable = false)
[info]  |-- goout: integer (nullable = false)
[info]  |-- dalc: integer (nullable = false)
[info]  |-- walc: integer (nullable = false)
[info]  |-- health: integer (nullable = false)
[info]  |-- absences: integer (nullable = false)
[info]  |-- g1: integer (nullable = false)
[info]  |-- g2: integer (nullable = false)
[info]  |-- g3: integer (nullable = false)
```

How it works...

The foundation of Spark is the **Resilient Distributed Dataset** (**RDD**). From a programmer's perspective, the composability of RDDs just like a regular Scala collection is a huge advantage. An RDD wraps three vital (and two subsidiary) pieces of information that help in the reconstruction of data. This enables fault tolerance. The other major advantage is that while RDDs can be composed into hugely complex graphs using RDD operations, the entire flow of data itself is not very difficult to reason with.

Other than optional optimization attributes (such as data location), at its core, RDD just wraps three vital pieces of information:

- The dependent/parent RDD (empty if not available)
- The number of partitions
- The function that needs to be applied to each element of the RDD

In simple words, RDDs are just collections of data elements that can exist in the memory or on the disk. These data elements must be serializable in order to have the capability to be moved across multiple machines (or be serialized on the disk). The number of partitions or blocks of data is primarily determined by the source of the input data (say, if the data is in HDFS, then each block would translate to a single partition), but there are also other ways of playing around with the number of partitions.

So, the number of partitions could be any of these:

- Dictated by the input data itself, for example, the number of blocks in the case of reading files from HDFS
- The number set by the `spark.default.parallelism` parameter (set while starting the cluster)
- The number set by calling `repartition` or `coalesce` on the RDD itself

Note that currently, for all our recipes, we are running our Spark application in the self-contained single JVM mode. While the programs work just fine, we are not yet exploiting the distributed nature of the RDDs. In *Chapter 6, Scaling Up*, we'll explore how to bundle and deploy our Spark application on a variety of cluster managers: YARN, Spark standalone clusters, and Mesos.

There's more...

In the previous chapter, we created a DataFrame from a `List` of `Employee` case classes:

```
val listOfEmployees =List(Employee(1,"Arun"), Employee(2, "Jason"),
Employee (3, "Abhi"))

val empFrame=sqlContext.createDataFrame(listOfEmployees)
```

However, in this recipe, we loaded a file, converted them to `RDD[String]`, transformed them into case classes, and finally converted them into a DataFrame.

There are subtle, yet powerful, differences in these approaches. In the first approach (converting a `List` of case classes into a DataFrame), we have the entire collection in the memory of the driver (we'll look at drivers and workers in *Chapter 6, Scaling Up*). Except for playing around with Spark, for all practical purposes, we don't have our dataset as a collection of case classes. We generally have it as a text file or read from a database. Also, requiring to hold the entire collection in a single machine before converting it into a distributed dataset (RDD) will unfold itself as a memory issue.

In this recipe, we loaded an HDFS distributed file as an `RDD[String]` that is distributed across a cluster of worker nodes, and then serialized each `String` into a case class, making the `RDD[String]` into an `RDD[Student]`. So, each worker node that holds some partitions of the dataset handles the computation around transforming `RDD[String]` to the case class, while making the resulting dataset conform to a fixed schema enforced by the case class itself. Since the computation and the data itself are distributed, we don't need to worry about a single machine requiring a lot of memory to store the entire dataset.

Loading JSON into DataFrames

JSON has become the most common text-based data representation format these days. In this recipe, we'll see how to load data represented as JSON into our DataFrame. To make it more interesting, let's have our JSON in HDFS instead of our local filesystem.

The **Hadoop Distributed File System** (**HDFS**) is a highly distributed filesystem that is both scalable and fault tolerant. It is a critical part of the Hadoop ecosystem and is inspired by the Google File System paper (`http://research.google.com/archive/gfs.html`). More details about the architecture and communication protocols on HDFS can be found at `http://hadoop.apache.org/docs/r1.2.1/hdfs_design.html`.

How to do it...

In this recipe, we'll see three subrecipes:

▶   How to create a schema-inferenced DataFrame from JSON using `sqlContext.jsonFile`

▶   Alternatively, if we prefer to preprocess the input file before parsing it into JSON, we'll parse the input file as text and convert it into JSON using `sqlContext.jsonRDD`

▶   Finally, we'll take a look at declaring an explicit schema and using it to create a `DataFrame`

Reading a JSON file using SQLContext.jsonFile

This recipe consists of three steps:

1. Storing our `json` (`profiles.json`) in HDFS: A copy of the data file is added to our project repository, and it can be downloaded from `https://github.com/arunma/ScalaDataAnalysisCookbook/blob/master/chapter3-data-loading/profiles.json`:

    ```
    hadoop fs -mkdir -p /data/scalada
    hadoop fs -put profiles.json /data/scalada/profiles.json
    hadoop fs -ls /data/scalada
    -rw-r--r--   1 Gabriel supergroup      176948 2015-05-16 22:13 /
    data/scalada/profiles.json
    ```

The following screenshot shows the HDFS file explorer available at `http://localhost:50070`, which confirms that our upload is successful:

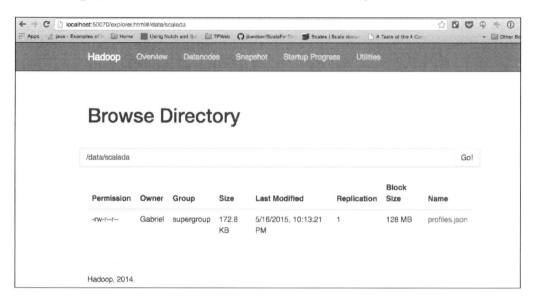

2. Creating contexts: We do the regular stuff—create `SparkConfig`, `SparkContext`, and then `SQLContext`:

```
val conf = new
SparkConf().setAppName("DataFromJSON").setMaster("local[2]")

    val sc = new SparkContext(conf)

    val sqlContext = new SQLContext(sc)
```

3. Creating a DataFrame from JSON: In this step, we use the `jsonFile` function of `SQLContext` to create a DataFrame. This is very similar to the `sqlContext.csvFile` function that we used in *Chapter 2, Getting Started with Apache Spark DataFrames*. There's just one thing that we need to watch out here; our `.json` should be formatted as one line per record. It is unusual to store JSON as one line per record considering that it is a structured format, but the `jsonFile` function treats every single line as one record, failing to do which it would throw a `scala.MatchError` error while parsing:

```
  val
dFrame=sqlContext.jsonFile("hdfs://localhost:9000/data/scalada/
profiles.json")
```

That's it! We are done! Let's just print the schema and sample the data:

```
dFrame.printSchema()
dFrame.show()
```

The following screenshot shows the schema that is inferenced from the JSON file. Note that now the age is resolved as long and tags are resolved as an array of string, as you can see here:

```
[info] root
[info]  |-- _id: string (nullable = true)
[info]  |-- about: string (nullable = true)
[info]  |-- address: string (nullable = true)
[info]  |-- age: long (nullable = true)
[info]  |-- company: string (nullable = true)
[info]  |-- email: string (nullable = true)
[info]  |-- eyeColor: string (nullable = true)
[info]  |-- favoriteFruit: string (nullable = true)
[info]  |-- gender: string (nullable = true)
[info]  |-- name: string (nullable = true)
[info]  |-- phone: string (nullable = true)
[info]  |-- registered: string (nullable = true)
[info]  |-- tags: array (nullable = true)
[info]  |      |-- element: string (containsNull = true)
```

The next screenshot shows you a sample of the dataset:

```
+--------------------+--------------------+--------------------+---+---------+--------------------+--------+-------------+------+
|                 _id|               about|             address|age|  company|               email|eyeColor|favoriteFruit|gender|
+--------------------+--------------------+--------------------+---+---------+--------------------+--------+-------------+------+
|55578ccb0cc5b350d...|Eu excepteur esse...|694 Oriental Cour...| 30|  ENDIPIN|tracynguyen@endip...|   brown|        apple|female|
|55578ccb6975c4e2a...|Proident exercita...|267 Amber Street,...| 23|  WARETEL|leannagarrett@war...|   brown|   strawberry|female|
|55578ccb33399a615...|Aute proident Lor...|243 Bridgewater S...| 24| IMPERIUM|blairwhite@imperi...|   brown|       banana|  male|
|55578ccb0f1d5ab09...|Officia cillum nu...|647 Loring Avenue...| 24|  BEADZZA|andrearay@beadzza...|    blue|        apple|female|
|55578ccb591a45d4e...|Sit fugiat mollit...|721 Bijou Avenue,...| 27|  AUSTECH|penningtongilbert...|   green|        apple|  male|
|55578ccb9f0cd20c4...|Minim do eiusmod ...|694 Llama Court, ...| 21|  PYRAMIA|shelleyburns@pyra...|   green|       banana|female|
|55578ccb8d0accc28...|Qui proident ulla...|498 Perry Terrace...| 40|  EDECINE|nicolefigueroa@ed...|   green|        apple|female|
|55578ccbd682cca21...|Labore exercitati...|243 Stillwell Ave...| 32|SINGAVERA|galealvarado@sing...|    blue|       banana|female|
|55578ccb0d9025ddd...|Velit cillum Lore...|649 Beard Street,...| 36|FURNITECH|melindaparker@fur...|    blue|   strawberry|female|
|55578ccb5be70de0d...|Laborum tempor mi...|972 Marconi Place...| 36|   DIGIAL|byerscarson@digia...|    blue|        apple|  male|
|55578ccbc5a1050a5...|Duis fugiat Lorem...|483 Hanson Place,...| 31| ASSURITY|kristiemckinney@a...|   green|       banana|female|
|55578ccb07fa02369...|Consequat fugiat ...|540 Woodpoint Roa...| 40|MICROLUXE|salazarburks@micr...|   brown|   strawberry|  male|
|55578ccb809e55bf0...|Lorem culpa Lorem...|442 Ainslie Stree...| 32| VIOCULAR|hopkinspatterson@...|   green|        apple|  male|
|55578ccb204ff8ee6...|Qui ad cillum mag...|444 Argyle Road, ...| 23|    IMKAN|maysrosario@imkan...|   green|        apple|  male|
|55578ccb4b062fc61...|Duis ex velit dui...|571 Sunnyside Ave...| 38|   HELIXO|atkinshancock@hel...|    blue|   strawberry|  male|
|55578ccba5ff361a9...|Et magna laboris ...|385 Meeker Avenue...| 40|  SLOFAST|edwinarobertson@s...|    blue|   strawberry|female|
|55578ccb386940ac3...|Labore sit mollit...|936 Cheever Place...| 37| FLEETMIX|elsienoel@fleetmi...|    blue|        apple|female|
|55578ccbfc41ff7fe...|Consequat eiusmod...|406 Lake Place, M...| 36|EVENTAGE|mirandamarsh@even...|   green|        apple|female|
|55578ccbfa6b6c300...|Duis fugiat conse...|364 Metropolitan ...| 31|  BALOOBA|sharronmcconnell@...|   brown|        apple|female|
|55578ccbdd6650d81...|Consequat et magn...|113 Applegate Cou...| 29|    EURON|mcdowellwelch@eur...|    blue|   strawberry|  male|
+--------------------+--------------------+--------------------+---+---------+--------------------+--------+-------------+------+
```

Reading a text file and converting it to JSON RDD

In the previous section, we saw how we can directly import a `textFile` containing JSON records as a DataFrame using `sqlContext.jsonFile`. Now, we'll see an alternate approach, wherein we construct an `RDD[String]` from the same `profiles.json` file and then convert them into a DataFrame. This has a distinct advantage from the previous approach—we can have more control over the schema instead of relying on the one that is inferenced:

```
val strRDD=sc.textFile("hdfs://localhost:9000/data/scalada/profiles.json")

val jsonDf=sqlContext.jsonRDD(strRDD)

jsonDf.printSchema()
```

The following is the output of the preceding command:

```
[info] root
[info]  |-- _id: string (nullable = true)
[info]  |-- about: string (nullable = true)
[info]  |-- address: string (nullable = true)
[info]  |-- age: long (nullable = true)
[info]  |-- company: string (nullable = true)
[info]  |-- email: string (nullable = true)
[info]  |-- eyeColor: string (nullable = true)
[info]  |-- favoriteFruit: string (nullable = true)
[info]  |-- gender: string (nullable = true)
[info]  |-- name: string (nullable = true)
[info]  |-- phone: string (nullable = true)
[info]  |-- registered: string (nullable = true)
[info]  |-- tags: array (nullable = true)
[info]  |      |-- element: string (containsNull = true)
```

Explicitly specifying your schema

Using `jsonRDD` and letting it resolve the schema by itself is clean and simple. However, it gives less control over the types; for example, the `age` field must be `Integer` and not `Long`. Similarly, the `registered` column is inferenced as a `String` while it is actually a `TimeStamp`. In order to achieve this, let's go ahead and declare our own schema. The way we do this is by constructing a `StructType` and `StructField`:

```
val profilesSchema = StructType(
    Seq(
    StructField("_id",StringType, true),
  StructField("about",StringType, true),
  StructField("address",StringType, true),
  StructField("age",IntegerType, true),
```

```
StructField("company",StringType, true),

StructField("email",StringType, true),

StructField("eyeColor",StringType, true),

StructField("favoriteFruit",StringType, true),

StructField("gender",StringType, true),

StructField("name",StringType, true),

StructField("phone",StringType, true),

StructField("registered",TimestampType, true),

StructField("tags",ArrayType(StringType), true)

   )

)


val jsonDfWithSchema=sqlContext.jsonRDD(strRDD, profilesSchema)


jsonDfWithSchema.printSchema() //Has timestamp

jsonDfWithSchema.show()
```

 Another advantage of specifying our own schema is that all the columns need not be specified in the `StructType`. We just need to specify the columns that we are interested in, and only those columns will be available in the target DataFrame. Also, any column that is declared in the schema but is not available in the dataset will be filled in with null values.

The following is the output.

We can see that the `registered` feature is considered to have a `timestamp` data type and `age` as `integer`:

```
[info] root
[info]  |-- id: string (nullable = true)
[info]  |-- about: string (nullable = true)
[info]  |-- address: string (nullable = true)
[info]  |-- age: integer (nullable = true)
[info]  |-- company: string (nullable = true)
[info]  |-- email: string (nullable = true)
[info]  |-- eyeColor: string (nullable = true)
[info]  |-- favoriteFruit: string (nullable = true)
[info]  |-- gender: string (nullable = true)
[info]  |-- name: string (nullable = true)
[info]  |-- phone: string (nullable = true)
[info]  |-- registered: timestamp (nullable = true)
[info]  |-- tags: array (nullable = true)
[info]  |    |-- element: string (containsNull = true)
```

Finally, just for kicks, let's fire a filter query based on the timestamp. This involves three steps:

1. Register the schema as a temporary table for querying, as has been done several times in previous recipes. The following line of code registers a table by the name of `profilesTable`:

```
jsonRDDWithSchema.registerTempTable("profilesTable")
```

2. Let's fire away our filter query. The following query returns all profiles that have been registered after August 26, 2014. Since the registered field is a timestamp, we require an additional minor step of casting the parameter into a `TimeStamp`:

```
val filterCount = sqlContext.sql("select * from profilesTable
where registered> CAST('2014-08-26 00:00:00' AS TIMESTAMP)").count
```

3. Let's print the count:

```
println("Filtered based on timestamp count : " + filterCount)
//106
```

There's more...

If you aren't comfortable with having the schema in the code and would like to save the schema in a file, it's just a one-liner for you:

```
import scala.reflect.io.File
import scala.io.Source
//Writes schema as JSON to file
File("profileSchema.json").writeAll(profilesSchema.json)
```

Obviously, you would want to reconstruct the schema from JSON, and that's also a one-liner:

```
val loadedSchema = DataType.fromJson(Source.fromFile("profileSchema.
json").mkString)
```

Let's check whether the `loadedSchema` and the `profileSchema` encapsulate the same schema by doing an equality check on their json:

```
println ("ProfileSchema == loadedSchema :"+(loadedSchema.
json==profilesSchema.json))
```

The output is shown as follows:

```
ProfileSchema == loadedSchema :true
```

If we would like to eyeball the `json`, we have a nice method called `prettyJson` that formats the `json`:

```
//Print loaded schema
println(loadedSchema.prettyJson)
```

The output is as follows:

```
[info] {
[info]    "type" : "struct",
[info]    "fields" : [ {
[info]      "name" : "id",
[info]      "type" : "string",
[info]      "nullable" : true,
[info]      "metadata" : { }
[info]    }, {
[info]      "name" : "about",
[info]      "type" : "string",
[info]      "nullable" : true,
[info]      "metadata" : { }
[info]    }, {
[info]      "name" : "address",
[info]      "type" : "string",
[info]      "nullable" : true,
[info]      "metadata" : { }
[info]    }, {
[info]      "name" : "age",
[info]      "type" : "integer",
[info]      "nullable" : true,
[info]      "metadata" : { }
[info]    }, {
[info]      "name" : "company",
[info]      "type" : "string",
[info]      "nullable" : true,
[info]      "metadata" : { }
[info]    }, {
[info]      "name" : "email",
[info]      "type" : "string",
[info]      "nullable" : true,
[info]      "metadata" : { }
[info]    }, {
[info]      "name" : "eyeColor",
[info]      "type" : "string",
[info]      "nullable" : true,
[info]      "metadata" : { }
[info]    }, {
[info]      "name" : "favoriteFruit",
```

Storing data as Parquet files

Parquet (`https://parquet.apache.org/`) is rapidly becoming the go-to data storage format in the world of big data because of the distinct advantages it offers:

> ▸ It has a column-based representation of data. This is better represented in a picture, as follows:

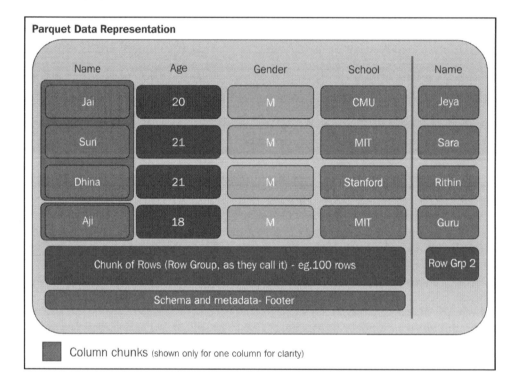

As you can see in the preceding screenshot, Parquet stores data in chunks of rows, say 100 rows. In Parquet terms, these are called **RowGroups**. Each of these RowGroups has chunks of columns inside them (or column chunks). Column chunks can hold more than a single unit of data for a particular column (as represented in the blue box in the first column). For example. **Jai, Suri,** and **Dhina** form a single chunk even though they are composed of three single units of data for **Name**.

Another unique feature is that these column chunks (groups of a single column's information) can be read independently. Let's consider the following image:

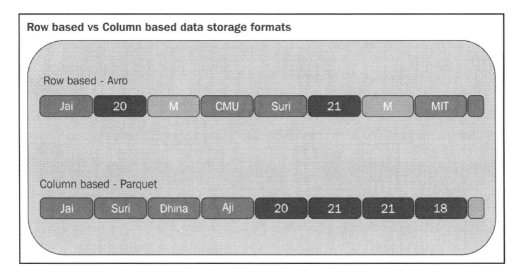

We can see that the items of column data are stored next to each other in a sequence. Since our queries are focused on just a few columns (a projection) most of the time and not on the entire table, this storage mechanism enables us to retrieve data much faster than reading the entire row data that is stored and filtering for columns. Also, with Spark's in-memory computations, the memory requirements are reduced in this way.

▶ The second advantage is that there is very little that is needed for our transition from the existing data models that we already use to represent the data. While Parquet has its own native object model, we are pretty much free to choose Avro, ProtoBuf, Thrift, and a variety of existing object models, and use an intermediate converter to serialize our data in Parquet. Most of these converters are readily available at the `Parquet-MR` project (`https://github.com/Parquet/parquet-mr`).

In this recipe, we'll cover the following steps:

1. Load a simple CSV file and convert it into a DataFrame.
2. Save it as a Parquet file.
3. Install Parquet tools.
4. Use the tools to inspect the Parquet file.
5. Enable compression for the Parquet file.

The entire code for this recipe can be found at `https://github.com/arunma/ScalaDataAnalysisCookbook/tree/master/chapter3-data-loading-parquet`.

How to do it...

Before we dive into the steps, let's briefly look at our `build.sbt` file, specifically the library dependencies and Avro settings (which we'll talk about in the following sections):

```
organization := "com.packt"

name := "chapter3-data-loading-parquet"

scalaVersion := "2.10.4"

val sparkVersion="1.4.1"

libraryDependencies ++= Seq(
  "org.apache.spark" %% "spark-core" % sparkVersion,
  "org.apache.spark" %% "spark-sql" % sparkVersion,
  "org.apache.spark" %% "spark-mllib" % sparkVersion,
  "org.apache.spark" %% "spark-hive" % sparkVersion,
  "org.apache.avro" % "avro" % "1.7.7",
  "org.apache.parquet" % "parquet-avro" % "1.8.1",
  "com.twitter" %% "chill-avro" % "0.6.0"
)

resolvers ++= Seq(
  "Apache HBase" at
"https://repository.apache.org/content/repositories/releases",
  "Typesafe repository" at
"http://repo.typesafe.com/typesafe/releases/",
  "Twitter" at "http://maven.twttr.com/"
)

fork := true

seq( sbtavro.SbtAvro.avroSettings : _*)

(stringType in avroConfig) := "String"

javaSource in sbtavro.SbtAvro.avroConfig <<= (sourceDirectory in
Compile)(_ / "java")
```

Now that we have `build.sbt` out of the way, let's go ahead and look at the code behind each of the listed steps.

Load a simple CSV file, convert it to case classes, and create a DataFrame from it

We can actually create a DataFrame directly from CSV using the `com.databricks/spark-csv` file, as we saw in *Chapter 2*, *Getting Started with Apache Spark DataFrames*, but for this recipe, we'll just tokenize the CSV and create classes from it. The input CSV has a header column. So, the conversion process involves skipping the first row.

 The class file that we will discuss in this section is the `https://github.com/arunma/ScalaDataAnalysisCookbook/blob/master/chapter3-data-loading-parquet/src/main/scala/com/packt/dataload/ParquetCaseClassMain.scala`.

There are just two interesting things that you might notice in the code:

```
sqlContext.setConf("spark.sql.parquet.binaryAsString","true")
```

Some Parquet producing systems, such as Impala, binary encode the strings. In order to work around this issue, we set the following configuration, which says that if it sees binary data, it should be treated as a string:

Instead of using `sqlContext.createDataFrame`, we just use a `toDF()` on the `RDD[Student]`. The `SQLContext.Implicits` object has a number of implicit conversions that help us convert an `RDD[T]` to a DataFrame directly. The only requirement for us, as expected, is to import the implicits:

```
import sqlContext.implicits._
```

The rest of the code is the same as we saw earlier:

```
val conf = new
SparkConf().setAppName("CaseClassToParquet").setMaster("local[2]")
  val sc = new SparkContext(conf)
  val sqlContext = new SQLContext(sc)

  //Treat binary encoded values as Strings
  sqlContext.setConf("spark.sql.parquet.binaryAsString","true")

  import sqlContext.implicits._

  //Convert each line into Student
  val rddOfStudents = convertCSVToStudents("StudentData.csv", sc)

  //Convert RDD[Student] to a Dataframe using sqlContext.implicits
  val studentDFrame = rddOfStudents.toDF()
```

The `convertCSVToStudents` method, which converts each line into a `Student` object, looks like this:

```
def convertCSVToStudents(filePath: String, sc: SparkContext):
RDD[Student] = {
    val rddOfStudents: RDD[Student]
=sc.textFile(filePath).flatMap(line => {
        val data = line.split("\\|")
        if (data(0) == "id") None else Some(Student(data(0),
data(1), data(2), data(3)))
    })
    rddOfStudents
}
```

Save it as a Parquet file

This is just a one-liner once we have the DataFrame. This can be done using either the `saveAsParquetFile` or the `save` method. If you wish to save it in a Hive table (https://hive.apache.org/), then there is also a `saveAsTable` method for you:

```
//Save DataFrame as Parquet using saveAsParquetFile
studentDFrame.saveAsParquetFile("studentPq.parquet")


//OR


//Save DataFrame as Parquet using the save method
studentDFrame.save("studentPq.parquet", "parquet",
SaveMode.Overwrite)
```

 The `save` method allows the usage of `SaveMode`, which has the following alternatives: `Append`, `ErrorIfExists`, `Ignore`, or `Overwrite`.

The `save` methods create a directory in the location that you specify (here, we simply store it in our project directory). The directory holds the files that represent the serialized data. It is not entirely human readable, but you may notice that the data of a single column is stored together.

Just as we do for the rest of the recipes, let's read the file and sample the data for confirmation:

```
//Read data for confirmation
  val pqDFrame=sqlContext.parquetFile("studentPq.parquet")
  pqDFrame.show()
```

The following is the output:

```
+--+-----------+--------------+--------------------+
|id|       name|         phone|               email|
+--+-----------+--------------+--------------------+
|51|      Baker|1-754-775-9024|enim@atortorNunc....|
|52|       Xena|1-527-990-8606|in.faucibus.orci@...|
|53|     Kasper|1-155-575-9346|velit.eget@pedeCu...|
|54|     Hannah|1-712-794-8145|Phasellus.libero....|
|55|      Reese|1-106-653-2899|aliquet.magna.a@l...|
|56|Buckminster|1-352-299-2056|cursus.Nunc.mauri...|
|57|    Richard|1-461-925-7084|fringilla.cursus@...|
|58|    Shafira|1-786-210-7819| a@magnamalesuada.ca|
|59|    Frances|1-312-680-5112|enim.consequat.pu...|
|60|        Ava|1-816-439-4739|ipsum.Phasellus.v...|
|61|     Maxine|1-422-863-3041|aliquet.molestie....|
|62|       Kirk|1-782-749-4287|fringilla@luctusv...|
|63|      Dylan|1-417-943-8961|vehicula.aliquet@...|
|64|  Francesca|1-425-876-2200|nec.euismod.in@co...|
|65|      Tiger|1-316-930-7880|nec@mollisnoncurs...|
|66|      Vance|1-268-680-0857|pellentesque@netu...|
|67|   Hermione|1-673-268-1156|eu.dolor@aauctorn...|
|68|    Candice|1-701-263-8889|sit.amet.ornare@a...||
|69|       Aiko|1-682-230-7013|turpis.vitae.puru...|
|70|     Quemby|1-380-414-6915|interdum.ligula@e...|
+--+-----------+--------------+--------------------+
```

Install Parquet tools

Other than using the `printSchema` method of the DataFrame to inspect the schema, we can use some interesting parquet tools provided as part of the parquet project to get a variety of other information.

 The `parquet-tools` is a subproject of Parquet and is available at `https://github.com/Parquet/parquet-mr/tree/master/parquet-tools`.

Since Spark 1.4.1 uses Parquet 1.6.0rc3, we'll need to download that version of the tools from the Maven repository. The executables and the JARs can be downloaded as one bundle from `https://repo1.maven.org/maven2/com/twitter/parquet-tools/1.6.0rc3/parquet-tools-1.6.0rc3-bin.tar.gz`.

Using the tools to inspect the Parquet file

Let's put the tools into action. Specifically, we'll do three things in this step:

▶ Display the schema in Parquet format

▶ Display the meta information that is stored in Parquet's footer

▸ Sample the data using `head` and `cat`

▸ **Displaying the schema**: This can be achieved by calling the `parquet-tools` command with `schema` and the `parquet` file as the parameter. As an example, let's print the schema using one of the part files:

```
bash-3.2$ parquet-tools-1.6.0rc3/parquet-tools meta part-r-00000-
20a8b58c-fe1d-43e7-b148-f874b78eb5ec.gz.parquet


message root {

  optional binary id (UTF8);

  optional binary name (UTF8);

  optional binary phone (UTF8);

  optional binary email (UTF8);

}
```

We see that the schema is indeed available in Parquet format and is derived from our case classes.

▸ **Displaying the meta information of a particular Parquet file**: As we saw earlier, meta information is stored in the footer. Let's print it to see it.

We see that the `extra` information has the schema that is specific to the data model we used. This information is used when the data is deserialized. The `meta` parameter of `parquet-tools` will help achieve this:

```
bash-3.2$  parquet-tools-1.6.0rc3/parquet-tools meta part-r-00000-
20a8b58c-fe1d-43e7-b148-f874b78eb5ec.gz.parquet

creator:      parquet-mr version 1.6.0rc3 (build
d4d5a07ec9bd262ca1e93c309f1d7d4a74ebda4c)

extra:        org.apache.spark.sql.parquet.row.metadata = {"type"
:"struct","fields":[{"name":"id","type":"string","nullable":true
,"metadata":{}},{"name":"name","type":"string","nullable":true,
[more]...


file schema: root
------------------------------------------------------------------
------------------------------------------------------------------
------------------------------------------------------------------
---
id:           OPTIONAL BINARY O:UTF8 R:0 D:1

name:         OPTIONAL BINARY O:UTF8 R:0 D:1

phone:        OPTIONAL BINARY O:UTF8 R:0 D:1
```

```
email:          OPTIONAL BINARY O:UTF8 R:0 D:1


row group 1: RC:50 TS:3516

-------------------------------------------------------------
-------------------------------------------------------------
-------------------------------------------------------------
---
id:             BINARY GZIP DO:0 FPO:4 SZ:140/326/2.33 VC:50
ENC:RLE,BIT_PACKED,PLAIN
name:           BINARY GZIP DO:0 FPO:144 SZ:313/483/1.54 VC:50
ENC:RLE,BIT_PACKED,PLAIN
phone:          BINARY GZIP DO:0 FPO:457 SZ:454/961/2.12 VC:50
ENC:RLE,BIT_PACKED,PLAIN
email:          BINARY GZIP DO:0 FPO:911 SZ:929/1746/1.88 VC:50
ENC:RLE,BIT_PACKED,PLAIN
```

▶ **Sampling data using head and cat**: Let's now have a sneak peek at the first few rows of the data. The head function will help us do that. It accepts an additional -n parameter, where you can specify the number of records to be displayed:

```
bash-3.2$ parquet-tools-1.6.0rc3/parquet-tools head -n 2
part-r-00001.parquet
```

The preceding command will display only two rows because of the additional -n 2 parameter.

The following is the output of this command:

```
id = 1
name = Burke
phone = 1-300-746-8446
email = ullamcorper.velit.in@ametnullaDonec.co.uk

id = 2
name = Kamal
phone = 1-668-571-5046
email = pede.Suspendisse@interdumenim.edu
```

Optionally, if you wish to display all the records in the file, you can use the cat parameter with the parquet-tools command:

```
parquet-tools cat part-r-00001.parquet
```

Enable compression for the Parquet file

As you can see from the meta information, the data is `gzipped` by default. In order to use **Snappy** compression, all that we need to do is set a configuration to our `SQLContext` (actually the `SQLConf` of `SQLContext`). There's just one catch with regard to enabling **Lempel–Ziv–Oberhumer** (**LZO**) compression—we are required to install `native-lzo` on all the machines where this data is stored. Otherwise, we get a `"native-lzo library not available"` error message.

Let's enable Snappy (`http://google.github.io/snappy/`) compression by passing the configuration parameter of Parquet compression to Snappy:

```
sqlContext.setConf("spark.sql.parquet.compression.codec", "snappy")
```

After running the program, let's use the `parquet-tools meta` command to verify it:

```
parquet-tools meta part-r-00000-aee54b77-288e-44b2-8f36-53b38a489e8d.
snappy.parquet
```

```
creator:    parquet-mr version 1.6.0rc3 (build d4d5a07ec9bd262ca1e93c309f1d7d4a74ebda4c)
extra:      org.apache.spark.sql.parquet.row.metadata = {"type":"struct","fields":[{"name":"id","type":"string","nullable":true,"metadata":{}},{"name":"name
","type":"string","nullable":true, [more]...

file schema: root
--------------------------------------------------------------------------------------------------------------

id:         OPTIONAL BINARY O:UTF8 R:0 D:1
name:       OPTIONAL BINARY O:UTF8 R:0 D:1
phone:      OPTIONAL BINARY O:UTF8 R:0 D:1
email:      OPTIONAL BINARY O:UTF8 R:0 D:1

row group 1: RC:50 TS:3516
--------------------------------------------------------------------------------------------------------------

id:         BINARY SNAPPY DO:0 FPO:4 SZ:245/326/1.33 VC:50 ENC:BIT_PACKED,RLE,PLAIN
name:       BINARY SNAPPY DO:0 FPO:249 SZ:423/483/1.14 VC:50 ENC:BIT_PACKED,RLE,PLAIN
phone:      BINARY SNAPPY DO:0 FPO:672 SZ:748/961/1.28 VC:50 ENC:BIT_PACKED,RLE,PLAIN
email:      BINARY SNAPPY DO:0 FPO:1420 SZ:1375/1746/1.27 VC:50 ENC:BIT_PACKED,RLE,PLAIN
```

Using the Avro data model in Parquet

Parquet is a kind of highly efficient columnar storage, but it is also relatively new. Avro (`https://avro.apache.org`) is a widely used row-based storage format. This recipe showcases how we can retain the older and flexible Avro schema in our code but still use the Parquet format during storage.

The Spark MR project (yes, the one that has the Parquet tools we saw in the previous recipe) has converters for almost all the popular data formats. These model converters take your format and convert it into Parquet format before causing it to persist.

How to do it...

In this recipe, we'll use the Avro data model and serialize the data in a Parquet file. The recipe involves the following steps:

1. Create the Avro Model.

2. Generate Avro objects using the `sbt avro` plugin.

3. Construct the RDD of your generated object (`StudentAvro`) from `Students.csv`.

4. Save the `RDD[StudentAvro]` in a Parquet file.

5. Read the file back for verification.

6. Use `Parquet-tools` to verify.

Creation of the Avro model

The Avro schema is defined using JSON. In our case, we'll just use the same `Student.csv` as the input file. So, let's code the four fields— `id`, `name`, `phone`, and `email`—in the schema:

```
{"namespace": "studentavro.avro",
 "type": "record",
 "name": "StudentAvro",
 "fields": [
     {"name": "id", "type": ["string", "null"]},
     {"name": "name",  "type": ["string", "null"]},
     {"name": "phone", "type": ["string", "null"]},
     {"name": "email", "type": ["string", "null"]}
 ]
}
```

Probably, you are already familiar with Avro, or you have already understood the schema just by taking a look at it, but let me bore you with some explanation of the schema anyway.

The `namespace` and `name` attributes in the JSON translate into our package name and class name in our world, respectively. So, our generated class will have a fully qualified name as `studentavro.avro.StudentAvro`. The `"record"` (of the `type` attribute) is one of the complex types in Avro (`http://avro.apache.org/docs/1.7.6/spec.html#schema_complex`). Let me rephrase this again. A record roughly translates to classes in Java/Scala. It is at the topmost level in the schema hierarchy. A record can have multiple fields encapsulated inside it, and these fields can be primitives (`https://avro.apache.org/docs/1.7.7/spec.html#schema_primitive`) or other complex types. The last bit about the `type` having an array of types is interesting (`"type": ["string", "null"]`). It just means that the field can be more than one `type`. In Avro terms, it is called a union.

Now that we are done with the schema, let's save this file with an extension of `.avsc`. I have saved it as `student.avsc` in the `src/main/avro` directory.

Generation of Avro objects using the sbt-avro plugin

The next step is to generate a class from the schema. The reason we stored the `avro` schema file in the `src/main/avro` folder is this: we'll be using an `sbt-avro` plugin (`https://github.com/cavorite/sbt-avro`) to generate a Java class from the schema. Configuring the plugin is as easy as configuring any other plugin for SBT:

- Let's add the plugin to `project/plugins.sbt`:

  ```
  addSbtPlugin("com.cavorite" % "sbt-avro" % "0.3.2")
  ```

- Add the default settings of the plugin to our `build.sbt`:

  ```
  seq( sbtavro.SbtAvro.avroSettings : _*)
  ```

- Let's generate the Java class now. We can do this by calling `sbt avro:generate`. You can see the generated Java file at `target/scala-2.10/src_managed/main/compiled_avro/studentavro/avro/StudentAvro.java`.

```
Gabriel@Gabriels-MacBook-Pro ~/D/a/S/C/s/chapter3-data-loading-parquet> sbt avro:generate
[info] Loading global plugins from /Users/Gabriel/.sbt/0.13/plugins
[info] Loading project definition from /Users/Gabriel/Dropbox/arun/ScalaDataAnalysis/Code/scaladataanalysisCB-tower/chapter3-dat
a-loading-parquet/project
[warn] Multiple resolvers having different access mechanism configured with same name 'sbt-plugin-releases'. To avoid conflict,
Remove duplicate project resolvers (`resolvers`) or rename publishing resolver (`publishTo`).
[info] Set current project to chapter3-data-loading-parquet (in build file:/Users/Gabriel/Dropbox/arun/ScalaDataAnalysis/Code/sc
aladataanalysisCB-tower/chapter3-data-loading-parquet/)
[info] Avro compiler using stringType=String
[info] Compiling Avro schema /Users/Gabriel/Dropbox/arun/ScalaDataAnalysis/Code/scaladataanalysisCB-tower/chapter3-data-loading-
parquet/src/main/avro/student.avsc
[success] Total time: 1 s, completed Sep 20, 2015 9:07:21 AM
```

▶ We also need the following library dependencies. Finally, let's perform an SBT compile to compile the class so that the rest of the project picks up the generated Java file:

```
libraryDependencies ++= Seq(
  "org.apache.spark" %% "spark-core" % sparkVersion,
  "org.apache.spark" %% "spark-sql" % sparkVersion,
  "org.apache.spark" %% "spark-mllib" % sparkVersion,
  "org.apache.spark" %% "spark-hive" % sparkVersion,
  "org.apache.avro" % "avro" % "1.7.7",
  "org.apache.parquet" % "parquet-avro" % "1.8.1",
  "com.twitter" %% "chill-avro" % "0.6.0"
)
  sbt compile
```

Constructing an RDD of our generated object from Students.csv

This step is very similar to the previous recipe in the sense that we use the convertCSVToStudents function to generate an RDD of the StudentAvro object. Also, since this isn't a Scala class and the generated Java object comes up with a builder inside it, we use the builder to construct the class fluently (http://en.wikipedia.org/wiki/Fluent_interface):

```
val conf = new
SparkConf().setAppName("AvroModelToParquet").setMaster("local[2]")

  val sc = new SparkContext(conf)
  val sqlContext = new SQLContext(sc)
  sqlContext.setConf("spark.sql.parquet.binaryAsString", "true")
  val rddOfStudents = convertCSVToStudents("StudentData.csv", sc)


//The CSV has a header row.  Zipping with index and skipping the
first row
  def convertCSVToStudents(filePath: String, sc: SparkContext):
RDD[StudentAvro] = {
    val rddOfStudents:
RDD[StudentAvro]=sc.textFile(filePath).flatMap(eachLine => {
      val data = eachLine.split("\\|")
      if (data(0) == "id") None
      else Some(StudentAvro.newBuilder()
        .setId(data(0))
        .setName(data(1))
        .setPhone(data(2))
        .setEmail(data(3)).build())
    })
    rddOfStudents
  }
```

Saving RDD[StudentAvro] in a Parquet file

This is a tricky step and involves multiple substeps. Let's decipher this step backwards. We fall back to RDD[StudentAvro] in this example instead of a DataFrame because DataFrames can be constructed only from an RDD of case classes (or classes that extend Product, as we saw earlier in this chapter) or from RDD[org.apache.spark.sql.Row]. If you prefer to use DataFrames, you can read the CSV as an array of values, and use RowFactory.create for each array of values. Once an RDD[Row] is available, we can use sqlContext.createDataFrame to convert it to a DataFrame:

- In order to save the RDD as a Hadoop SequenceFile, we can use saveAsNewAPIHadoopFile. A sequence file is simply a text file that holds key-value pairs. We could have chosen one of the Student attributes as a key, but for the sake of it, let's have it as a Void in this example.

  To represent a pair (key-value) in Spark, we use PairRDD (https://spark. apache.org/docs/1.4.1/api/scala/index.html#org.apache.spark. rdd.PairRDDFunctions). Not surprisingly, saveAsNewAPIHadoopFile is available only for PairRDDs. To convert the existing RDD[StudentAvro] to a PairRDD[Void, StudentAvro], we use the map function:

  ```
  val pairRddOfStudentsWithNullKey = rddOfStudents.map(each
  => (null, each))
  ```

- Spark uses Java serialization by default to serialize the RDD to be distributed across the cluster. However, the Avro model doesn't implement the serializable interface, and hence it won't be able to leverage Java serialization. That's no reason for worry, however, because Spark provides another 10x performant serialization mechanism called **Kryo**. The only downside is that we need to explicitly register our serialization candidates:

  ```
    val conf = new
  SparkConf().setAppName("AvroModelToParquet").setMaster("local[2]")
    conf.set("spark.kryo.registrator",
  classOf[StudentAvroRegistrator].getName)
      conf.set("spark.serializer",
  "org.apache.spark.serializer.KryoSerializer")
  ```

  So, we say using the "spark.serializer" configuration that we intend to use KryoSerializer, and that our registrator is StudentAvroRegistrator. As you may expect, what the Registrator does is register our StudentAvro class as a candidate for Kryo serialization. The twitter-chill project (https://github. com/twitter/chill) provides a nice extension to delegate the Kryo serializer to use the Avro serialization:

  ```
  class StudentAvroRegistrator extends KryoRegistrator {
    override def registerClasses(kryo: Kryo) {
  ```

```
    kryo.register(classOf[StudentAvro],
AvroSerializer.SpecificRecordBinarySerializer[StudentAvro])
  }
}
```

▶ The intent of this recipe is to write a Parquet file, but the data model (schema) is Avro. Since we are going to write this down as a sequence file, we'll be using a bunch of Hadoop APIs. The `org.apache.hadoop.mapreduce.OutputFormat` specifies the output format of the file that we are going to write, and as expected, we use `ParquetOutputFormat` (this is available in the `parquet-hadoop` subproject in the `parquet-mr` project). There are two things that an `OutputFormat` requires:

  ❑ The `WriteSupport` class, which knows how to convert the Avro data model to the actual format. This is achieved with the following line:

```
ParquetOutputFormat.setWriteSupportClass(job,
classOf[AvroWriteSupport])
```

  ❑ The schema needs to be written to the footer of the Parquet file too. The schema of `StudentAvro` is accessible by using the `getClassSchema` function. This line of code achieves that:

```
AvroParquetOutputFormat.setSchema(job, StudentAvro.
getClassSchema)
```

Now, what's that `job` parameter doing here in these two lines of code? The `job` object is just an instance of `org.apache.hadoop.mapreduce.Job`:

```
val job = new Job()
```

When we call the `setWriteSupportClass` and `setSchema` methods of `ParquetOutputFormat` and `AvroParquetOutputFormat`, the resulting configuration is captured inside the `JobConf` encapsulated inside the `Job` object. We'll be using this `job` configuration while saving the data in a sequence file.

▶ Finally, we save the file by calling `saveAsNewAPIHadoopFile`. The `save` method requires a bunch of parameters, each of which we have already discussed. The first parameter is the filename, followed by the key and the value classes. The fourth is the `OutputFormat` of the file, and finally comes the `job` configuration itself:

```
pairRddOfStudentsWithNullKey.saveAsNewAPIHadoopFile("studentAvro
Pq",
    classOf[Void],
    classOf[StudentAvro],
    classOf[AvroParquetOutputFormat],
    job.getConfiguration())
```

We saw the entire program in bits and pieces, so for the sake of completion, let's see it completely:

```scala
object ParquetAvroSchemaMain extends App {

  val conf = new
SparkConf().setAppName("AvroModelToParquet").setMaster("local[2]")
  conf.set("spark.kryo.registrator",
classOf[StudentAvroRegistrator].getName)
  conf.set("spark.serializer",
"org.apache.spark.serializer.KryoSerializer")

  val job = new Job()

  val sc = new SparkContext(conf)
  val sqlContext = new SQLContext(sc)
  sqlContext.setConf("spark.sql.parquet.binaryAsString",
"true")
  val rddOfStudents =
convertCSVToStudents("StudentData.csv", sc)

  ParquetOutputFormat.setWriteSupportClass(job,
classOf[AvroWriteSupport])
  AvroParquetOutputFormat.setSchema(job,
StudentAvro.getClassSchema)

  val pairRddOfStudentsWithNullKey = rddOfStudents.map(each
=>
(null, each))

pairRddOfStudentsWithNullKey.saveAsNewAPIHadoopFile("studentAvro
Pq",
    classOf[Void],
    classOf[StudentAvro],
    classOf[AvroParquetOutputFormat],
    job.getConfiguration())

  //The CSV has a header row.  Zipping with index and
skipping the first row
  def convertCSVToStudents(filePath: String, sc:
SparkContext):
RDD[StudentAvro] = {
    val rddOfStudents:
RDD[StudentAvro]=sc.textFile(filePath).flatMap(eachLine =>
{
      val data = eachLine.split("\\|")
```

```
          if (data(0) == "id") None
          else Some(StudentAvro.newBuilder()
            .setId(data(0))
            .setName(data(1))
            .setPhone(data(2))
            .setEmail(data(3)).build())
        })
        rddOfStudents
      }

    }

    class StudentAvroRegistrator extends KryoRegistrator {
      override def registerClasses(kryo: Kryo) {
        kryo.register(classOf[StudentAvro],
    AvroSerializer.SpecificRecordBinarySerializer[StudentAvro])
      }
    }
```

Reading the file back for verification

As always, let's read the file back for confirmation. The function to be called
for this is `newAPIHadoopFile`, which accepts a similar set of parameters as
`saveAsNewAPIHadoopFile`: the name of the file, InputFormat, the key class, the value
class, and finally the job configuration. Note that we are using `newAPIHadoopFile` instead
of the previously used the `parquetFile` method. This is because we are reading from a
Hadoop sequence file:

```
//Reading the file back for confirmation.
  ParquetInputFormat.setReadSupportClass(job, classOf[AvroWriteSupport])

  val readStudentsPair = sc.newAPIHadoopFile("studentAvroPq", classOf[Av
roParquetInputFormat[StudentAvro]], classOf[Void], classOf[StudentAvro],
job.getConfiguration())

  val justStudentRDD: RDD[StudentAvro] = readStudentsPair.map(_._2)

  val studentsAsString = justStudentRDD.collect().take(5).mkString("\n")

  println(studentsAsString)
```

This is the output:

```
[info] {"id": "1", "name": "Burke", "phone": "1-300-746-8446", "email": "ullamcorper.velit.in@ametnullaDonec.co.uk"}
[info] {"id": "2", "name": "Kamal", "phone": "1-668-571-5046", "email": "pede.Suspendisse@interdumenim.edu"}
[info] {"id": "3", "name": "Olga", "phone": "1-956-311-1686", "email": "Aenean.eget.metus@dictumcursusNunc.edu"}
[info] {"id": "4", "name": "Belle", "phone": "1-246-894-6340", "email": "vitae.aliquet.nec@neque.co.uk"}
[info] {"id": "5", "name": "Trevor", "phone": "1-300-527-4967", "email": "dapibus.id@acturpisegestas.net"}
```

Using Parquet tools for verification

We'll also use Parquet tools to confirm that the schema that is stored in the Parquet file is indeed an `avro` schema:

```
/Users/Gabriel/Dropbox/arun/ScalaDataAnalysis/git/parquet-mr/parquet-
tools/target/parquet-tools-1.6.0rc3/parquet-tools meta /Users/Gabriel/
Dropbox/arun/ScalaDataAnalysis/Code/scaladataanalysisCB-tower/chapter3-
data-loading-parquet/studentAvroPq
```

Yup! Looks like it is! The `extra` section in `meta` does confirm that the `avro` schema is stored:

```
creator:        parquet-mr

extra:          parquet.avro.schema = {"type":"record","name":"StudentAvro",
"namespace":"studentavro.avro","fields":[{"name":"id","type":[{"type":"st
ring","avro.java.string":"Stri [more] ...
```

```
creator:     parquet-mr
extra:       parquet.avro.schema = {"type":"record","name":"StudentAvro","namespace":"studentavro.avro","fields":[{"name":"id","

file schema: studentavro.avro.StudentAvro
--------------------------------------------------------------------------------
id:          OPTIONAL BINARY O:UTF8 R:0 D:1
name:        OPTIONAL BINARY O:UTF8 R:0 D:1
phone:       OPTIONAL BINARY O:UTF8 R:0 D:1
email:       OPTIONAL BINARY O:UTF8 R:0 D:1

row group 1: RC:50 TS:3382
--------------------------------------------------------------------------------
id:          BINARY UNCOMPRESSED DO:0 FPO:4 SZ:316/316/1.00 VC:50 ENC:PLAIN,RLE,BIT_PACKED
name:        BINARY UNCOMPRESSED DO:0 FPO:320 SZ:470/470/1.00 VC:50 ENC:PLAIN,RLE,BIT_PACKED
phone:       BINARY UNCOMPRESSED DO:0 FPO:790 SZ:925/925/1.00 VC:50 ENC:PLAIN,RLE,BIT_PACKED
email:       BINARY UNCOMPRESSED DO:0 FPO:1715 SZ:1671/1671/1.00 VC:50 ENC:PLAIN,RLE,BIT_PACKED
```

Loading from RDBMS

As the final recipe on loading, let's try to load data from an RDBMS data source, which is MySQL in our case. This recipe assumes that you have already installed MySQL in your machine.

How to do it...

Let's go through the prerequisite steps first. If you already have a MySQL table to play with, you can safely ignore this step. We are just going to create a new database and a table and load some sample data into it.

The prerequisite step (optional):

1. Creating a database and a table: This is achieved in MySQL by using the create database and the create table DDL:

```
create database scalada;

use scalada
```

```
CREATE TABLE student (
id varchar(20),
`name` varchar(200),
phone varchar(50),
email varchar(200),
PRIMARY KEY (id));
```

2. Loading data into the table: Let's dump some data into the table. I wrote a very simple app to do this. Alternatively, you can use the `load data infile` command if you have `"local-infile=1"` enabled on your server and the client. Refer to `https://dev.mysql.com/doc/refman/5.1/en/load-data.html` for details about this command.

As you can see, the program loads the `Student.csv` that we saw in *Chapter 2, Getting Started with Apache Spark DataFrames,* when we saw how to use DataFrames with Spark using the `databricks.csv` connector. Then, for each line, the data is inserted into the table using the plain old JDBC insert. As you might have already figured out, we need to add the MySQL connector `java` dependency to our `build.sbt` too:

```
"mysql" % "mysql-connector-java" % "5.1.34"


object LoadDataIntoMySQL extends App {

  val conf = new
SparkConf().setAppName("LoadDataIntoMySQL").setMaster("local[2]")
  val config=ConfigFactory.load()
  val sc = new SparkContext(conf)
  val sqlContext = new SQLContext(sc)

  val students = sqlContext.csvFile(filePath =
"StudentData.csv", useHeader = true, delimiter = '|')

  students.foreachPartition { iter=>
      val conn =
DriverManager.getConnection(config.getString("mysql.connection.
url"))
      val statement = conn.prepareStatement("insert into
scalada.student (id, name, phone, email) values (?,?,?,?)
")

      for (eachRow <- iter) {
        statement.setString(1, eachRow.getString(0))
        statement.setString(2, eachRow.getString(1))
        statement.setString(3, eachRow.getString(2))
        statement.setString(4, eachRow.getString(3))
```

```
        statement.addBatch()
    }

    statement.executeBatch()
    conn.close()
    println ("All rows inserted successfully")
}

}
```

A "`select * from scalada.student`" on the MySQL client should confirm this, as shown here:

id	name	phone	email
▶ 10	Maya	1-271-683-2698	accumsan.convallis@ornarelectusjusto.edu
100	Mannix	1-804-635-5645	rutrum@per.org
11	Emi	1-467-270-1337	est@nunc.com
12	Caleb	1-683-212-0896	Suspendisse@Quisque.edu
13	Florence	1-603-575-2444	sit.amet.dapibus@lacusAliquamrutrum.ca
14	Anika	1-856-828-7883	euismod@ligulaelit.co.uk
15	Tarik	1-398-171-2268	turpis@felisorci.com

Steps for loading RDBMS data into DataFrame:

The recommended approach to loading data from RDBMS databases is using the SQLContext's `load` method:

1. Creating the Spark and `SQLContext`: You may have already become familiar with this step by looking at the previous recipes:

    ```
    val conf = new
    SparkConf().setAppName("DataFromRDBMS").setMaster("local[2]")
    val sc = new SparkContext(conf)
    val sqlContext = new SQLContext(sc)
    ```

2. Constructing a map of options: This map is expected to have not only the driver and the connection URL, but also the query to be invoked in order to load the data. In this example, we'll store the parameter values in an external `Typesafe config` file and load the values into our program.

    The Typesafe `application.conf` is located at `src/main/resources` as per standard SBT/Maven conventions. Here is a screenshot that shows the contents of `application.conf`:

```
application.conf ⊠
1 mysql.driver="com.mysql.jdbc.Driver"
2 mysql.connection.url="jdbc:mysql://localhost:3306/scalada?user=root&password=orange123"
```

Now let's look at the code that constructs the map:

```
val config = ConfigFactory.load()

val options = Map(
  "driver" -> config.getString("mysql.driver"),
  "url" -> config.getString("mysql.connection.url"),
  "dbtable" -> "(select * from student) as student",
  "partitionColumn" -> "id",
  "lowerBound" -> "1",
  "upperBound" -> "100",
  "numPartitions"-> "2")
```

The first three parameters are straightforward. The numPartitions specifies the number of partitions for this job, and partitionColumn specifies the column in the table based on which the job has to be partitioned. The lowerBound and upperBound are values of the "id" field. The amount of data to be handled by a single partition is calculated using the number of partitions and the lower and upper bounds.

3. Loading data from the table: The load function of SQLContext expects two parameters. The first one specifies that the source of the data is through "jdbc", and the second parameter is the options that we constructed in step 2. Let's now print the schema and show the first 20 rows, as we always do:

```
val dFrame=sqlContext.load("jdbc", options)
dFrame.printSchema()
dFrame.show()
```

This is the output:

```
root
 |-- id: string (nullable = false)
 |-- name: string (nullable = true)
 |-- phone: string (nullable = true)
 |-- email: string (nullable = true)
 |-- gender: string (nullable = true)
```

We see that the schema of the DataFrame is derived from the MySQL table definition by examining the not nullable constraint of the id field.

The output is as follows:

```
[info] id   name     phone          email
[info] 10   Maya     1-271-683-2698 accumsan.convalli...
[info] 100  Mannix   1-804-635-5645 rutrum@per.org
[info] 11   Emi      1-467-270-1337 est@nunc.com
[info] 12   Caleb    1-683-212-0896 Suspendisse@Quisq...
[info] 13   Florence 1-603-575-2444 sit.amet.dapibus@...
[info] 14   Anika    1-856-828-7883 euismod@ligulaeli...
[info] 15   Tarik    1-398-171-2268 turpis@felisorci.com
[info] 16   Amena    1-878-250-3129 lorem.luctus.ut@s...
[info] 17   Blossom  1-154-406-9596 Nunc.commodo.auct...
[info] 18   Guy      1-869-521-3230 senectus.et.netus...
[info] 19   Malachi  1-608-637-2772 Proin.mi.Aliquam@...
[info] 2    Kamal    1-668-571-5046 pede.Suspendisse@...
[info] 20   Edward   1-711-710-6552 lectus@aliquetlib...
[info] 21            1-598-439-7549 consectetuer.adip...
[info] 22   Talon    1-880-986-1269 nec.malesuada.ut@...
[info] 23   Julie    1-430-807-5430 turpis.Nulla.aliq...
[info] 24   Marsden  1-477-629-7528 Donec.dignissim.m...
[info] 25   Igor     1-903-815-5364 conubia@tellus.co.uk
[info] 26   Amela    1-526-909-2605 in@vitaesodales.edu
[info] 27   Bianca   1-842-558-2906 posuere.cubilia@s...
```

Preparing data in Dataframes

Other than filtering, conversions, and transformations (with DataFrames which we saw in *Chapter 2, Getting Started with Apache Spark DataFrames*) , let's see a few more data preparation tricks in this recipe. We'll also be looking at specific data preparation in *Chapter 5, Learning from Data*, where we will focus on using various machine learning algorithms.

How to do it...

While preprocessing data, we may be required to:

- ▶ Merge two different datasets
- ▶ Perform set operations on two datasets
- ▶ Sort the DataFrame by casting an attribute value
- ▶ Choose a member from one dataset over another based on the predicate
- ▶ Parse arbitrary date/time inputs

We'll use the StudentPrep1.csv and StudentPrep2.csv datasets for the first four tasks, and for the last one, we'll use StrangeDate.json, a JSON-based dataset. The CSV and the JSON dataset are chosen primarily for convenience—the input data could be anything.

The `StudentPrep1.csv` dataset is shown in this screenshot:

```
1|Burke|1-300-746-8446|ullamcorper.velit.in@ametnullaDonec.co.uk
2|Kamal|1-668-571-5046|pede.Suspendisse@interdumenim.edu
3|Olga|1-956-311-1686|Aenean.eget.metus@dictumcursusNunc.edu
4|Belle|1-246-894-6340|vitae.aliquet.nec@neque.co.uk
5|Trevor|1-300-527-4967|dapibus.id@acturpisegestas.net
6|Laurel|1-691-379-9921|adipiscing@consectetueripsum.edu
7|Sara|1-608-140-1995|Donec.nibh@enimEtiamimperdiet.edu
8|Kaseem|1-881-586-2689|cursus.et.magna@euismod.org
9|Lev|1-916-367-5608|Vivamus.nisi@ipsumdolor.com
10|Maya|1-271-683-2698|accumsan.convallis@ornarelectusjusto.edu
```

The `StudentPrep2.csv` dataset is shown in the following screenshot:

```
id|studentName|phone|email
1|BurkeDifferentName|1-300-746-8446|ullamcorper.velit.in@ametnullaDonec.co.uk
2|KamalDifferentName|1-668-571-5046|pede.Suspendisse@interdumenim.edu
3|Olga|1-956-311-1686|Aenean.eget.metus@dictumcursusNuncDifferentEmail.edu
4|BelleDifferentName|1-246-894-6340|vitae.aliquet.nec@neque.co.uk
5|Trevor|1-300-527-4967|dapibusDifferentEmail.id@acturpisegestas.net
6|LaurelInvalidPhone|000000000|adipiscing@consectetueripsum.edu
7|Sara|1-608-140-1995|Donec.nibh@enimEtiamimperdiet.edu
8|Kaseem|1-881-586-2689|cursus.et.magna@euismod.org
9|Lev|1-916-367-5608|Vivamus.nisi@ipsumdolor.com
10|Maya|1-271-683-2698|accumsan.convallis@ornarelectusjusto.edu
999|LevUniqueToSecondRDD|1-916-367-5608|Vivamus.nisi@ipsumdolor.com
```

 The code for this recipe can be found at `https://github.com/arunma/ScalaDataAnalysisCookbook/tree/master/chapter3-data-loading`.

Let's convert them into a DataFrame using the `databricks/spark-csv` library, which we used in *Chapter 2, Getting Started with Apache Spark DataFrames*, when we talked about loading DataFrames from CSV:

```
import com.databricks.spark.csv.CsvContext

val students1=sqlContext.csvFile(filePath="StudentPrep1.csv",
useHeader=true, delimiter='|')
val students2=sqlContext.csvFile(filePath="StudentPrep2.csv",
useHeader=true, delimiter='|')
```

1. **Merging datasets**: The DataFrame provides a convenient way to merge another DataFrame—`unionAll`. The `unionAll` accepts another DataFrame as an argument. Not surprisingly, the merged DataFrame maintains duplicates inside it:

```
val allStudents=students1.unionAll(students2)

allStudents.show(allStudents.count().toInt)
```

The output is shown as follows:

```
+---+--------------------+--------------+--------------------+
| id|         studentName|         phone|               email|
+---+--------------------+--------------+--------------------+
|  1|               Burke|1-300-746-8446|ullamcorper.velit...|
|  2|               Kamal|1-668-571-5046|pede.Suspendisse@...|
|  3|                Olga|1-956-311-1686|Aenean.eget.metus...|
|  4|               Belle|1-246-894-6340|vitae.aliquet.nec...|
|  5|              Trevor|1-300-527-4967|dapibus.id@acturp...|
|  6|              Laurel|1-691-379-9921|adipiscing@consec...|
|  7|                Sara|1-608-140-1995|Donec.nibh@enimEt...|
|  8|              Kaseem|1-881-586-2689|cursus.et.magna@e...|
|  9|                 Lev|1-916-367-5608|Vivamus.nisi@ipsu...|
| 10|                Maya|1-271-683-2698|accumsan.convalli...|
|  1| BurkeDifferentName|1-300-746-8446|ullamcorper.velit...|
|  2| KamalDifferentName|1-668-571-5046|pede.Suspendisse@...|
|  3|                Olga|1-956-311-1686|Aenean.eget.metus...|
|  4| BelleDifferentName|1-246-894-6340|vitae.aliquet.nec...|
|  5|              Trevor|1-300-527-4967|dapibusDifferentE...|
|  6|   LaurelInvalidPhone|     000000000|adipiscing@consec...|
|  7|                Sara|1-608-140-1995|Donec.nibh@enimEt...|
|  8|              Kaseem|1-881-586-2689|cursus.et.magna@e...|
|  9|                 Lev|1-916-367-5608|Vivamus.nisi@ipsu...|
| 10|                Maya|1-271-683-2698|accumsan.convalli...|
|999|LevUniqueToSecondRDD|1-916-367-5608|Vivamus.nisi@ipsu...|
+---+--------------------+--------------+--------------------+
```

2. **Performing set operations**: Just like `unionAll`, the DataFrame has functions for various set operations.

The intersection of two DataFrames would just entail calling the `intersect` function:

```
val intersection=students1.intersect(students2)

intersection.foreach(println)
```

```
[7,Sara,1-608-140-1995,Donec.nibh@enimEtiamimperdiet.edu]

[8,Kaseem,1-881-586-2689,cursus.et.magna@euismod.org]

[10,Maya,1-271-683-2698,accumsan.convallis@ornarelectusjusto.edu]

[9,Lev,1-916-367-5608,Vivamus.nisi@ipsumdolor.com]
```

Deriving the difference of one DataFrame from another is done by calling the `except()` function with another DataFrame as the parameter:

```
val subtraction=students1.except(students2)

subtraction.foreach(println)
```

Here is the output:

```
[6,Laurel,1-691-379-9921,adipiscing@consectetueripsum.edu]

[4,Belle,1-246-894-6340,vitae.aliquet.nec@neque.co.uk]

[2,Kamal,1-668-571-5046,pede.Suspendisse@interdumenim.edu]

[5,Trevor,1-300-527-4967,dapibus.id@acturpisegestas.net]

[3,Olga,1-956-311-1686,Aenean.eget.metus@dictumcursusNunc.edu]

[1,Burke,1-300-746-8446,ullamcorper.velit.in@ametnullaDonec.co.uk]
```

If there are duplicates in the data, the `distinct` function will ignore them and return a DataFrame with only unique data:

```
val distinctStudents=allStudents.distinct

distinctStudents.foreach(println)

println(distinctStudents.count())
```

The following is the output:

```
[4,BelleDifferentName,1-246-894-6340,vitae.aliquet.nec@neque.
co.uk]

[1,Burke,1-300-746-8446,ullamcorper.velit.in@ametnullaDonec.co.uk]

[2,KamalDifferentName,1-668-571-5046,pede.Suspendisse@
interdumenim.edu]

[999,LevUniqueToSecondRDD,1-916-367-5608,Vivamus.nisi@ipsumdolor.
com]

[1,BurkeDifferentName,1-300-746-8446,ullamcorper.velit.in@
ametnullaDonec.co.uk]

[2,Kamal,1-668-571-5046,pede.Suspendisse@interdumenim.edu]

[3,Olga,1-956-311-1686,Aenean.eget.metus@dictumcursusNunc.edu]

[7,Sara,1-608-140-1995,Donec.nibh@enimEtiamimperdiet.edu]

[8,Kaseem,1-881-586-2689,cursus.et.magna@euismod.org]

[5,Trevor,1-300-527-4967,dapibus.id@acturpisegestas.net]

[4,Belle,1-246-894-6340,vitae.aliquet.nec@neque.co.uk]

[6,Laurel,1-691-379-9921,adipiscing@consectetueripsum.edu]

[6,LaurelInvalidPhone,000000000,adipiscing@consectetueripsum.edu]

[9,Lev,1-916-367-5608,Vivamus.nisi@ipsumdolor.com]
```

```
[3,Olga,1-956-311-1686,Aenean.eget.metus@
dictumcursusNuncDifferentEmail.edu]
```

```
[5,Trevor,1-300-527-4967,dapibusDifferentEmail.id@acturpisegestas.
net]
```

```
[10,Maya,1-271-683-2698,accumsan.convallis@ornarelectusjusto.edu]
```

Count output:

17

3. **Sorting the DataFrame by casting an attribute value**: Sometimes, our DataFrame inferences an integer attribute as a string. Since, DataFrames are immutable, the correct way of converting an attribute from one type to another is by creating another DataFrame. In this recipe, we'll not only cast one attribute type to another, but also sort the DataFrame based on that attribute. The simplest way to achieve this is by using the Spark SQL expression:

```
val sortedCols=allStudents.selectExpr("cast(id as int) as id",
"studentName", "phone", "email").sort("id")

  println ("sorting")

  sortedCols.show(sortedCols.count.toInt)
```

The output is shown here:

```
+---+-------------------+-------------+-------------------+
| id|        studentName|        phone|              email|
+---+-------------------+-------------+-------------------+
|  1|              Burke|1-300-746-8446|ullamcorper.velit...|
|  1| BurkeDifferentName|1-300-746-8446|ullamcorper.velit...|
|  2|              Kamal|1-668-571-5046|pede.Suspendisse@...|
|  2| KamalDifferentName|1-668-571-5046|pede.Suspendisse@...|
|  3|               Olga|1-956-311-1686|Aenean.eget.metus...|
|  3|               Olga|1-956-311-1686|Aenean.eget.metus...|
|  4|              Belle|1-246-894-6340|vitae.aliquet.nec...|
|  4| BelleDifferentName|1-246-894-6340|vitae.aliquet.nec...|
|  5|             Trevor|1-300-527-4967|dapibusDifferentE...|
|  5|             Trevor|1-300-527-4967|dapibus.id@acturp...|
|  6|             Laurel|1-691-379-9921|adipiscing@consec...|
|  6| LaurelInvalidPhone|    000000000|adipiscing@consec...|
|  7|               Sara|1-608-140-1995|Donec.nibh@enimEt...|
|  7|               Sara|1-608-140-1995|Donec.nibh@enimEt...|
|  8|             Kaseem|1-881-586-2689|cursus.et.magna@e...|
|  8|             Kaseem|1-881-586-2689|cursus.et.magna@e...|
|  9|                Lev|1-916-367-5608|Vivamus.nisi@ipsu...|
|  9|                Lev|1-916-367-5608|Vivamus.nisi@ipsu...|
| 10|               Maya|1-271-683-2698|accumsan.convalli...|
| 10|               Maya|1-271-683-2698|accumsan.convalli...|
|999|LevUniqueToSecondRDD|1-916-367-5608|Vivamus.nisi@ipsu...|
+---+-------------------+-------------+-------------------+
```

4. **Choosing a member from one dataset over another based on predicate**: Let's assume that for a given student ID across two different datasets, you would like to pick only the one that has a longer name (or matches some predicate). The result would be just one row per ID.

This involves three mini-steps:

1. Map the merged DataFrame (using `unionAll`) and spit out an RDD of pairs with the key as the ID (or any other field based on which you would like to merge):

```
val
idStudentPairs=allStudents.rdd.map(eachRow=>(eachRow.
getString(0),eachRow))
```

2. The next step is to use a function called `reduceByKey`. It accepts a function that takes two rows and returns a single row. In our case, we simply write the logic to choose the row with the longer name:

```
//Removes duplicates by id and holds on to the row with
the longest name

val idStudentPairs=allStudents.rdd.map(eachRow=>(eachRow.
getString(0),eachRow))

val longestNameRdd=idStudentPairs.reduceByKey((row1, row2)
=>

    if (row1.getString(1).length()>row2.getString(1).
length()) row1 else row2

    )
```

3. Let's print the output:

```
longestNameRdd.values.foreach(println)
```

The output is as follows:

```
[4,BelleDifferentName,1-246-894-6340,vitae.aliquet.nec@neque.
co.uk]

[8,Kaseem,1-881-586-2689,cursus.et.magna@euismod.org]

[6,LaurelInvalidPhone,000000000,adipiscing@consectetueripsum.edu]

[2,KamalDifferentName,1-668-571-5046,pede.Suspendisse@
interdumenim.edu]

[7,Sara,1-608-140-1995,Donec.nibh@enimEtiamimperdiet.edu]

[5,Trevor,1-300-527-4967,dapibusDifferentEmail.id@acturpisegestas.
net]

[9,Lev,1-916-367-5608,Vivamus.nisi@ipsumdolor.com]

[3,Olga,1-956-311-1686,Aenean.eget.metus@
dictumcursusNuncDifferentEmail.edu]
```

```
[999,LevUniqueToSecondRDD,1-916-367-5608,Vivamus.nisi@ipsumdolor.
com]

[1,BurkeDifferentName,1-300-746-8446,ullamcorper.velit.in@
ametnullaDonec.co.uk]

[10,Maya,1-271-683-2698,accumsan.convallis@ornarelectusjusto.edu]
```

5. **Parsing arbitrary date/time inputs and convert an array into a comma-separated string**: While preparing the data, we see that, particularly, the date and time appear in some crazy formats. As always, our aim is to standardize them. For this subrecipe, we'll be using a JSON that looks like this:

```
{"name":"Cecelia Duke","dob":"09/06/2014 05:25:39","tags":["reprehenderit","cupidatat","elit","esse","exercitation","enim","sunt"]},
{"name":"Conrad Lucas","dob":"04/08/2014 05:54:02","tags":["occaecat","amet","adipisicing","in","est","reprehenderit","reprehenderit"]},
{"name":"Tasha Duran","dob":"02/10/2014 00:29:27","tags":["voluptate","consectetur","esse","ad","et","dolor","ea"]},
{"name":"Faulkner Jackson","dob":"07/03/2014 15:13:08","tags":["anim","eiusmod","commodo","consequat","aliqua","ad","non"]},
{"name":"Reed Joseph","dob":"03/07/2014 00:19:31","tags":["voluptate","enim","ullamco","incididunt","cillum","consectetur","velit"]}
```

As we saw in previous recipes, we could bring in this JSON as a DataFrame, but the date format isn't ISO 8601, which means that it won't be considered as a timestamp and would be treated as plain string. In this subrecipe, let's see how to convert a string into a date format. This subrecipe involves four steps:

> Performing arbitrary transformations is a work in progress (https://issues.apache.org/jira/browse/SPARK-4190).

1. Import JSON as a text file:

    ```
    val stringRDD = sc.textFile("StrangeDate.json")
    ```

2. Create a new `org.joda.time.format.DateTimeFormat` for the specific pattern that our input is in:

    ```
    val formatter = DateTimeFormat.forPattern("MM/dd/yyyy
    HH:mm:ss")
    ```

3. We add `json4s` as our dependency in `build.sbt`:

    ```
    "org.json4s" % "json4s-core_2.10" % "3.2.11",

    "org.json4s" % "json4s-jackson_2.10" % "3.2.11"
    ```

4. For each line of the JSON string, parse, and convert the string to `org.json4s.JsonValue`. The advantage of `JsonValue` is that we can traverse the JSON object with XPath-like expressions.

Chaining the compact and render function will help us convert `JsonValue` to `String`. In the following code, we extract the `name` field as is, convert an array of tags into a comma-separated string using the `extract` function, parse the date string using the `DateTimeFormat` that we created earlier, and construct a `Timestamp` object. Finally, we yield a case class called `JsonDataModel` out of the for comprehension that wraps around the name, date, and tags:

```
case class JsonDateModel (name:String, dob:Timestamp, tags:String)
  import org.json4s._
  import org.json4s.jackson.JsonMethods._
  implicit val formats = DefaultFormats

val dateModelRDD = for {
    json <- stringRDD
    jsonValue = parse(json)
    name = compact(render(jsonValue \ "name"))
    dateAsString=compact(render(jsonValue \ "dob")).replace("\"","")
    date = new Timestamp(formatter.parseDateTime(dateAsString).
getMillis())
    tags = render(jsonValue \ "tags").extract[List[String]].
mkString(",")
  } yield JsonDateModel(name, date, tags)
```

After that, we construct a DataFrame out of this case class RDD and print the schema to confirm:

```
import sqlContext.implicits._

val df=dateModelRDD.toDF()

df.printSchema()

df.show(df.count.toInt)
```

The output is as follows:

▸ Schema:

```
[info] root
[info]  |-- name: string (nullable = true)
[info]  |-- dob: timestamp (nullable = true)
[info]  |-- tags: string (nullable = true)
```

▸ Data:

```
[info] name                dob                    tags
[info] "Cecelia Duke"      2014-09-06 05:25:...   ["reprehenderit",...
[info] "Conrad Lucas"      2014-04-08 05:54:...   ["occaecat","amet...
[info] "Tasha Duran"       2014-02-10 00:29:...   ["voluptate","con...
[info] "Faulkner Jackson"  2014-07-03 15:13:...   ["anim","eiusmod"...
[info] "Reed Joseph"       2014-03-07 00:19:...   ["voluptate","eni...
```

4
Data Visualization

In this chapter, we will cover the following recipes:

- ▸ Visualizing using Zeppelin
- ▸ Creating scatter plots with Bokeh-Scala
- ▸ Creating a time series MultiPlot with Bokeh-Scala

Introduction

In all honesty, free / open source data visualization tools in Scala aren't that rich compared to those in other mature data analysis languages, such as R or Python. We might partly attribute this to the lack of rich charting frameworks in Java, and visualization has never been a strong point for big data analytics.

That said, Scala (or more specifically the Hadoop world, including Spark) is catching up with the presence of the Apache incubator project Zeppelin and the highly active Scala bindings (`https://github.com/bokeh/bokeh-scala`) for the Bokeh project (`http://bokeh.pydata.org/en/latest/`). With R becoming the first-class citizen in Spark—with the availability of SparkR DataFrames from 1.4 onwards—Spark gets additional visualization from R other than the already existing Python APIs.

As a side note, all existing Java libraries are accessible from Scala. Hence, we are free to borrow any visualization library from Java.

Visualizing using Zeppelin

Apache Zeppelin is a nifty web-based tool that helps us visualize and explore large datasets. From a technical standpoint, Apache Zeppelin is a web application on steroids. We aim to use this application to render some neat, interactive, and shareable graphs and charts.

The interesting part of Zeppelin is that it has a bunch of built-in interpreters—ones that can interpret and invoke all API functions in Spark (with a `SparkContext`) and Spark SQL (with a `SQLContext`). The other interpreters that are built in are for Hive, Flink, Markdown, and Scala. It also has the ability to run remote interpreters (outside of Zeppelin's own JVM) via Thrift. To look at the list of built-in interpreters, you can go through `conf/interpreter.json` in the `zeppelin` installation directory. Alternatively, you can view and customize the interpreters from `http://localhost:8080/#/interpreter` once you start the `zeppelin` daemon.

How to do it...

In this recipe, we'll be using the built-in `SparkContext` and `SQLContext` inside Zeppelin and transform data using Spark. At the end, we'll register the transformed data as a table and use Spark SQL to query the data and visualize it.

The list of subrecipes in this section is as follows:

- ▸ Installing Zeppelin
- ▸ Customizing Zeppelin's server and websocket port
- ▸ Visualizing data on HDFS – parameterizing inputs
- ▸ Using custom functions during visualization
- ▸ Adding external dependencies to Zeppelin
- ▸ Pointing to an external Spark cluster

Installing Zeppelin

Zeppelin (`http://zeppelin-project.org/`) doesn't have a binary bundle yet. However, just as its project site claims, it is pretty easy to build from source. We just ought to run one command to install it on our local machine. At the end of this recipe, we'll take a look at how to point our Zeppelin to an external Spark master:

```
git clone https://github.com/apache/incubator-zeppelin.git

cd incubator-zeppelin

mvn clean package -Pspark-1.4 -Dhadoop.version=2.2.0 -Phadoop-2.2
-DskipTests
```

```
[INFO] Reactor Summary:
[INFO]
[INFO] Zeppelin ........................................... SUCCESS [3.364s]
[INFO] Zeppelin: Interpreter ............................. SUCCESS [15.299s]
[INFO] Zeppelin: Zengine ................................. SUCCESS [6.053s]
[INFO] Zeppelin: Spark ................................... SUCCESS [36.770s]
[INFO] Zeppelin: Markdown interpreter .................... SUCCESS [2.342s]
[INFO] Zeppelin: Angular interpreter ..................... SUCCESS [2.430s]
[INFO] Zeppelin: Shell interpreter ....................... SUCCESS [2.055s]
[INFO] Zeppelin: Hive interpreter ........................ SUCCESS [3.454s]
[INFO] Zeppelin: Tajo interpreter ........................ SUCCESS [2.624s]
[INFO] Zeppelin: web Application ......................... SUCCESS [31.395s]
[INFO] Zeppelin: Server .................................. SUCCESS [16.905s]
[INFO] Zeppelin: Packaging distribution .................. SUCCESS [0.546s]
[INFO] ------------------------------------------------------------------------
[INFO] BUILD SUCCESS
[INFO] ------------------------------------------------------------------------
[INFO] Total time: 2:03.650s
[INFO] Finished at: Fri May 29 23:10:52 SGT 2015
[INFO] Final Memory: 97M/1323M
[INFO] ------------------------------------------------------------------------
```

Once built, we can start the Zeppelin daemon using the following command:

```
bin/zeppelin-daemon.sh start
```

```
Gabriel@Gabriels-MacBook-Pro ~/A/incubator-zeppelin> bin/zeppelin-daemon.sh start
Log dir doesn't exist, create /Users/Gabriel/Apps/incubator-zeppelin/logs
Pid dir doesn't exist, create /Users/Gabriel/Apps/incubator-zeppelin/run
Zeppelin start                                          [ OK ]
```

To stop the daemon, we can use this command:

```
bin/zeppelin-daemon.sh stop
```

If you come across the following error, you can check with `rat.txt`, only to find that it complains about your data file:

Failed to execute goal org.apache.rat:apache-rat-plugin:0.11:check (verify.rat) on project zeppelin: Too many files with unapproved license: 3

Simply move your data file to a different location and initiate the build again.

Customizing Zeppelin's server and websocket port

Zeppelin runs on port `8080` by default, and it has a websocket port enabled at the +1 port (`8081`) by default. We can customize the port by copying `conf/zeppelin-site.xml.template` to `conf/zeppelin-site.xml` and changing the ports and various other properties, if necessary. Since the Spark standalone cluster master web UI also runs on `8080`, when we are running Zeppelin on the same machine as the Spark master, we have to change the ports to avoid conflicts.

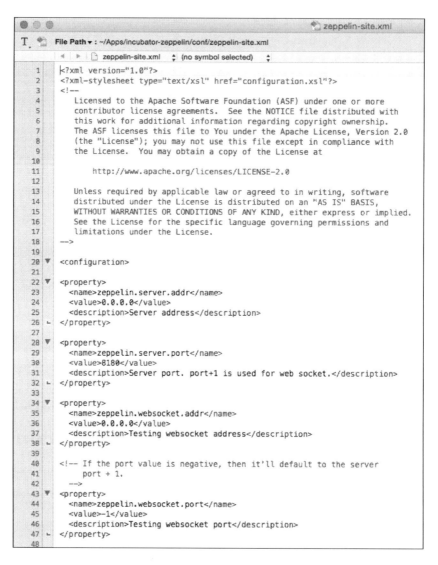

1. For now, let's change the port to `8180`. In order for this to take effect, let's restart Zeppelin using `bin/zeppelin-daemon restart`

Visualizing data on HDFS – parameterizing inputs

Once we start the daemon, we can point our browser to `http://localhost:8080` (change the port as per your modified port configuration) to view the Zeppelin UI. Zeppelin organizes its contents as notes and paragraphs. A note is simply a list of all the paragraphs on a single web page.

Using data from HDFS simply means that we point to the HDFS location instead of the local filesystem location.

Before we consume the file from HDFS, let's quickly check the Spark version that Zeppelin uses. This can be achieved by issuing `sc.version` on a paragraph. The `sc` is an implicit variable representing the `SparkContext` inside Zeppelin, which simply means that we need not programmatically create a `SparkContext` within Zeppelin.

```
sc.version
res0: String = 1.4.0
Took 1 seconds
```

Next, let's load the `profiles.json` sample data file, convert it into a DataFrame, and print the schema and the first 20 rows (show) for verification. Let's also finally register the DataFrame as a table. Just like the implicit variable for `SparkContext`, `SQLContext` is represented by the `sqlc` implicit variable inside Zeppelin:

```
val profilesJsonRdd = sqlc.jsonFile("hdfs://localhost:9000/data/scalada/
profiles.json")
val profileDF=profilesJsonRdd.toDF()
profileDF.printSchema()
profileDF.show()
profileDF.registerTempTable("profiles")
```

The output looks like this:

```
val profilesJsonRdd = sqlc.jsonFile(s"hdfs://localhost:9000/data/scalada/profiles.json")
val profileDF=profilesJsonRdd.toDF()

profileDF.printSchema()

profileDF.show()

profileDF.registerTempTable("profiles")
```

```
profilesJsonRdd: org.apache.spark.sql.DataFrame = [_id: string, about: string, address: string, age: bigint, c
ing, phone: string, registered: string, tags: array<string>]
profileDF: org.apache.spark.sql.DataFrame = [_id: string, about: string, address: string, age: bigint, company
hone: string, registered: string, tags: array<string>]
root
 |-- _id: string (nullable = true)
 |-- about: string (nullable = true)
 |-- address: string (nullable = true)
 |-- age: long (nullable = true)
 |-- company: string (nullable = true)
 |-- email: string (nullable = true)
 |-- eyeColor: string (nullable = true)
 |-- favoriteFruit: string (nullable = true)
 |-- gender: string (nullable = true)
 |-- name: string (nullable = true)
 |-- phone: string (nullable = true)
 |-- registered: string (nullable = true)
 |-- tags: array (nullable = true)
 |    |-- element: string (containsNull = true)
```

```
_id                 about            address          age company   email                eyeColor fav
55578ccb0cc5b350d... Eu excepteur esse... 694 Oriental Cour... 30  ENDIPIN   tracynguyen@endip... brown    app
55578ccb6975c4e2a... Proident exercita... 267 Amber Street,... 23  WARETEL   leannagarrett@war... brown    str
55578ccb33399a615... Aute proident Lor... 243 Bridgewater S... 24  IMPERIUM  blairwhite@imperi... brown    ban
55578ccb0f1d5ab09... Officia cillum nu... 647 Loring Avenue... 24  BEADZZA   andrearay@beadzza... blue     app
55578ccb591a45d4e... Sit fugiat mollit... 721 Bijou Avenue,... 27  AUSTECH   penningtongilbert... green    app
55578ccb9f0cd20c4... Minim do eiusmod ... 694 Llama Court, ... 21  PYRAMIA   shelleyburns@pyra... green    ban
55578ccb8d0accc28... Qui proident ulla... 498 Perry Terrace... 40  EDECINE   nicolefigueroa@ed... green    app
55578ccbd682cca21... Labore exercitati... 243 Stillwell Ave... 32  SINGAVERA galealvarado@sing... blue     ban
55578ccb0d9025ddd... Velit cillum Lore... 649 Beard Street,... 36  FURNITECH melindaparker@fur... blue     str
55578ccb5be70de0d... Laborum tempor mi... 972 Marconi Place... 36  DIGIAL    byerscarson@digia... blue     app
55578ccbc5a1050a5... Duis fugiat Lorem... 483 Hanson Place,... 31  ASSURITY  kristiemckinney@a... green    ban
55578ccb07fa02369... Consequat fugiat ... 540 Woodpoint Roa... 40  MICROLUXE salazarburks@micr... brown    str
55578ccb809e55bf0... Lorem culpa Lorem... 442 Ainslie Stree... 32  VIOCULAR  hopkinspatterson@... green    app
55578ccb204ff8ee6... Qui ad cillum mag... 444 Argyle Road, ... 23  IMKAN     maysrosario@imkan... green    app
55578ccb4b062fc61... Duis ex velit dui... 571 Sunnyside Ave... 38  HELIXO    atkinshancock@hel... blue     str
55578ccba5ff361a9... Et magna laboris ... 385 Meeker Avenue... 40  SLOFAST   edwinarobertson@s... blue     str
55578ccb386940ac3... Labore sit mollit... 936 Cheever Place... 37  FLEETMIX  elsienoel@fleetmi... blue     app
55578ccbfc41ff7fe... Consequat eiusmod... 406 Lake Place, M... 36  EVENTAGE  mirandamarsh@even... green    app
55578ccbfa6b6c300... Duis fugiat conse... 364 Metropolitan ... 31  BALOOBA   sharronmcconnell@... brown    app
55578ccbdd6650d81... Consequat et magn... 113 Applegate Cou... 29  EURON     mcdowellwelch@eur... blue     str
Took 1 seconds
```

 Be careful not to explicitly create `SQLContext` or `SparkContext`. If we create a `SQLContext` explicitly and register our temporary tables to it, it won't be accessible from the SQL queries that we execute. We'll get this error:

no such table List ([YOUR TEMP TABLE NAME])

Let's now run a simple query to understand eye colors and their counts for men in the dataset:

```
%sql select eyeColor, count(eyeColor) as count from profiles where
gender='male' group by eyeColor
```

The %sql at the beginning of the paragraph indicates to Zeppelin that we are about to execute a Spark SQL query in this paragraph.

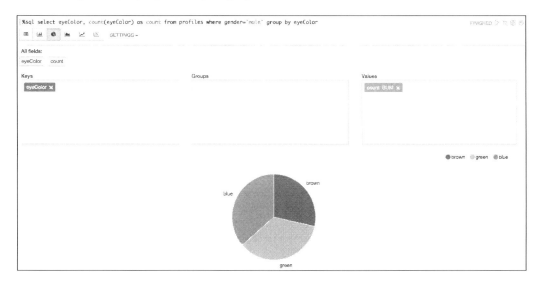

Now, if we wish to share this chart with someone or link it to an external website, we can do so by clicking on the gear icon in this paragraph and then clicking on **Link this paragraph**, as shown in the following screenshot:

We can actually parameterize the input for gender instead of altering our query every time. This is achieved by the use of ${PARAMETER PLACEHOLDER}:

```
%sql select eyeColor, count(eyeColor) as count from profiles where
gender="${gender}" group by eyeColor
```

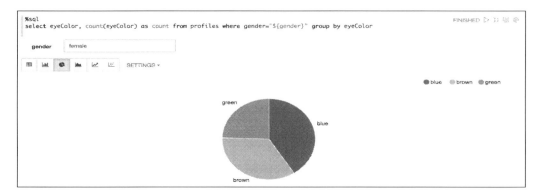

Finally, if parameterizing using free-form text isn't enough, we can use a dropdown instead:

```
%sql select eyeColor, count(eyeColor) as count from profiles where gender
="${gender=male,male|female}" group by eyeColor
```

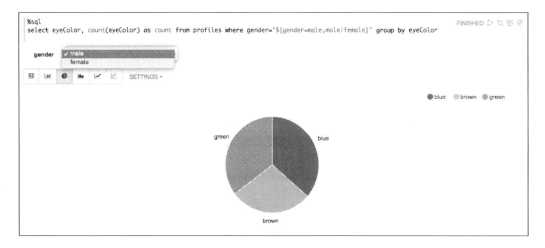

Running custom functions

While Spark SQL doesn't support a range of functions as wide as ANSI SQL does, it has an easy and powerful mechanism for registering a normal Scala function and using it inside the SQL context.

Let's say we would like to find out how many profiles fall under each age group. We have a simple function called `ageGroup`. Given an age, it returns a string representing the age group:

```
def ageGroup(age: Long) = {
    val buckets = Array("0-10", "11-20", "20-30", "31-40", "41-50", "51-
60", "61-70", "71-80", "81-90", "91-100", ">100")
    buckets(math.min((age.toInt - 1) / 10, buckets.length - 1))
}
```

Now, in order to register this function to be used inside Spark SQL, all that we need to do is give it a name and call the register method of the SQLContext's user-defined function object:

```
sqlc.udf.register("ageGroup", (age:Long)=>ageGroup(age.toInt))
```

Let's fire our query and see the use of the function in action:

```
%sql select ageGroup(age) as group,
          count(1) as total
from profiles
where gender='${gender=male,male|female}' group by ageGroup(age)
order by group
```

Here is the output:

Adding external dependencies to Zeppelin

Sooner or later, we would be depending on external libraries than that come bundled with Zeppelin, say for an efficient CSV import or RDBMS data import. Let's see how to load a MySQL database driver and visualize data from a table.

In order to load a `mysql` connector `java` driver, we just need to specify the group ID, artifact ID, and version number, and the JAR gets downloaded from the `maven` repository. `%dep` indicates that the paragraph adds a dependency, and the `z` implicit variable represents the Zeppelin context:

```
%dep
z.load("mysql:mysql-connector-java:5.1.35")
```

If we would like to point to our enterprise Maven repository or some other custom repository, we can add them by calling the `addRepo` method of the Zeppelin context available via the same `z` implicit variable:

```
%dep
z.addRepo("RepoName").url("RepoURL")
```

Alternatively, we can load the `jar` from the local filesystem using the overloaded `load` method:

```
%dep
z.load("/path/to.jar")
```

The only thing that we need to watch out for while using `%dep` is that the dependency paragraph should be used before using the libraries that are being loaded. So, it is generally advised to load the dependencies at the top of the Notebook.

Let's see the use in action:

  ▸ Loading the dependency:

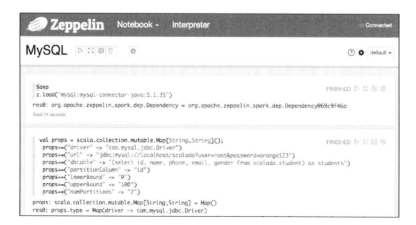

Once we have loaded the dependencies, we need to construct the options required to connect to the MySQL database:

```
val props = scala.collection.mutable.Map[String,String]();
  props+=("driver" -> "com.mysql.jdbc.Driver")
  props+=("url" -> "jdbc:mysql://localhost/scalada?user=root&passw
ord=orange123")
  props+=("dbtable" -> "(select id, name, phone, email, gender
from scalada.student) as students")
  props+=("partitionColumn" -> "id")
  props+=("lowerBound" -> "0")
  props+=("upperBound" -> "100")
  props+=("numPartitions" -> "2")
```

▸   Using the connection to create a DataFrame:

```
import scala.collection.JavaConverters._                                    FINISHED ▷ ✕ ▦ ⚙

  val studentDf = sqlContext.load("jdbc", props.asJava)
  studentDf.printSchema()
  studentDf.show()
  studentDf.registerTempTable("students")
import scala.collection.JavaConverters._
warning: there were 1 deprecation warning(s); re-run with -deprecation for details
studentDf: org.apache.spark.sql.DataFrame = [id: string, name: string, phone: string, email: string, gender: s
tring]
root
 |-- id: string (nullable = false)
 |-- name: string (nullable = true)
 |-- phone: string (nullable = true)
 |-- email: string (nullable = true)
 |-- gender: string (nullable = true)

+---+--------+--------------+--------------------+------+
|id |  name  |    phone     |              email|gender|
+---+--------+--------------+--------------------+------+
|10 |   Maya |1-271-683-2698|accumsan.convalli...|    F |
|11 |    Emi |1-467-270-1337|        est@nunc.com|    F |
|12 |  Caleb |1-683-212-0896|Suspendisse@Quisq...|    M |
|13 |Florence|1-603-575-2444|sit.amet.dapibus@...|    F |
```

```
import scala.collection.JavaConverters._
  val studentDf = sqlContext.load("jdbc", props.asJava)
    studentDf.printSchema()
    studentDf.show()
    studentDf.registerTempTable("students")
```

▸ Visualizing the data:

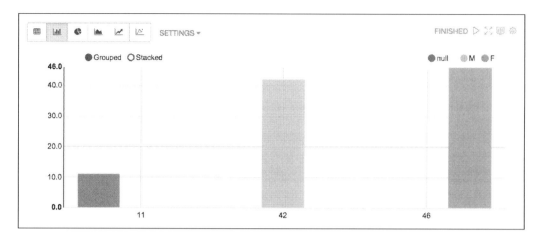

Pointing to an external Spark cluster

Running Zeppelin with built-in Spark is all good, but in most of our cases, we'll be executing the Spark jobs initiated by Zeppelin on a cluster of workers. Achieving this is pretty simple; we need to configure Zeppelin to point its Spark `master` property to an external Spark master URL. We'll be looking at how to install and run a Spark cluster on AWS, or a truly distributed cluster, in a later chapter (*Chapter 6, Scaling Up*), but for this example, I have a simple and standalone external Spark cluster running on my local machine. Please note that we will have to run Zeppelin on a different port because of the Zeppelin UI port's conflict with the Spark standalone cluster master web UI over `8080`:

For this example, let's download the Spark source for 1.4.1 and build it for Hadoop version 2.2:

```
build/mvn -Pyarn -Phadoop-2.2 -Dhadoop.version=2.2.0 -DskipTests clean
package
```

Similarly, let's download the `zeppelin` incubator and build it, specifying the Hadoop version to be 2.2:

```
mvn clean install -Pspark-1.4 -Dhadoop.version=2.2.0 -Phadoop-2.2
-DskipTests -Pyarn
```

Let's bring up the Spark cluster. From inside your Spark source, execute this:

```
sbin/start-all.sh
```

Finally, let's modify `conf/interpreter.json` and `conf/zeppelin-env.sh` to point the `master` property to the host on which the Spark VM is running. In this case, it will be my `localhost`, with the port being `7077`, which is the default master port.

1. The `conf/interpreter.json` file:

```
"ZARAAA1GU": {
    "id": "ZARAAA1GU",
    "name": "spark",
    "group": "spark",
    "properties": {
        "spark.cores.max": "",
        "spark.yarn.jar": "",
        "master": "spark://Gabriels-MacBook-Pro.local:7077",
        "zeppelin.spark.maxResult": "1000",
        "zeppelin.dep.localrepo": "local-repo",
        "spark.app.name": "Zeppelin",
        "spark.executor.memory": "512m",
        "zeppelin.spark.useHiveContext": "true",
        "zeppelin.spark.concurrentSQL": "false",
        "spark.home": "",
        "args": "",
```

2. The `conf/zeppelin-env.sh` file:

```
# export JAVA_HOME=
export MASTER=spark://Gabriels-MacBook-Pro.local:7077
```

Now, when we rerun Spark SQL from Zeppelin, we can see that the job runs on the external Spark instance, as shown here:

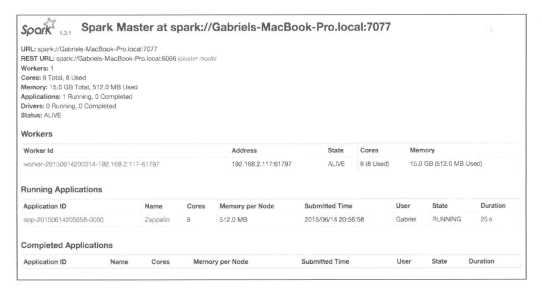

Creating scatter plots with Bokeh-Scala

While Zeppelin is powerful enough to quickly execute our Spark SQLs and visualize data, it is still an evolving platform. In this section, we'll take a brief look at the most popular visualizing framework in Python, called Bokeh, and use its (also fast evolving) Scala bindings to the framework. Breeze also has a visualization API called **breeze-viz**, which is built on JFreeChart. Unfortunately, at the time of writing this book, the API is not actively maintained, and therefore we won't be discussing it here.

The power of Zeppelin lies in the ability to share and view graphics on the browser. This is brought forth by the backing of the D3.js JavaScript visualization library. Bokeh is also backed by another JavaScript visualization library, called BokehJS. The Scala bindings library (`bokeh-scala`) not only gives an easier way to construct glyphs (lines, circles, and so on) out of Scala objects, but also translates glyphs into a format that is understandable by the BokehJS JavaScript components.

There is a warning here: the Bokeh-Scala bindings are still evolving and act at a lower level. Sometimes, this is more cumbersome than its Python counterpart. That said, I am still sure that we all would be able to appreciate the amazing graphs that we can create right out of Scala.

How to do it...

In this recipe, we will be creating a scatter plot using iris data (`https://archive.ics.uci.edu/ml/datasets/Iris`), which has the length and width attributes of flowers belonging to three different species of the same plant. Drawing a scatter plot on this dataset involves a series of interesting substeps.

For the purpose of representing the iris data in a Breeze matrix, I have naïvely transformed the species categories into numbers:

- *Iris setosa*: 0
- *Iris versicolor*: 1
- *Iris virginica*: 2

This is available in `irisNumeric.csv`. Later, we'll see how we can load the original iris data (`iris.data`) into a Spark DataFrame and use that as a source for plotting.

For the sake of clarity, let's define what the various terms in Bokeh actually mean:

- **Glyph**: All geometric shapes that we can think of—circles, squares, lines, and so on—are glyphs. This is just the UI representation and doesn't hold any data. All the properties related to this object just help us modify the UI properties: `color`, `x`, `y`, `width`, and so on.

▸ **Plot**: A plot is like a canvas on which we arrange various objects relevant to the visualization, such as the legend, *x* and *y* axes, grid, tools, and obviously, the core of the graph—the data itself. We construct various accessory objects and finally add them to the list of renderers in the plot object.

▸ **Document**: The document is the component that does the actual rendering. It accepts the plot as an argument, and when we call the `save` method in the document, it uses all the child renderers in the plot object and constructs a JSON from the wrapped elements. This JSON is eventually read by the BokehJS widgets to render the data in a visually pleasing manner. More than one plot can be rendered in the document by adding it to a grid plot (we'll look at how this is done in the next recipe, *Creating a time series MultiPlot with Bokeh-Scala*).

A plot is a composition of multiple widgets/glyphs.

This consists of a series of steps:

1. Preparing our data.
2. Creating the Plot and Document objects.
3. Creating a point (marker object) and a renderer for it.
4. Setting the x and y axes' data range for the plot.
5. Drawing the x and the y axes.
6. Viewing the marker objects with varying colors.
7. Adding Grid lines.
8. Adding a legend to the plot.

Preparing our data

Bokeh plots require our data to be in a format that it understands, but it's really easy to do it. All that we need to do is create a new source object that inherits from `ColumnDataSource`. The other options are `AjaxDataSource` and `RemoteDataSource`.

So, let's overlay our Breeze data source on `ColumnDataSource`:

```
import breeze.linalg._

object IrisSource extends ColumnDataSource {

  private val colormap = Map[Int, Color](0 -> Color.Red, 1 ->
Color.Green, 2 -> Color.Blue)

  private val iris = csvread(file = new File("irisNumeric.csv"),
separator = ',')
```

```
    val sepalLength = column(iris(::, 0))
    val sepalWidth = column(iris(::, 1))
    val petalLength = column(iris(::, 2))
    val petalWidth = column(iris(::, 3))
    val species = column(iris(::, 4))
}
```

The first line just reads `irisNumeric.csv` using the `csvread` function of the Breeze library. The color map is something that we'll be using later while plotting. The purpose of this map is to translate each species of flower into a different color. The final piece is where we convert the Breeze matrix into `ColumnDataSource`. As required by `ColumnDataSource`, we select and map specific columns in the Breeze matrix to corresponding columns.

Creating Plot and Document objects

Let's have our image's title as `Iris Petal Length vs Width` and create a document object so that we can save the final HTML by the name `IrisBokehBreeze.html`. Since we haven't specified the full path of the target file in the `save` method, the file will be saved in the same directory as the project itself:

```
val plot = new Plot().title("Iris Petal Length vs Width")


val document = new Document(plot)
val file = document.save("IrisBokehBreeze.html")


println(s"Saved the chart as ${file.url}")
```

Creating a marker object

Our plot has neither data nor any glyphs. Let's first create a marker object that marks the data point. There are a variety of marker objects to choose from: `Asterisk`, `Circle`, `CircleCross`, `CircleX`, `Cross`, `Diamond`, `DiamondCross`, `InvertedTriangle`, `PlainX`, `Square`, `SquareCross`, `SquareX`, and `Triangle`.

Let's choose `Diamond` for our purpose:

```
val diamond = new Diamond()
    .x(petalLength)
    .y(petalWidth)
    .fill_color(Color.Blue)
    .fill_alpha(0.5)
    .size(5)


val dataPointRenderer = new GlyphRenderer().data_source(IrisSource).
glyph(diamond)
```

While constructing the marker object, other than the UI attributes, we also say what the *x* and the *y* coordinates for it are. Note that we have also mentioned that the color of this marker is blue. We'll change that in a while using the color map.

Setting the X and Y axes' data range for the plot

The plot needs to know what the x and y data ranges of the plot are before rendering. Let's do that by creating two `DataRange` objects and setting them to the plot:

```
val xRange = new DataRange1d().sources(petal_length :: Nil)
val yRange = new DataRange1d().sources(petal_width :: Nil)


plot.x_range(xRange).y_range(yRange)
```

Let's try and run the first cut of this program.

The following is the output:

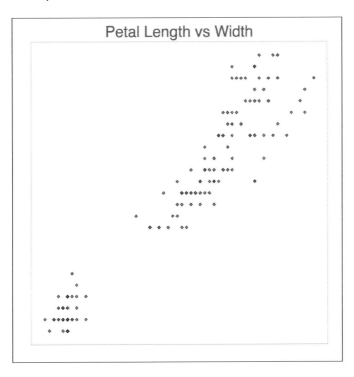

We see that this needs a lot of work to be done. Let's do it bit by bit.

Drawing the x and the y axes

Let's now draw the axes, set their bounds, and add them to the plot's renderers. We also need to let the plot know which location each axis belongs to:

```
//X and Y Axis
  val xAxis = new LinearAxis().plot(plot).axis_label("Petal Length").
bounds((1.0, 7.0))

  val yAxis = new LinearAxis().plot(plot).axis_label("Petal Width").
bounds((0.0, 2.5))

  plot.below <<= (listRenderer => (xAxis :: listRenderer))

  plot.left <<= (listRenderer => (yAxis :: listRenderer))


  //Add the renderer to the plot
  plot.renderers := List(xAxis, yAxis, dataPointRenderer)
```

Here is the output:

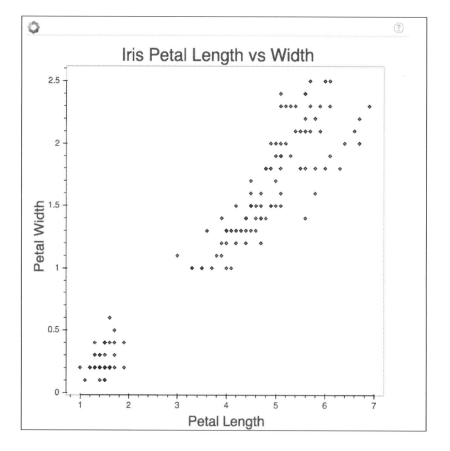

Viewing flower species with varying colors

All the data points are marked with blue as of now, but we would really like to differentiate the species visually. This is a simple two-step process:

1. Add new derived data (`speciesColor`) into our `ColumnDataSource` to hold colors that represent the species:

```
object IrisSource extends ColumnDataSource {

  private val colormap = Map[Int, Color](0 -> Color.Red, 1
-> Color.Green, 2 -> Color.Blue)

  private val iris = csvread(file = new
File("irisNumeric.csv"), separator = ',')

  val sepalLength = column(iris(::, 0))
  val sepalWidth = column(iris(::, 1))
  val petalLength = column(iris(::, 2))
  val petalWidth = column(iris(::, 3))
val speciesColor = column(species.value.map(v =>
colormap(v.round.toInt)))
}
```

So, we assign red to Iris setosa, green to Iris versicolor and blue to Iris virginica.

2. Modify the `diamond` marker to take this as input instead of accepting a static blue:

```
val diamond = new Diamond()
    .x(petalLength)
    .y(petalWidth)
    .fill_color(speciesColor)
    .fill_alpha(0.5)
    .size(10)
```

The output is as follows:

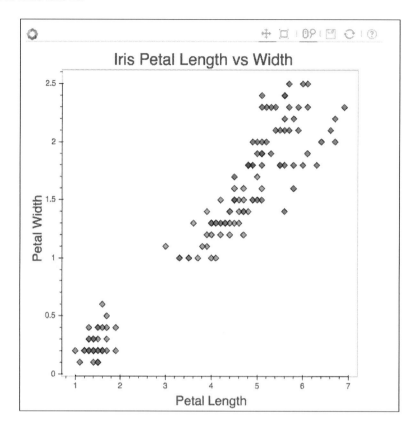

It looks fairly okay now. Let's add some tools to the image. Bokeh has some nice tools that can be attached to the image: `BoxSelectTool`, `BoxZoomTool`, `CrosshairTool`, `HoverTool`, `LassoSelectTool`, `PanTool`, `PolySelectTool`, `PreviewSaveTool`, `ResetTool`, `ResizeTool`, `SelectTool`, `TapTool`, `TransientSelectTool`, and `WheelZoomTool`.

Let's add a few of them to see them for fun:

```
val panTool = new PanTool().plot(plot)
  val wheelZoomTool = new WheelZoomTool().plot(plot)
  val previewSaveTool = new PreviewSaveTool().plot(plot)
  val resetTool = new ResetTool().plot(plot)
  val resizeTool = new ResizeTool().plot(plot)
  val crosshairTool = new CrosshairTool().plot(plot)


plot.tools := List(panTool, wheelZoomTool, previewSaveTool, resetTool,
resizeTool, crosshairTool)
```

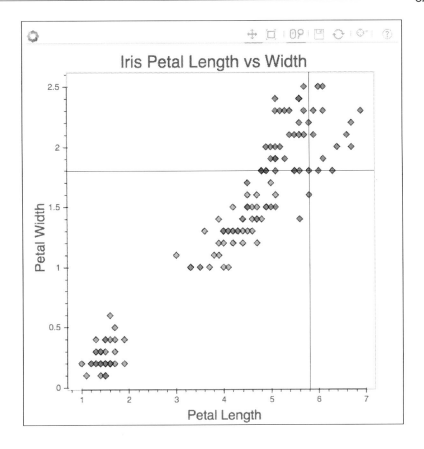

Adding grid lines

While we have the crosshair tool, which helps us locate the exact x and y values of a particular data point, it would be nice to have a data grid too. Let's add two data grids, one for the x axis and one for the y axis:

```
val xAxis = new LinearAxis().plot(plot).axis_label("Petal Length").
bounds((1.0, 7.0))
```

```
val yAxis = new LinearAxis().plot(plot).axis_label("Petal Width").
bounds((0.0, 2.5))
```

```
val xgrid = new Grid().plot(plot).axis(xAxis).dimension(0)
```

```
val ygrid = new Grid().plot(plot).axis(yAxis).dimension(1)
```

Next, let's add the grids to the plot renderer list too:

```
plot.renderers := List(xAxis, yAxis, dataPointRenderer, xgrid, ygrid)
```

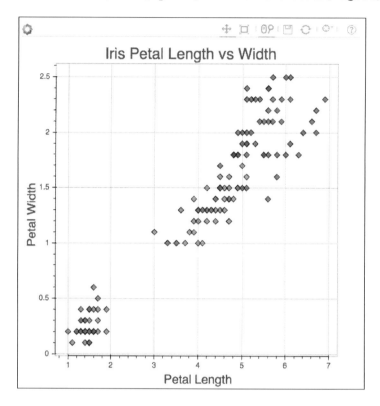

Adding a legend to the plot

This step is a bit tricky in the Scala binding of Bokeh due to the lack of high-level graphing objects, such as scatter. For now, let's cook up our own legend. The legends property of the Legend object accepts a list of tuples - a label and a GlyphRenderer pair. Let's explicitly create three GlyphRenderer wrapping diamonds of three colors, which represent the species. We then add them to the plot:

```
val setosa = new Diamond().fill_color(Color.Red).size(10).fill_alpha(0.5)

  val setosaGlyphRnd=new GlyphRenderer().glyph(setosa)

  val versicolor = new Diamond().fill_color(Color.Green).size(10).fill_
alpha(0.5)

  val versicolorGlyphRnd=new GlyphRenderer().glyph(versicolor)

  val virginica = new Diamond().fill_color(Color.Blue).size(10).fill_
alpha(0.5)

  val virginicaGlyphRnd=new GlyphRenderer().glyph(virginica)
```

```
val legends = List("setosa" -> List(setosaGlyphRnd),
        "versicolor" -> List(versicolorGlyphRnd),
        "virginica" -> List(virginicaGlyphRnd))
```

```
val legend = new Legend().orientation(LegendOrientation.TopLeft).
plot(plot).legends(legends)
```

```
plot.renderers := List(xAxis, yAxis, dataPointRenderer, xgrid, ygrid,
legend, setosaGlyphRnd, virginicaGlyphRnd, versicolorGlyphRnd)
```

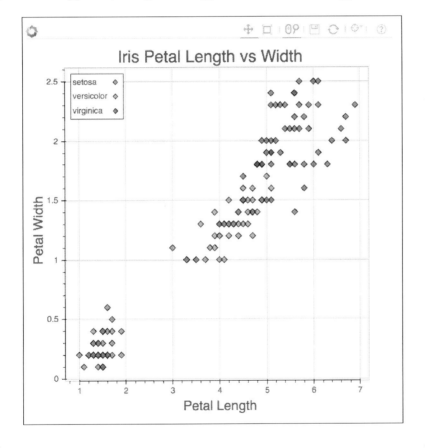

The code for this recipe can be found at `https://github.com/arunma/ScalaDataAnalysisCookbook/blob/master/chapter4-visualization/src/main/scala/com/packt/scalada/viz/breeze`.

Creating a time series MultiPlot with Bokeh-Scala

In this second recipe on plotting using Bokeh, we'll see how to plot a time series graph with a dataset borrowed from `https://archive.ics.uci.edu/ml/datasets/ Dow+Jones+Index`. We will also see how to plot multiple charts in a single document.

How to do it...

We'll be using only two fields from the dataset: the closing price of the stock at the end of the week, and the last business day of the week. Our dataset is comma separated. Let's take a look at some samples, as shown here:

```
quarter,stock,date,open,high,low,close,volume,percent_change_price,percent_change_volume_over_last_wk,previous_weeks_vol
1,AA,1/7/2011,$15.82,$16.72,$15.78,$16.42,239655616,3.79267,,,$16.71,$15.97,-4.42849,26,0.182704
1,AA,1/14/2011,$16.71,$16.71,$15.64,$15.97,242963398,-4.42849,1.380223028,239655616,$16.19,$15.79,-2.47066,19,0.187852
1,AA,1/21/2011,$16.19,$16.38,$15.60,$15.79,138428495,-2.47066,-43.02495926,242963398,$15.87,$16.13,1.63831,12,0.189994
1,AA,1/28/2011,$15.87,$16.63,$15.82,$16.13,151379173,1.63831,9.355500109,138428495,$16.18,$17.14,5.93325,5,0.185989
1,AA,2/4/2011,$16.18,$17.39,$16.18,$17.14,154387761,5.93325,1.987451735,151379173,$17.33,$17.37,0.230814,97,0.175029
1,AA,2/11/2011,$17.33,$17.48,$16.97,$17.37,114691279,0.230814,-25.71219489,154387761,$17.39,$17.28,-0.632547,90,0.172712
1,AA,2/18/2011,$17.39,$17.68,$17.28,$17.28,80023895,-0.632547,-30.22669579,114691279,$16.98,$16.68,-1.76678,83,0.173611
1,AA,2/25/2011,$16.98,$17.15,$15.96,$16.68,132981863,-1.76678,66.17769355,80023895,$16.81,$16.58,-1.36823,76,0.179856
1,AA,3/4/2011,$16.81,$16.94,$16.13,$16.58,109493077,-1.36823,-17.66315005,132981863,$16.58,$16.03,-3.31725,69,0.180941
1,AA,3/11/2011,$16.58,$16.75,$15.42,$16.03,114332562,-3.31725,4.419900447,109493077,$15.95,$16.11,1.00313,62,0.187149
1,AA,3/18/2011,$15.95,$16.33,$15.43,$16.11,130374108,1.00313,14.03060136,114332562,$16.38,$17.09,4.33455,55,0.18622
1,AA,3/25/2011,$16.38,$17.24,$16.26,$17.09,95550392,4.33455,-26.71060729,130374108,$17.13,$17.47,1.98482,48,0.175541
```

Preparing our data

In contrast to the previous recipe, where we used the Breeze matrix to construct the Bokeh `ColumnDataSource`, we'll use the Spark DataFrame to construct the source this time. The `getSource` method accepts a ticker (MSFT-Microsoft and CAT-Caterpillar) and a `SQLContext`. It runs a Spark SQL, fetches the data from the table, and constructs a `ColumnDataSource` from it:

```scala
import org.joda.time.format.DateTimeFormat

object StockSource {

  val formatter = DateTimeFormat.forPattern("MM/dd/yyyy");

  def getSource(ticker: String, sqlContext: SQLContext) = {
    val stockDf = sqlContext.sql(s"select stock, date, close from
stocks where stock= '$ticker'")
    stockDf.cache()
```

```
    val dateData: Array[Double] =
stockDf.select("date").collect.map(eachRow =>
formatter.parseDateTime(eachRow.getString(0)).getMillis().toDouble)
    val closeData: Array[Double] =
stockDf.select("close").collect.map(eachRow =>
eachRow.getString(0).drop(1).toDouble)

    object source extends ColumnDataSource {
      val date = column(dateData)
      val close = column(closeData)
    }
    source
  }
}
```

Earlier, we constructed SQLContext and registered the dataset as a table, like this:

```
val conf = new SparkConf().setAppName("csvDataFrame").
setMaster("local[2]")

val sc = new SparkContext(conf)

val sqlContext = new SQLContext(sc)

val stocks = sqlContext.csvFile(filePath = "dow_jones_index.data",
useHeader = true, delimiter = ',')

stocks.registerTempTable("stocks")
```

The only tricky thing that we do here is convert the date value into milliseconds. This is because the Plot point requires a double. We use the **Joda-Time** API to achieve this.

Creating a plot

Let's go ahead and create the Plot object from the source:

```
//Create Plot
val plot = new Plot().title(ticker).x_range(xdr).y_range(ydr).width(800).
height(400)
```

Let's have our image's title as the ticker name of the stock and create a Document object so that we can save the final HTML by the name ClosingPrices.html:

```
    val msDocument = new Document(microsoftPlot)
    val msHtml = msDocument.save("ClosingPrices.html")
```

Creating a line that joins all the data points

As we saw earlier with the `Diamond` marker, we'll have to pass the x and the y positions of the data points. Also, we will need to wrap the `Line` glyph into a renderer so that we can add it to `Plot`:

```
val line = new Line().x(date).y(close).line_color(color).line_width(2)

val lineGlyph = new GlyphRenderer().data_source(source).glyph(line)
```

Setting the x and y axes' data range for the plot

The plot needs to know what the x and y data ranges of the plot are before rendering. Let's do that by creating two `DataRange` objects and setting them to the plot:

```
val xdr = new DataRange1d().sources(List(date))

val ydr = new DataRange1d().sources(List(close))


plot.x_range(xdr).y_range(ydr)
```

Drawing the axes and the grids

Drawing the axes and the grids is the same as before. We added some labels to the axis, formatted the display of the *x* axis, and then added them to the `Plot`:

```
val xformatter = new DatetimeTickFormatter().formats(Map(DatetimeUnits.
Months -> List("%b %Y")))

val xaxis = new DatetimeAxis().plot(plot).formatter(xformatter).axis_
label("Month")

val yaxis = new LinearAxis().plot(plot).axis_label("Price")

plot.below <<= (xaxis :: _)

plot.left <<= (yaxis :: _)

val xgrid = new Grid().plot(plot).dimension(0).axis(xaxis)

val ygrid = new Grid().plot(plot).dimension(1).axis(yaxis)
```

Adding tools

As before, let's add some tools to the image—and to the `plot`:

```
//Tools
val panTool = new PanTool().plot(plot)
val wheelZoomTool = new WheelZoomTool().plot(plot)
val previewSaveTool = new PreviewSaveTool().plot(plot)
val resetTool = new ResetTool().plot(plot)
val resizeTool = new ResizeTool().plot(plot)
```

```
val crosshairTool = new CrosshairTool().plot(plot)


plot.tools := List(panTool, wheelZoomTool, previewSaveTool,
resetTool, resizeTool, crosshairTool)
```

Adding a legend to the plot

Since we already have the `Glyph` renderer for the `line`, all we need to do is add it to the legend. The properties of the line automatically propagate to the legend:

```
//Legend
    val legends = List(ticker -> List(lineGlyph))
    val legend = new Legend().plot(plot).legends(legends)
```

Next, let's add all the renderers that we created before to the plot:

```
plot.renderers <<= (xaxis :: yaxis :: xgrid :: ygrid :: lineGlyph ::
legend :: _)
```

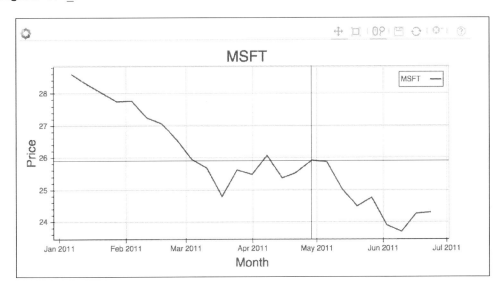

As the final step, let's try plotting multiple plots in the same document.

Multiple plots in the document

Creating multiple plots in the same document is child's play. All that we need to do is create all our plots and then add them into a grid. Finally, instead of passing our individual plot object into the document, we pass in `GridPlot`:

```
val children = List(List(microsoftPlot, bofaPlot), List(caterPillarPlot,
mmmPlot))

val grid = new GridPlot().children(children)


val document = new Document(grid)

val html = document.save("DJClosingPrices.html")
```

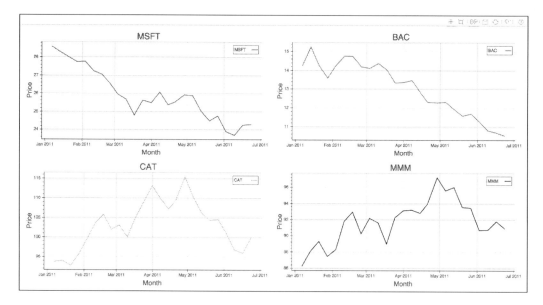

 The code for this recipe can be found at `https://github.com/arunma/ScalaDataAnalysisCookbook/blob/master/chapter4-visualization/src/main/scala/com/packt/scalada/viz/breeze.`

In this chapter, we explored two methods of visualization and built some basic graphs and charts using Scala. As I mentioned earlier, the visualization libraries in Scala are actively being developed and cannot be compared to advanced visualizations that can be generated using R or, for that sake, Tableau.

5
Learning from Data

In this chapter, we will cover the following recipes:

- ▸ Predicting continuous values using linear regression
- ▸ Binary classification using LogisticRegression and SVM
- ▸ Binary classification using LogisticRegression with the Pipeline API
- ▸ Clustering using K-means
- ▸ Feature reduction using principal component analysis

Introduction

In previous chapters, we saw how to load, prepare, and visualize data. Now, let's start doing some interesting stuff with it. In this chapter, we'll be looking into applying various machine learning techniques on top of it. We'll look at a few examples for the two broad classifications of machine learning techniques: supervised and unsupervised learning. Before that, however, let's briefly see what these terms mean.

Supervised and unsupervised learning

If you are reading this book, you probably already know what supervised and unsupervised learning are, but for the sake of completion, let's briefly summarize what they mean. In supervised learning, we train the algorithms with labeled data. Labeled data is nothing but input data along with the outcome variable. For example, if our intention is to predict whether a website is about news, we would be preparing a sample dataset of website content with "news" and "not news" as labels. This dataset is called the training dataset.

With supervised learning, our end goal is to use the training dataset and come up with a function that maps our input variables to an output variable with least margin of error. We call input variables (or *x* variables) features or explanatory variables, and the output variable (also known as the *y* variable or label) the target or dependent variable. In the news website example, the text content in the website would be the input variable and "news" or "not news" would be the target variable. The function, along with its parameters (or weights or theta), is our hypothesis, or model.

In the case of unsupervised learning, we aim to find a structure within the data— groups and relationships among these groups or the participants of a group. Unlike supervised learning, we don't know any information about the data or even its subset. An example would be to see whether there are similar buying patterns among a group of people (which helps cross-selling) or to see which group of people is more likely to buy pizza from our newly opened store.

Gradient descent

With supervised learning, in order for the algorithm to learn the relationship between the input and the output features, we provide a set of manually curated values for the target variable (*y*) against a set of input variables (*x*). We call it the training set. The learning algorithm then has to go over our training set, perform some optimization, and come up with a model that has the least cost—deviation from the true values. So technically, we have two algorithms for every learning problem: an algorithm that comes up with the function and (an initial set of) weights for each of the *x* features, and a supporting algorithm (also called cost minimization or optimization algorithm) that looks at our function parameters (feature weights) and tries to minimize the cost as much as possible.

There are a variety of cost minimization algorithms, but one of the most popular is gradient descent. Imagine gradient descent as climbing down a mountain. The height of the mountain represents the cost, and the plain represents the feature weights. The highest point is your function with the maximum cost, and the lowest point has the least cost. Therefore, our intention is to walk down the mountain. What gradient descent does is as follows: for every single step down the slope that it takes of a particular size (the step size), it goes through the entire dataset (!) and updates all the values of the weights for *x* features. This goes on until it reaches a state where the cost is the minimum. This flavor of gradient descent, in which it sees all of the data per iteration and updates all the parameters during every iteration, is called batch gradient descent. The trouble with using this algorithm against the size of the data that Spark aims to handle is that going through millions of rows per iteration is definitely not optimal. So, Spark uses a variant of gradient descent, called **Stochastic Gradient Descent (SGD)**, wherein the parameters are updated for each training example as it looks at it one by one. In this way, it starts making progress almost immediately, and therefore the computational effort is considerably reduced. The SGD settings can be customized using the `optimizer` attribute inside each of the ML algorithm. We'll look at this in detail in the recipes.

In the following recipes, we'll be looking at linear regression, logistic regression, and support vector machines as examples of supervised learning and K-means clustering, as well as dimensionality reduction using **Principal Component Analysis** (**PCA**) as an example of unsupervised learning. We'll also briefly look at the Stanford NLP toolkit and Scala NLP's Epic, popular natural language processing libraries, as examples of fitting a third-party library into Spark jobs.

Predicting continuous values using linear regression

At the risk of stating the obvious, linear regression aims to find the relationship between an output (y) based on an input (x) using a mathematical model that is linear to the input variables. The output variable, y, is a continuous numerical value. If we have more than one input/explanatory variable (x), as in the example that we are going to see, we call it multiple linear regression. The dataset that we'll use for this recipe, for lack of creativity, is lifted from the UCI website at `http://archive.ics.uci.edu/ml/machine-learning-databases/wine-quality/`. This dataset has 1599 instances of various red wines, their chemical composition, and their quality. We'll use it to predict the quality of a red wine.

How to do it...

Let's summarize the steps:

1. Importing the data.
2. Converting each instance into a LabeledPoint.
3. Preparing the training and test data.
4. Scaling the features.
5. Training the model.
6. Predicting against the test data.
7. Evaluating the model.
8. Regularizing the parameters.
9. Mini batching.

 The code for this recipe can be found at `https://github.com/arunma/ScalaDataAnalysisCookbook/tree/master/chapter5-learning/src/main/scala/com/packt/scalada/learning/LinearRegressionWine.scala`.

"Step zero" of this process is the creation of `SparkConfig` and the `SparkContext`. There is nothing fancy here:

```
val conf = new SparkConf().setAppName("linearRegressionWine").
setMaster("local[2]")

val sc = new SparkContext(conf)
```

Importing the data

We then import the semicolon-separated text file. We map each line into an `Array[String]` by splitting each of them using semicolons. We end up with RDD[Array[String]]:

```
val rdd = sc.textFile("winequality-red.csv").map(line => line.split(";"))
```

Converting each instance into a LabeledPoint

As we discussed earlier, supervised learning requires training data to be provided. We are also are required to test the model that we create for its accuracy against another set of data—the test data. If we have two different datasets for this, we can import them separately and mark them as a training set and a test set. In our example, we'll use a single dataset and split it into training and test sets.

```
7.4;0.7;0;1.9;0.076;11;34;0.9978;3.51;0.56;9.4;5
7.8;0.88;0;2.6;0.098;25;67;0.9968;3.2;0.68;9.8;5
7.8;0.76;0.04;2.3;0.092;15;54;0.997;3.26;0.65;9.8;5
11.2;0.28;0.56;1.9;0.075;17;60;0.998;3.16;0.58;9.8;6
7.4;0.7;0;1.9;0.076;11;34;0.9978;3.51;0.56;9.4;5
7.4;0.66;0;1.8;0.075;13;40;0.9978;3.51;0.56;9.4;5
7.9;0.6;0.06;1.6;0.069;15;59;0.9964;3.3;0.46;9.4;5
7.3;0.65;0;1.2;0.065;15;21;0.9946;3.39;0.47;10;7
7.8;0.58;0.02;2;0.073;9;18;0.9968;3.36;0.57;9.5;7
7.5;0.5;0.36;6.1;0.071;17;102;0.9978;3.35;0.8;10.5;5
6.7;0.58;0.08;1.8;0.097;15;65;0.9959;3.28;0.54;9.2;5
7.5;0.5;0.36;6.1;0.071;17;102;0.9978;3.35;0.8;10.5;5
```

Each of our training samples has the following format: the last field is the quality of the wine, a rating from 1 to 10, and the first 11 fields are the properties of the wine. So, from our perspective, the quality of the wine is the *y* variable (the output) and the rest of them are *x* variables (input). Now, let's represent this in a format that Spark understands—a LabeledPoint. A LabeledPoint is a simple wrapper around the input features (our *x* variables) and our pre-predicted value (*y* variable) for these *x* input values:

```
val dataPoints=rdd.map(row=>new LabeledPoint(row.last.toDouble,Vectors.
dense(row.take(row.length-1).map(str=>str.toDouble))))
```

The first parameter to the constructor of the LabeledPoint is the label (*y* variable), and the second parameter is a vector of input variables.

Preparing the training and test data

As we discussed earlier, we can have two different independent datasets for training and testing. However, it is a common practice to split the dataset into training and test datasets. In this recipe, we will be splitting the dataset into training and test sets in the ratio of 80:20, with each of the elements being selected randomly. This random shuffling of data is one of the prerequisites for better performance of the SGD too:

```
val dataSplit = dataPoints.randomSplit(Array(0.8, 0.2))

val trainingSet = dataSplit(0)

val testSet = dataSplit(1)
```

Scaling the features

Running a quick summary statistics reveals that our features aren't in the same range:

```
val featureVector = rdd.map(row => Vectors.dense(row.take(row.length-1).
map(str => str.toDouble)))

print(s"Max : ${stats.max}, Min : ${stats.min}, and Mean : ${stats.mean}
and Variance : ${stats.variance}")

println ("Min "+ stats.min)

println ("Max "+ stats.max)
```

Here is the output:

```
Min [4.6,0.12,0.0,0.9,0.012,1.0,6.0,0.99007,2.74,0.33,8.4]

Max [15.9,1.58,1.0,15.5,0.611,72.0,289.0,1.00369,4.01,2.0,14.9]

Variance : [3.031416388997815,0.0320623776515516,0.0379
4748313440582,1.987897132985963,0.00215142653300991,10
9.41488383305895,1082.1023725325845,3.56202945332629E-
6,0.02383518054541292,0.02873261612976197,1.135647395000472]
```

It is always recommended that the input variables have a mean of 0. This is easily achieved with the help of the `StandardScaler` built into the Spark ML library itself. The one thing that we have to watch out for here is that we have to scale the training and the test sets uniformly. The way we do it is by creating a scaler for trainingSplit and using the same scaler to scale the test set. Another side note is that feature scaling helps with faster convergence in SGD:

```
val scaler = new StandardScaler(withMean = true, withStd = true).
fit(trainingSet.map(dp => dp.features))


val scaledTrainingSet = trainingSet.map(dp => new LabeledPoint(dp.label,
scaler.transform(dp.features))).cache()


val scaledTestSet = testSet.map(dp => new LabeledPoint(dp.label, scaler.
transform(dp.features))).cache()
```

Training the model

The next step is to use our training data to create a model. This just involves creating an instance of `LinearRegressionWithSGD` and passing in a few parameters: one for the LinearRegression algorithm and two for the SGD. The SGD parameters can be accessed through the use of the `optimizer` attribute inside `LinearRegressionWithSGD`:

- ▸ `setIntercept`: While predicting, we are more interested in the slope. This setting will force the algorithm to find the intercept too.

- ▸ `optimizer.setNumIterations`: This determines the number of iterations that our algorithm needs to go through on the training set before finalizing the hypothesis. An optimal number would be 10^6 divided by the number of instances in your dataset. In our case, we'll set it to `1000`.

- ▸ `setStepSize`: This tells the gradient descent algorithm while it tries to reduce the parameters how big a step it needs to take during every iteration. Setting this parameter is really tricky because we would like the SGD to take bigger steps in the beginning and smaller steps towards the convergence. Setting a fixed small number would slow down the algorithm, and setting a fixed bigger number would not give us a function that is a reasonable minimum. The way Spark handles our `setStepSize` input parameter is as follows: it divides the input parameter by a root of the iteration number. So initially, our step size is huge, and as we go further down, it becomes smaller and smaller. The default step size parameter is `1`.

```
val regression=new LinearRegressionWithSGD().setIntercept(true)
regression.optimizer.setNumIterations(1000).setStepSize(0.1)


//Let's create a model out of our training examples.
val model=regression.run(scaledTrainingSet)
```

Predicting against test data

This step is just a one-liner. We use the resulting model to predict the output (*y*) based on the features of the test set:

```
val predictions:RDD[Double]=model.predict(scaledTestSet.map(point=>point.
features))
```

Evaluating the model

Let's evaluate our model against one of the most popular regression evaluation metrics— **mean squared error**. Let's get the actual values that our test data has (the *y* variable prepared manually) and then compare it with the predictions from our model:

```
val actuals:RDD[Double]=scaledTestSet.map(_.label)
```

Mean squared error

The mean squared error is given by this formula:

$$MSE = \frac{1}{n} \sum_{i=1}^{n} (y_i - \tilde{y}_i)^2$$

So, we take the difference between the actual and the predicted values (errors), square them, and calculate the sum of them all. We then divide this sum by the number of values, thereby calculating the mean:

```
val predictsAndActuals: RDD[(Double, Double)] = predictions.zip(actuals)

val sumSquaredErrors=predictsAndActuals.map{case (pred,act)=>
  println (s"act, pred and difference $act, $pred ${act-pred}")
  math.pow(act-pred,2)
}.sum()

val meanSquaredError = sumSquaredErrors / scaledTestSet.count

println(s"SSE is $sumSquaredErrors")
println(s"MSE is $meanSquaredError")
```

Here is the output:

```
SSE is 162.21647197365706
MSE is 0.49607483783992984
```

In our example, we selected all the features that are present in our dataset. Later, we'll take a look at dimensionality reduction, which helps us reduce the number of features while still maintaining the variance of the dataset at a reasonably higher level.

Regularizing the parameters

Before we see what regularization is, let's briefly see what overfitting is. A model is said to be overfit (or having high variance) when it memorizes the training set. The result of this is that the algorithm fails to generalize and therefore performs badly with unseen datasets. One way to solve the problem of overfitting is to manually select the important features that will be used to create the model, but for a large-dimensional dataset, it is hard to decide which ones to keep and which ones to throw away.

The other popular option is to retain all the features but reduce the magnitudes of the feature weights. Thus, even with a model that is complex (with higher degree polynomials), if the feature weights are really small, the resulting model would be simple. In other words, given two equally (or almost equally) performing models, with one model being complex (with higher degree polynomial) and the other model being simple, regularization chooses the simple model. The reasoning behind this is that models with simple parameters have a higher probability of predicting unseen data (also known as generalization).

The Spark MLlib comes with implementations for the most common L1 and L2 regularizations. As a side note, `LinearRegressionWithSGD`, by default, uses a `SimpleUpdater`, which does not regularize the parameters. Interestingly, Spark has implementations of regression algorithms that are based on top of the L1 and L2 updaters; they are called the Lasso (that uses the L1 updater) and Ridge (that uses the L2 updater by default).

While the L1 regularizer offers some feature selection when the dataset that we have is sparse (or if the dataset's rows are smaller than the feature itself), most of the time, it is recommended is to use the L2 regularizer. The new Pipeline API also has out-of-the-box support for ElasticNet regularization, which uses both the L1 and L2 regularizations internally. Now, let's go over the code:

```scala
def algorithm(algo: String, iterations: Int, stepSize: Int) = algo
match {
    case "linear" => {
        val algo = new LinearRegressionWithSGD()
algo.setIntercept(true).optimizer.setNumIterations(iterations).
setStepSize(stepSize)
        algo
    }
    case "lasso" => {
        val algo = new LassoWithSGD()
algo.setIntercept(true).optimizer.setNumIterations(iterations).
setStepSize(stepSize)
        algo
    }
    case "ridge" => {
        val algo = new RidgeRegressionWithSGD()
algo.setIntercept(true).optimizer.setNumIterations(iterations).
setStepSize(stepSize)
        algo
    }
}
```

As discussed earlier, `LassoWithSGD` wraps an L1 updater and `RidgeRegessionWithSGD` wraps an L2 updater. From a code perspective, all that we need to do is change the name of the class. The optimizer (gradient descent) now accepts a regularization parameter that penalizes larger parameters for the features. The default value of the regularization parameter is 0.01 in Spark. A smaller regularization parameter would result in underfitting, and a large parameter would result in overfitting.

The following output shows that regularizing the parameters has reduced our error values:

```
************** Printing metrics for Linear Regression with SGD
*****************
SSE is 132.39124792957116
MSE is 0.4124337941731189
************** Printing metrics for Lasso Regression with SGD
*****************
SSE is 132.3943810653321
MSE is 0.4124435547206608
************** Printing metrics for Ridge Regression with SGD
*****************
SSE is 132.44011034123344
MSE is 0.4125860135240917
```

Mini batching

Instead of going through our dataset one by one in the case of SGD, or seeing the entire dataset for every iteration (in the case of batch gradient descent) while updating the parameter vector, we can settle for something in the middle. With the mini batch fraction parameter, for every single iteration, the SGD considers that fraction of the dataset to process for the parameter update. Let's set the batch size to 5 percent:

```
algo.setIntercept(true).optimizer.setNumIterations(iterations).
setStepSize(stepSize).setRegParam(0.001).setMiniBatchFraction(0.05)
```

The results are as follows:

```
************** Printing metrics for Linear Regression with SGD
*****************
SSE is 112.96958667767147
MSE is 0.3574986920179477
SST is 183.05305027649794
Residual sum of squares is 0.38285875866568087
************** Printing metrics for Lasso Regression with SGD
*****************
```

```
SSE is 112.95392101963424

MSE is 0.35744911715074124

SST is 183.05305027649794

Residual sum of squares is 0.3829443385454675

************** Printing metrics for Ridge Regression with SGD
*****************

SSE is 112.9218089913291

MSE is 0.3573474968080035

SST is 183.05305027649794

Residual sum of squares is 0.3831197632557175
```

The advantage that we get from using mini batches is that this obviously gives better performance than plain SGD without batches. This is because with plain SGD, for every iteration, only one example is considered to update the parameters. However, with mini batches, we consider a batch of examples. That said, the improvement in the mean squared error from the previous run is not the result of using batches, but just a feature of SGD—roaming around the minima and not converging at a fixed point.

Binary classification using LogisticRegression and SVM

Unlike linear regression, wherein we predicted continuous values for the outcome (the *y* variable), logistic regression and the **Support Vector Machine** (**SVM**) are used to predict just one out of the *n* possibilities for the outcome (the *y* variable). If the outcome is one of two possibilities, then the classification is called a binary classification.

Logistic regression, when used for binary classification, looks at each data point and estimates the probability of that data point falling under the positive case. If the probability is less than a threshold, then the outcome is negative (or 0); otherwise, the outcome is positive (or 1).

As with any other supervised learning techniques, we will be providing training examples for logistic regression. We then add a bit of code for feature extraction and let the algorithm create a model that encapsulates the probability of each of the features belonging to one of the binary outcomes.

What SVM tries to do is map all of the training data as points in the feature space. The algorithm comes up with a hyperplane that separates the positive and negative training examples in such a way that the distance (margin band) between them is maximum. This is better illustrated with a diagram:

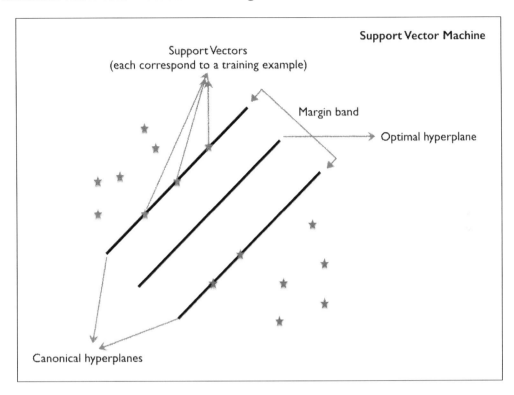

When a new and unseen data point comes up for prediction, the algorithm looks at that point and tries to find the closest point to the input data point. The label corresponding to that point will be predicted as the label for the input point as well.

How to do it...

Both the implementations of LogisticRegression and SVM in Spark use L2 regularization by default, but we are free to switch to L1 by setting the updater explicitly.

In this recipe, we'll classify a spam/ham dataset (https://archive.ics.uci.edu/ml/datasets/SMS+Spam+Collection) against three variants of classification algorithms:

► Logistic regression with SGD as the optimization algorithm

► Logistic regression with BFGS as the optimization algorithm

► Support vector machine with SGD as the optimization algorithm

The BFGS optimization algorithm provides the benefits of converging to the minimum faster than SGD. Also, for BFGS, we need not break our heads coming up with an optimal learning rate.

Let's summarize the steps:

1. Importing the data.
2. Tokenizing the data and converting it into LabeledPoints.
3. Factoring the Inverse Document Frequency (IDF).
4. Preparing the training and test data.
5. Constructing the algorithm.
6. Training the model and predicting the test data.
7. Evaluating the model.

 The code for this recipe can be found at `https://github.com/arunma/ScalaDataAnalysisCookbook/blob/master/chapter5-learning/src/main/scala/com/packt/scalada/learning/BinaryClassificationSpam.scala`.

Importing the data

As usual, our input data is in the form of a text file—SMSSpamCollection. The data file looks like this:

```
1 ham  Go until jurong point, crazy.. Available only in bugis n great world la e buffet... Cine there got amore wat...
2 ham  Ok lar... Joking wif u oni...
3 spam  Free entry in 2 a wkly comp to win FA Cup final tkts 21st May 2005. Text FA to 87121 to receive entry question(std txt rate)T&C's apply 08452810075over18's
4 ham  U dun say so early hor... U c already then say...
5 ham  Nah I don't think he goes to usf, he lives around here though
6 spam  FreeMsg Hey there darling it's been 3 week's now and no word back! I'd like some fun you up for it still? Tb ok! XxX std chgs to send, £1.50 to rcv
7 ham  Even my brother is not like to speak with me. They treat me like aids patent.
8 ham  As per your request 'Melle Melle (Oru Minnaminunginte Nurungu Vettam)' has been set as your callertune for all Callers. Press *9 to copy your friends Callertune
9 spam  WINNER!! As a valued network customer you have been selected to receiveo £900 prize reward! To claim call 09061701461. Claim code KL341. Valid 12 hours only.
10 spam  Had your mobile 11 months or more? U R entitled to Update to the latest colour mobiles with camera for Free! Call The Mobile Update Co FREE on 08002986030
11 ham  I'm gonna be home soon and i don't want to talk about this stuff anymore tonight, k? I've cried enough today.
12 spam  SIX chances to win CASH! From 100 to 20,000 pounds txt> CSH11 and send to 87575. Cost 150p/day, 6days, 16+ TsandCs apply Reply HL 4 info
13 spam  URGENT! You have won a 1 week FREE membership in our £100,000 Prize Jackpot! Txt the word: CLAIM to No: 81010 T&C www.dbuk.net LCCLTD POBOX 4403LDNW1A7RW18
14 ham  I've been searching for the right words to thank you for this breather. I promise i wont take your help for granted and will fulfil my promise. You have been wonder
15 ham  I HAVE A DATE ON SUNDAY WITH WILL!!
```

As we can see, the label and the data are separated by a tab. So, while reading each line, we split the label and the content, and then populate a simple case class named `Document`. This `Document` class is just a temporary placeholder. In the next step, we'll convert these documents into LabeledPoints:

```scala
//Frankly, we could make this a tuple but this looks neat
  case class Document(label: String, content: String)

  val docs = sc.textFile("SMSSpamCollection").map(line => {
    val words = line.split("\t")
    Document(words.head.trim(), words.tail.mkString(" "))
  })
```

Tokenizing the data and converting it into LabeledPoints

For the tokenization, instead of relying on the tokenizer provided inside Spark, we'll see how to plug in two external NLP libraries—the Stanford CoreNLP and Scala NLP's Epic libraries. These are the two most popular NLP libraries: one from the Java world and the other from Scala. However, one thing that we ought to watch out for while using external libraries is that the instantiation of these APIs, and therefore the creation of heavyweight objects required for the use of these APIs (such as a tokenizer), should be done at the partition level. If we do it at the level of a closure, such as a map over RDD, we'll end up creating new instance of the API object for every single instance of the data.

In the case of Epic, we just split the documents into sentences and then tokenize them into words. We also add two more restrictions. Only those tokens that contain letters or digits will be considered, and the tokens should be of at least two characters:

```
import epic.preprocess.TreebankTokenizer
import epic.preprocess.MLSentenceSegmenter
//Use Scala NLP - Epic
      val labeledPointsUsingEpicRdd: RDD[LabeledPoint] =
docs.mapPartitions { docIter =>

        val segmenter = MLSentenceSegmenter.bundled().get
        val tokenizer = new TreebankTokenizer()
        val hashingTf = new HashingTF(5000)

        docIter.map { doc =>
          val sentences = segmenter(doc.content)
          val tokens = sentences.flatMap(sentence =>
tokenizer(sentence))

          //consider only features that are letters or digits and
cut off all words that are less than 2 characters
          val filteredTokens=tokens.toList.filter(token =>
token.forall(_.isLetterOrDigit)).filter(_.length() > 1)

          new LabeledPoint(if (doc.label=="ham") 0 else 1,
hashingTf.transform(filteredTokens))
        }
      }.cache()
```

`MLSentenceSegmenter` splits the paragraph into sentences. The sentences are then split into terms (or words) using the tokenizer. `HashingTF` creates a map of terms with their frequency of occurrence. Finally, to construct a LabeledPoint for each document, we convert these terms into a term frequency vector for that document using the `transform` function of `HashingTF`. Also, we restrict the maximum number of interested terms to 5,000 by way of setting the `numFeatures` in `HashingTF`.

With Stanford CoreNLP, the process is a little more involved, in the sense that we reduce the tokens to lemmas (https://en.wikipedia.org/wiki/Lemmatisation). In order to do this, we create an NLP pipeline that splits sentences, tokenizes, and finally reduces the tokens to lemmas:

```scala
def corePipeline(): StanfordCoreNLP = {
        val props = new Properties()
        props.put("annotators", "tokenize, ssplit, pos, lemma")
        new StanfordCoreNLP(props)
    }

    def lemmatize(nlp: StanfordCoreNLP, content: String):
List[String] = {
        //We are required to prepare the text as 'annotatable'
before we annotate :-)
        val document = new Annotation(content)
        //Annotate
        nlp.annotate(document)
        //Extract all sentences
        val sentences =
document.get(classOf[SentencesAnnotation]).asScala

        //Extract lemmas from sentences
        val lemmas = sentences.flatMap { sentence =>
          val tokens =
sentence.get(classOf[TokensAnnotation]).asScala
            tokens.map(token =>
token.getString(classOf[LemmaAnnotation]))

        }
        //Only lemmas with letters or digits will be considered.
Also consider only those words which has a length of at least 2
        lemmas.toList.filter(lemma =>
lemma.forall(_.isLetterOrDigit)).filter(_.length() > 1)
        }

    val labeledPointsUsingStanfordNLPRdd: RDD[LabeledPoint] =
docs.mapPartitions { docIter =>
        val corenlp = corePipeline()
        val stopwords = Source.fromFile("stopwords.txt").getLines()
        val hashingTf = new HashingTF(5000)

        docIter.map { doc =>
          val lemmas = lemmatize(corenlp, doc.content)
          //remove all the stopwords from the lemma list
          lemmas.filterNot(lemma => stopwords.contains(lemma))
```

```
        //Generates a term frequency vector from the features
        val features = hashingTf.transform(lemmas)

        //example : List(until, jurong, point, crazy, available,
only, in, bugi, great, world, la, buffet, Cine, there, get, amore,
wat)
        new LabeledPoint(
          if (doc.label.equals("ham")) 0 else 1,
          features)


      }
    }.cache()
```

Factoring the inverse document frequency

With `HashingTF`, we have a map of terms along with their frequency of occurrence in the documents. Now, the problem with taking this metric is that common words such as "the" and "a" get higher rankings compared to rare words. The **inverse document frequency** (**IDF**) calculates the occurrences of a word in all the documents and gives higher weight to a term that is uncommon. We'll now factor in the inverse document frequency so that we have the TF-IDF score (https://en.wikipedia.org/wiki/Tf-idf) for each term. This is easily achievable in Spark with the availability of `org.apache.spark.mllib.feature.IDFModel`. We extract all term frequencies from LabeledPoints and pass them to the `transform` function `IDFModel` to generate the TF-IDF:

```
val labeledPointsUsingStanfordNLPRdd=getLabeledPoints(docs,
"STANFORD")
val lpTfIdf=withIdf(labeledPointsUsingStanfordNLPRdd).cache()


def withIdf(lPoints: RDD[LabeledPoint]): RDD[LabeledPoint] = {
    val hashedFeatures = labeledPointsWithTf.map(lp =>
lp.features)
    val idf: IDF = new IDF()
    val idfModel: IDFModel = idf.fit(hashedFeatures)

    val tfIdf: RDD[Vector] = idfModel.transform(hashedFeatures)

    val lpTfIdf= labeledPointsWithTf.zip(tfIdf).map {
      case (originalLPoint, tfIdfVector) => {
        new LabeledPoint(originalLPoint.label, tfIdfVector)
      }
    }

    lpTfIdf
  }

  val lpTfIdf=withIdf(labeledPointsWithTf).cache()
```

Prepare the training and test data

Our test data has a skewed distribution of spam and ham data. We just have to make sure that when we split the data into training and test data into 80% and 20%, we first split the training and test data into two subsets and then split it into the 80:20 ratio. At the end of this, the training data and test data will have a ratio of 4:1 spam and ham samples.

The spam and ham counts in our dataset are 747 and 4827, respectively:

```
//Split dataset
val spamPoints = lpTfIdf.filter(point => point.label ==
1).randomSplit(Array(0.8, 0.2))
  val hamPoints = lpTfIdf.filter(point => point.label ==
0).randomSplit(Array(0.8, 0.2))

  println ("Spam
count:"+(spamPoints(0).count)+"::"+(spamPoints(1).count))
  println ("Ham count:"+(hamPoints(0).count)+"::"+(hamPoints(1).
count))

  val trainingSpamSplit = spamPoints(0)
  val testSpamSplit = spamPoints(1)

  val trainingHamSplit = hamPoints(0)
  val testHamSplit = hamPoints(1)

  val trainingSplit = trainingSpamSplit ++ trainingHamSplit
  val testSplit = testSpamSplit ++ testHamSplit
```

Constructing the algorithm

Now that we have our training and test sets, the next obvious step is to train a model out of these examples. Let's create instances of the three variants of the algorithms that we would like to experiment with:

```
  val logisticWithSGD = getAlgorithm("logsgd", 100, 1, 0.001)
  val logisticWithBfgs = getAlgorithm("logbfgs", 100, Double.Nan,
0.001)
  val svmWithSGD = getAlgorithm("svm", 100, 1, 0.001)



  def getAlgorithm(algo: String, iterations: Int, stepSize:
Double, regParam: Double) = algo match {
    case "logsgd" => {
      val algo = new LogisticRegressionWithSGD()
```

```
algo.setIntercept(true).optimizer.setNumIterations(iterations).
setStepSize(stepSize).setRegParam(regParam)
      algo
    }
    case "logbfgs" => {
      val algo = new LogisticRegressionWithLBFGS()
algo.setIntercept(true).optimizer.setNumIterations(iterations).
setRegParam(regParam)
      algo
    }
    case "svm" => {
      val algo = new SVMWithSGD()
algo.setIntercept(true).optimizer.setNumIterations(iterations).
setStepSize(stepSize).setRegParam(regParam)
      algo
    }
  }
```

We can notice that the `stepSize` parameter isn't set for logistic regression with BFGS.

Training the model and predicting the test data

Like linear regression, training and predicting the labels for the test set is just a matter of calling the `run` and `predict` methods of the classification algorithm.

Soon after the prediction is done, the next logical step is to evaluate the model. In order to generate metrics for this, we extract the predicted and the actual labels. Our `runClassification` function trains the model using the training data and makes predictions against the test data. It then zips the predicted and the actual outcomes into a value called `predictsAndActuals`. This value is returned from the function.

The `runClassification` accepts a `GeneralizedLinearAlgorithm` as the parameter, which is the parent of `LinearRegressionWithSGD`, `LogisticRegressionWithSGD`, and `SVMWithSGD`:

```
val
logisticWithSGDPredictsActuals=runClassification(logisticWithSGD,
trainingSplit, testSplit)
val
logisticWithBfgsPredictsActuals=runClassification(logisticWithBfgs,
trainingSplit, testSplit)
val svmWithSGDPredictsActuals=runClassification(svmWithSGD,
trainingSplit, testSplit)
```

```
    def runClassification(algorithm: GeneralizedLinearAlgorithm[_ <:
GeneralizedLinearModel], trainingData:RDD[LabeledPoint],
testData:RDD[LabeledPoint]): RDD[(Double, Double)] = {
        val model = algorithm.run(trainingData)
        val predicted = model.predict(testData.map(point =>
point.features))
        val actuals = testData.map(point => point.label)
        val predictsAndActuals: RDD[(Double, Double)] =
predicted.zip(actuals)
        predictsAndActuals
    }
```

Evaluating the model

For generating the metrics, Spark has some inbuilt APIs. The two most common metrics used to evaluate a classification model are the area under curve and the confusion matrix. The `org. apache.spark.mllib.evaluation.BinaryClassificationMetrics` gives us the area under the curve, and `org.apache.spark.mllib.evaluation.MulticlassMetrics` gives us the confusion matrix. We also calculate the simple accuracy measure manually using the values of `predicated` and `actuals`. The accuracy is simply the result of dividing the correctly classified count of the test dataset by the total count of the test dataset. Refer to `https:// en.wikipedia.org/wiki/Accuracy_and_precision#In_binary_classification` for more details:

```
 def calculateMetrics(predictsAndActuals: RDD[(Double, Double)],
algorithm: String) {


    val accuracy = 1.0*predictsAndActuals.filter(predActs => predActs._1
== predActs._2).count() / predictsAndActuals.count()
    val binMetrics = new BinaryClassificationMetrics(predictsAndActuals)
    println(s"************** Printing metrics for $algorithm
***************")
    println(s"Area under ROC ${binMetrics.areaUnderROC}")
    //println(s"Accuracy $accuracy")


    val metrics = new MulticlassMetrics(predictsAndActuals)
    val f1=metrics.fMeasure
    println(s"F1 $f1")
    println(s"Precision : ${metrics.precision}")
    println(s"Confusion Matrix \n${metrics.confusionMatrix}")
    println(s"************** ending metrics for $algorithm
*****************")


}
```

As we can see from the output, `LogisticRegressionWithSGD` and `SVMWithSGD` have a slightly bigger area under curve than `LogisticRegressionWithBFGS`, which means that the two models perform a tad bit better.

This is a sample output (your output could vary):

```
************** Printing metrics for Logistic Regression with SGD
***************
Area under ROC 0.9208860759493671

Accuracy 0.9769585253456221

Confusion Matrix

927.0   0.0

25.0    133.0

************** ending metrics for Logistic Regression with SGD
*****************


************** Printing metrics for SVM with SGD **************
Area under ROC 0.9318656156156157

Precision : 0.9784845650140318

Confusion Matrix

921.0   4.0

19.0    125.0

************** ending metrics for SVM with SGD ****************


************** Printing metrics for Logistic Regression with BFGS
***************
Area under ROC 0.8790559620074445

Accuracy 0.9596136962247586

Confusion Matrix

971.0   9.0

37.0    122.0

************** ending metrics for Logistic Regression with BFGS ********
*************************
```

Binary classification using LogisticRegression with Pipeline API

Earlier, with the spam example on binary classification, we saw how we prepared the data, separated it into training and test data, trained the model, and evaluated it against test data before we finally arrived at the metrics. This series of steps can be abstracted in a simplified manner using Spark's Pipeline API.

In this recipe, we'll take a look at how to use the Pipeline API to solve the same classification problem. Imagine the pipeline to be a factory assembly line where things happen one after another. In our case, we'll pass our raw unprocessed data through various processors before we finally feed the data into the classifier.

How to do it...

In this recipe, we'll classify the same spam/ham dataset (https://archive.ics.uci. edu/ml/datasets/SMS+Spam+Collection) first using the plain Pipeline, and then using a cross-validator to select the best model for us given a grid of parameters.

Let's summarize the steps:

1. Importing and splitting data as test and training sets.
2. Constructing the participants of the Pipeline.
3. Preparing a pipeline and training a model.
4. Predicting against test data.
5. Evaluating the model without cross-validation.
6. Constructing parameters for cross-validation.
7. Constructing a cross-validator and fitting the best model.
8. Evaluating a model with cross-validation.

 The code for this recipe can be found at https://github.com/ arunma/ScalaDataAnalysisCookbook/blob/master/ chapter5-learning/src/main/scala/com/packt/scalada/ learning/BinaryClassificationSpamPipeline.scala.

Importing and splitting data as test and training sets

This process is a little different from the previous recipe, in the sense that we don't construct LabeledPoint now. Instead of an RDD of LabeledPoint, the pipeline requires a DataFrame. So, we convert each line of text into a `Document` object (with the label and the content) and then convert `RDD[Document]` into a DataFrame by calling the `toDF()` function on the RDD:

```
case class Document(label: Double, content: String)

  val docs = sc.textFile("SMSSpamCollection").map(line => {
    val words = line.split("\t")
    val label=if (words.head.trim()=="spam") 1.0 else 0.0
    Document(label, words.tail.mkString(" "))
  })


  //Split dataset
  val spamPoints = docs.filter(doc => doc.label==1.0).
randomSplit(Array(0.8, 0.2))
  val hamPoints = docs.filter(doc => doc.label==0.0).
randomSplit(Array(0.8, 0.2))


  println("Spam count:" + (spamPoints(0).count) + "::" + (spamPoints(1).
count))
  println("Ham count:" + (hamPoints(0).count) + "::" + (hamPoints(1).
count))


  val trainingSpamSplit = spamPoints(0)
  val testSpamSplit = spamPoints(1)


  val trainingHamSplit = hamPoints(0)
  val testHamSplit = hamPoints(1)


  val trainingSplit = trainingSpamSplit ++ trainingHamSplit
  val testSplit = testSpamSplit ++ testHamSplit


  import sqlContext.implicits._
  val trainingDFrame=trainingSplit.toDF()
  val testDFrame=testSplit.toDF()
```

Construct the participants of the Pipeline

In order to arrange the pipeline, we need to construct its participants. There are three unique participants (or pipeline stages) of this pipeline, and we have to line them up in the right order:

- ▸ **Tokenizer**: This disintegrates the sentence into tokens
- ▸ **HashingTF**: This creates a term frequency vector from the terms
- ▸ **IDF**: This creates an inverse document frequency vector from the terms
- ▸ **VectorAssembler**: This combines the TF-IDF vector and the label vector to form a single vector, which will form the input features for the classification algorithm
- ▸ **LogisticRegression**: This is the classification algorithm itself

Let's construct these first:

```
val tokenizer=new Tokenizer().setInputCol("content").
setOutputCol("tokens")

  val hashingTf=new HashingTF().setInputCol(tokenizer.getOutputCol).
setOutputCol("tf")

  val idf = new IDF().setInputCol(hashingTf.getOutputCol).
setOutputCol("tfidf")

  val assembler = new VectorAssembler().setInputCols(Array("tfidf",
"label")).setOutputCol("features")


val logisticRegression=new LogisticRegression().
setFeaturesCol("features").setLabelCol("label").setMaxIter(10)
```

When RDD [Document] is run against the first pipeline stage, that is, Tokenizer, the "content" field of the Document is taken as the input column, and the output of the tokenizer is a bag of words that is captured in the "tokens" output column. HashingTF takes the "tokens" and converts them into a TF vector. Notice that the input column of HashingTF is the same as the output column from the previous stage. IDF takes the tf vector and returns a tf-idf vector. VectorAssembler merges the tf-idf vector and the label to form a single vector. This will be used as an input to the classification algorithm. Finally, for the LogisticRegression stage, we specify the features column and the label column. However, if the input DataFrame has a column named "label" with a Double type and "features" of type Vector, there is no need to explicitly mention that. So, in our case, since we have "label" as an attribute of the Document case class and the output column of the HashingTF is named "features", there is no need for us to specify them explicitly. The following code would work just fine:

```
val logisticRegression=new LogisticRegression().setMaxIter(10)
```

Internally, this implementation of LogisticRegression constructs LabeledPoints for each instance of the data, and uses some advanced optimization algorithms to derive a model from the training data.

At every stage, each of these transformations occurs against the input DataFrame of that particular stage, and the transformed DataFrame gets passed along until the final stage.

Preparing a pipeline and training a model

As the next step, we just need to form a pipeline out of the various pipeline stages that we constructed in the previous step. We then train a model by calling the `pipeline.fit` function:

```
val pipeline=new Pipeline()
```

```
pipeline.setStages(Array(tokenizer, hashingTf, logisticRegression))
```

```
val model=pipeline.fit(trainingDFrame)
```

 If you are getting `java.lang.IllegalArgumentException:` `requirement failed: Column label must be of type` `DoubleType but was actually StringType`, it just means that your label isn't of the Double type.

Predicting against test data

Using the newly constructed model to predict the data is just a matter of calling the transform method of the model. Then, we also extract the actual label and the predicted value to calculate the metrics:

```
  val predictsAndActualsNoCV:RDD[(Double,Double)]=model.
transform(testDFrame).map(r => (r.getAs[Double]("label"), r.getAs[Double]
("prediction"))).cache
```

Evaluating a model without cross-validation

Cross-validation is a multiple-iteration model validation technique in which our training and test sets are split into different partitions. The entire dataset is split into subsets, and for each iteration, analysis is done on one subset and validation on a different subset. For this recipe, we'll run the algorithm first without cross-validation, and then with cross-validation.

Firstly, we'll use the same validation metric and method that we used in the previous recipe. We will simply calculate the area under the ROC curve, the precision, and the confusion matrix:

```
def calculateMetrics(predictsAndActuals: RDD[(Double, Double)],
algorithm: String) {


    val accuracy = 1.0 * predictsAndActuals.filter(predActs =>
predActs._1 == predActs._2).count() / predictsAndActuals.count()
    val binMetrics = new BinaryClassificationMetrics(predictsAndActuals)
    println(s"************** Printing metrics for $algorithm
**************")
    println(s"Area under ROC ${binMetrics.areaUnderROC}")
    println(s"Accuracy $accuracy")


    val metrics = new MulticlassMetrics(predictsAndActuals)
    println(s"Precision : ${metrics.precision}")
    println(s"Confusion Matrix \n${metrics.confusionMatrix}")
    println(s"************** ending metrics for $algorithm
**************")

 }
```

A sample output of this pipeline without cross-validation is as follows:

```
************** Printing metrics for Without Cross validation
**************
Area under ROC 0.9676924738149228
Accuracy 0.9656357388316151
Confusion Matrix
993.0   36.0
4.0     131.0
************** ending metrics for Without Cross validation
**************
```

Constructing parameters for cross-validation

Before we use the cross-validator to choose the best model that fits the data, we would want to provide each of the parameters a set of alternate values that the validator can choose from.

The way we provide alternate values is in the form of a parameter grid:

```
val paramGrid=new ParamGridBuilder()
    .addGrid(hashingTf.numFeatures, Array(1000, 5000, 10000))
```

```
.addGrid(logisticRegression.regParam, Array(1, 0.1, 0.03, 0.01))
.build()
```

So, we say that the number of term frequency vectors that we want HashingTF to generate could be one of 1,000, 5,000, and 10,000, and the regularization parameter for logistic regression could be one of 1, 0.1, 0.03, and 0.01. Thus, in essence, we are passing a 3 x 4 matrix as the parameter grid.

Constructing cross-validator and fit the best model

Next, we construct a cross-validator and pass in the following parameters:

- ▸ The parameter grid that we constructed in the previous step.
- ▸ The pipeline that we constructed in step 3.
- ▸ An evaluator for the cross-validator to decide which model is better.
- ▸ The number of folds. Say, if we set the number of folds to 10, the training data would be split into 10 blocks. For each iteration (10 iterations), the first block would be selected as the cross-validation set, and the other nine would be the training sets:

```
val crossValidator=new CrossValidator()
    .setEstimator(pipeline)
    .setEvaluator(new BinaryClassificationEvaluator())
    .setEstimatorParamMaps(paramGrid)
    .setNumFolds(10)
```

We finally let the cross-validator run against the training dataset and derive the best model out of it. Contrast the following line with `pipeline.fit`, where we skipped cross-validation:

```
val bestModel=crossValidator.fit(trainingDFrame)
```

Evaluating the model with cross-validation

Now, let's evaluate the model that is generated against the actual test data set (rather than the test dataset that the cross-validator uses internally):

```
  val predictsAndActualsWithCV:RDD[(Double,Double)]=bestModel.
transform(testDFrame).map(r => (r.getAs[Double]("label"), r.getAs[Double]
("prediction"))).cache


 calculateMetrics(predictsAndActualsWithCV, "Cross validation")
```

A sample output of this pipeline with cross-validation is as follows:

```
************** Printing metrics for Cross validation **************
Area under ROC 0.9968220338983051
```

```
Accuracy 0.994579945799458

Confusion Matrix

938.0   6.0

0.0     163.0

************* ending metrics for Cross validation *****************
```

As we can see, the area under ROC is far better for this model than for any of our previously generated models.

Clustering using K-means

Clustering is a class of unsupervised learning algorithms wherein the dataset is partitioned into a finite number of clusters in such a way that the points within a cluster are similar to each other in some way. This, intuitively, also means that the points of two different clusters should be dissimilar.

K-means is one of the popular clustering algorithms, and in this recipe, we'll be looking at how Spark implements K-means and how to use the algorithm to cluster a sample dataset. Since the number of clusters is a crucial input for the K-means algorithm, we'll also see the most common method of arriving at the optimal number of clusters for the data.

How to do it...

Spark provides two initialization modes for cluster center (centroid) initialization: the original Lloyd's method (https://en.wikipedia.org/wiki/K-means_clustering), and a parallelizable and scalable variant of K-means++ (https://en.wikipedia.org/wiki/K-means%2B%2B). K-means++ itself is a variant of the original K-means and differs in the way in which the initial centroids of the clusters are picked up. We can switch between the original and the parallelized K-means++ versions by passing KMeans.RANDOM or KMeans.PARALLEL as the initialization mode. Let's first look at the details of the implementation.

KMeans.RANDOM

In the regular K-means (the KMeans.RANDOM initialization mode in the case of Spark), the algorithm randomly selects *k* points (equal to the number of clusters that we expect to see) and marks them as cluster centers (centroids). Then it iteratively does the following:

> ▶ It marks all the points as belonging to a cluster based on the distance between a point and its nearest centroid.

> ▶ The mean of all the points in a cluster is calculated. This mean is now set as the new centroid of that cluster.

> ▶ The rest of the data points are reassigned their clusters based on this new centroid.

Since we generally deal with more than one feature in a dataset, each instance of the data and the centroids are vectors. In Spark, we represent them as `org.apache.spark.mllib.linalg.Vector`.

KMeans.PARALLEL

Scalable K-means or K-means|| is a variant of K-means++. Let's look at what these variants of K-means actually do.

K-means++

Instead of choosing all the centroids randomly, the K-means++ algorithm does the following:

1. It chooses the first centroid randomly (uniform)

2. It calculates the distance squared of each of the rest of the points from the current centroid

3. A probability is attached to each of these points based on how far they are. The farther the centroid candidate is, the higher is its probability.

4. We choose the second centroid from the distribution that we have in step 3.

5. On the *i*th iteration, we have *1+i* clusters. Find the new centroid by going over the entire dataset and forming a distribution out of these points based on how far they are from all the precomputed centroids.

These steps are repeated over *k-1* iterations until *k* centroids are selected. K-means++ is known for considerably increasing the quality of centroids. However, as we see, in order to select the initial set of centroids, the algorithm goes through the entire dataset *k* times. Unfortunately, with a large dataset, this becomes a problem.

K-means||

With K-means parallel (K-means||), for each iteration, instead of choosing a single point after calculating the probability distribution of each of the points in the dataset, a lot more points are chosen. In the case of Spark, the number of samples that are chosen per step is *2 * k*. Once these initial centroid candidates are selected, a K-means++ is run against these data points (instead of going through the entire dataset).

Let's now look at the most important parameters that are passed to the algorithm.

Max iterations

There are worst-case scenarios for both random and parallel. In the case of random, since the points in K-means are chosen at random, there is a distinct possibility that the model identifies two centroids from the same cluster. Say with *k=3*, there is a possibility of two clusters becoming a part of a single cluster and a single cluster being separated into two. A similar case applies to K-means++ with a bad choice of the initial set of centroids.

The following figure proves that though we can see three clusters, a bad choice of centroids separates a single cluster into two and makes two clusters one:

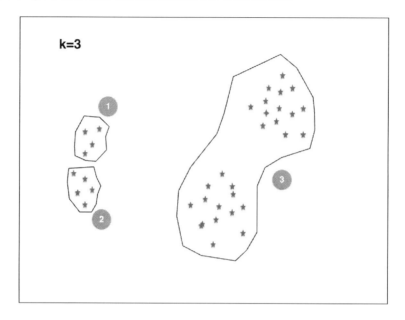

To solve this problem, we run the same algorithm with a different set of randomly initialized centroids. This is determined by the `maxIterations` parameter. The distance between the centroid and the points in the cluster is calculated (a mean squared difference in distances). This will be the cost of the model. The iteration with the least cost is chosen and returned. The metric that Spark uses to calculate the distance is the Euclidean distance.

Epsilon

How does the K-means algorithm know when to stop? There will always be a small distance that the centroid can move if the clusters aren't separated by a huge margin. If all the centroids have moved by a distance less than the epsilon parameter, it's the cue to the algorithm that it has converged. In other words, the epsilon is nothing but a **convergence threshold**.

Now that we have the parameters that need to be passed to the K-means cluster out of the way, let's look at the steps needed to run this algorithm to find the clusters:

1.   Importing the data and converting it into a vector.
2.   Feature scaling the data.
3.   Deriving the number of clusters.
4.   Constructing the model.
5.   Evaluating the model.

The code for this recipe can be found at `https://github.com/arunma/ScalaDataAnalysisCookbook/blob/master/chapter5-learning/src/main/scala/com/packt/scalada/learning/KMeansClusteringIris.scala`.

Importing the data and converting it into a vector

As usual, our input data is in the form of a text file—`iris.data`. Since we are clustering, we can ignore the label (species) in the data. The data file looks like this:

```
5.1,3.5,1.4,0.2,Iris-setosa
4.9,3.0,1.4,0.2,Iris-setosa
4.7,3.2,1.3,0.2,Iris-setosa
4.6,3.1,1.5,0.2,Iris-setosa
5.0,3.6,1.4,0.2,Iris-setosa
5.4,3.9,1.7,0.4,Iris-setosa
4.6,3.4,1.4,0.3,Iris-setosa
5.0,3.4,1.5,0.2,Iris-setosa
4.4,2.9,1.4,0.2,Iris-setosa
4.9,3.1,1.5,0.1,Iris-setosa
5.4,3.7,1.5,0.2,Iris-setosa
4.8,3.4,1.6,0.2,Iris-setosa
4.8,3.0,1.4,0.1,Iris-setosa
```

```scala
val data = sc.textFile("iris.data").map(line => {
    val dataArray = line.split(",").take(4)
    Vectors.dense(dataArray.map(_.toDouble))
})
```

Feature scaling the data

When we look at the summary statistics of the data, the data looks alright, but it is always advisable perform do feature scaling before running a K-means:

```scala
val stats = Statistics.colStats(data)
println("Statistics before scaling")
print(s"Max : ${stats.max}, Min : ${stats.min}, and Mean : ${stats.mean} and Variance : ${stats.variance}")
```

Here is the statistics before scaling:

```
Max : [7.9,4.4,6.9,2.5]
Min : [4.3,2.0,1.0,0.1]
```

```
Mean : [5.843333333333332,3.0540000000000003,3.7586666666666666,1.1986666
666666668]
```

```
Variance : [0.685693512304251,0.18800402684563744,3.113179418344516,0.582
4143176733783]
```

We run the data using `StandardScaler` and cache the resulting RDD. Since K-means goes through the dataset multiple times, caching the data is strongly recommended to avoid recomputation:

```
//Scale data
  val scaler = new StandardScaler(withMean = true, withStd = true).
fit(data)
  val scaledData = scaler.transform(data).cache()
```

The following is the statistics after scaling:

```
Max : [2.483698580557868,3.1042842692548858,1.7803768862629268,1.70518904
10833728]
```

```
Min : [-1.8637802962695154,-2.4308436996988485,-1.5634973589465175,-
1.4396268133736672], and Mean : [1.6653345369377348E-15,-
7.216449660063518E-16,-1.1102230246251565E-16,-3.3306690738754696E-16]
```

```
Variance : [0.9999999999999997,1.0000000000000007,1.0000000000000013,0.99
99999999999997]
```

Deriving the number of clusters

Many times, we already know the number of clusters that are there in the dataset. But at times, if we aren't sure, the general method is to plot the number of clusters against the cost and watch out for the point from which the cost stops falling drastically. If the data is large, running the entire set of data just to obtain the number of clusters is computationally expensive. Instead, we can take a random sample and come up with the k value. In this example, we have taken a random 20% sample, but the sample percentage depends entirely on your dataset:

```
 //Take a sample to come up with the number of clusters
val sampleData = scaledData.sample(false, 0.2).cache()
  //Decide number of clusters
  val clusterCost = (1 to 7).map { noOfClusters =>

    val kmeans = new KMeans()
      .setK(noOfClusters)
      .setMaxIterations(5)
      .setInitializationMode(KMeans.K_MEANS_PARALLEL) //KMeans||

    val model = kmeans.run(sampleData)
```

```
    (noOfClusters, model.computeCost(sampleData))

}

println ("Cluster cost on sample data")
clusterCost.foreach(println)
```

Cluster	Cost
1	98.34739863322832
2	38.07068957755217
3	20.357460464958457
4	14.755544266868153
5	15.923133807959202
6	11.165034661812456
7	7.794137577588026

When we plot this, we can see that after cluster **3**, the cost does not reduce drastically. This point is called an **Elbow bend**, as shown here:

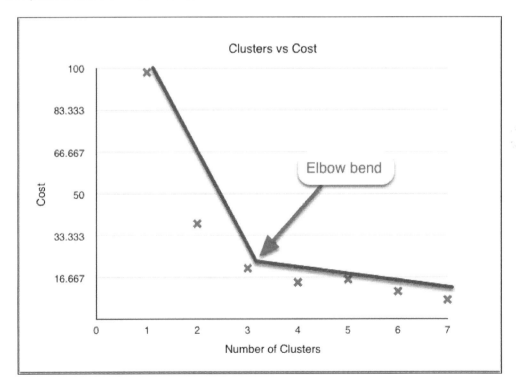

Constructing the model

Now that we have figured out the number of clusters, let's run the algorithm against the entire dataset:

```
//Let's do the real run for 3 clusters
val kmeans = new KMeans()
  .setK(3)
  .setMaxIterations(5)
  .setInitializationMode(KMeans.K_MEANS_PARALLEL) //KMeans||

val model = kmeans.run(scaledData)
```

Evaluating the model

The last step is to evaluate the model by printing the cost of this model. The cost is nothing but the square of the distance between all points in a cluster to its centroid. Therefore, a good model must have the least cost:

```
//Cost
println("Total cost " + model.computeCost(scaledData))
printClusterCenters(model)

def printClusterCenters(model:KMeansModel) {
  //Cluster centers
  val clusterCenters: Array[Vector] = model.clusterCenters
  println("Cluster centers")
  clusterCenters.foreach(println)

}
```

Here is the output:

```
Total cost 34.98320617204239
Cluster centers
[-0.011357501034038157,-
0.8699705596441868,0.3756258413625911,0.3106129627676019]
[1.1635361185919766,0.1532643388373168,0.999796072473665,1.02619470887105
72]
[-1.0111913832028123,0.839494408624649,-1.3005214861029282,-
1.250937862106244]
```

Feature reduction using principal component analysis

Quoting the curse of dimensionality (`https://en.wikipedia.org/wiki/Curse_of_dimensionality`), large number of features are computationally expensive. One way of reducing the number of features is by manually choosing and ignoring certain features. However, identification of the same features (represented differently) or highly correlated features is laborious when we have a huge number of features. Dimensionality reduction is aimed at reducing the number of features in the data while still retaining its variability.

Say, we have a dataset of housing prices and there are two features that represent the area of the house in feet and meters; we can always drop one of these two. Dimensionality reduction is very useful when dealing with text where the number of features easily runs into a few thousands.

In this recipe, we'll be looking into **Principal Component Analysis** (**PCA**) as a means to reduce the dimensions of data that is meant for both supervised and unsupervised learning.

How to do it...

As we have seen earlier, the only difference between the data for supervised and unsupervised learning is that the training and the test data for supervised learning have labels attached to them. This brings in a little complication, considering that we are interested only in reducing the dimensions of the feature vector and would like to retain the labels as they are.

Dimensionality reduction of data for supervised learning

The only thing that we have to watch out for while reducing the dimensions of data to be used as training data for supervised learning is that PCA must be applied on training data only. The test set must not be used to extract the components. Using test data for PCA would bleed the information in the test data into the components. This may result in higher accuracy numbers while testing, but it could perform poorly on unseen production data.

The least number of components that can be chosen while maintaining a sufficiently high variance is facilitated by the singular value vector available in the `SingularValueDecomposion` object. The singular values, available by calling the `svd.s`, show the amount of variance captured by the components. The first component will be the most important (by contributing the highest variance), and the importance will slowly diminish.

In order to come up with the probable number of dimensions, we can watch out for the difference and the extent to which the singular values diminish. Alternatively, we can just use simple heuristics and come up with a reasonable number if the features extend to a few thousand:

```
val dimensionDecidingSample=new RowMatrix((trainingSplit.
randomSplit(Array(0.8,0.2))(1)).map(lp=>lp.features))
```

```
val svd = dimensionDecidingSample.computeSVD(500, computeU = false)

val sum = svd.s.toArray.sum

//Calculate the number of principal components which retains a variance
of 95%
val featureRange=(0 to 500)


val placeholder=svd.s.toArray.zip(featureRange).foldLeft(0.0) {

  case (cum, (curr, component)) =>

    val percent = (cum + curr) / sum

    println(s"Component and percent ${component + 1} :: $percent ::::
Singular value is : $curr")

    cum + curr

}
```

The steps that are involved are as follows:

1. Mean-normalizing the training data.
2. Extracting the principal components.
3. Preparing the labeled data.
4. Preparing the test data.
5. Classify and evaluate the metrics.

 The code for this recipe can be found at `https://github.com/ arunma/ScalaDataAnalysisCookbook/blob/master/ chapter5-learning/src/main/scala/com/packt/ scalada/learning/PCASpam.scala`.

Mean-normalizing the training data

It is highly recommended that the data be centered before running it by PCA. We achieve this using the `fit` and `transform` functions of `StandardScaler`. However, since the scaler in Spark accepts a `DenseVector` as the argument, we'll use the `Vectors.dense` factory method to convert the features in the labeled point into a `DenseVector`:

```
val docs = sc.textFile("SMSSpamCollection").map(line => {
    val words = line.split("\t")
    Document(words.head.trim(), words.tail.mkString(" "))
  }).cache()


val labeledPointsWithTf = getLabeledPoints(docs)
val lpTfIdf = withIdf(labeledPointsWithTf).cache()


  //Split dataset
val spamPoints = lpTfIdf.filter(point => point.label ==
1).randomSplit(Array(0.8, 0.2))

val hamPoints = lpTfIdf.filter(point => point.label ==
0).randomSplit(Array(0.8, 0.2))


val trainingSpamSplit = spamPoints(0)
val trainingHamSplit = hamPoints(0)


val trainingData = trainingSpamSplit ++ trainingHamSplit


val unlabeledTrainData = trainingData.map(lpoint => Vectors.dense(lpoint.
features.toArray)).cache()


  //Scale data - Does not support scaling of SparseVector.
  val scaler = new StandardScaler(withMean = true, withStd = false).
fit(unlabeledTrainData)
  val scaledTrainingData = scaler.transform(unlabeledTrainData).cache()
```

Extracting the principal components

The `computePrincipalComponents` function is available in `RowMatrix`. So, we wrap our scaled training data into a `RowMatrix` and then extract 100 principal components out of it (as shown earlier, the number 100 is based on a run against a sample set of data and on investigating the singular value vector of the SVD). Our training data is currently a 4419 x 5000 matrix—4419 instances of data * 5000 features restricted by us while generating the term frequency using `HashingTF`. We then multiply this training matrix (4419 x 5000) by the principal component matrix (5000 x 100) to arrive at a 4419 * 100 matrix—4419 instances of data by 100 features (principal components). We can extract the feature vectors from this matrix by calling the `rows()` function:

```
val trainMatrix = new RowMatrix(scaledTrainingData)
val pcomp: Matrix = trainMatrix.computePrincipalComponents(100)

val reducedTrainingData = trainMatrix.multiply(pcomp).rows.cache()
```

Preparing the labeled data

Now that we have reduced the data fifty-fold, the next step that we have to take is to use this reduced data in our algorithm to see how it fares. The classification algorithm (in this case, `LogisticRegressionWithBFGS`) requires an RDD of LabeledPoints. To construct the LabeledPoint, we extract the label from the original `trainingData` and the feature vector from the dimension-reduced dataset:

```
val reducedTrainingSplit = trainingData.zip(reducedTrainingData).map {
case (labeled, reduced) => new LabeledPoint(labeled.label, reduced) }
```

Preparing the test data

Before predicting our test data against the algorithm, we need to bring the test data to the same dimension as the training data. This is achieved by multiplying the principal components with the test matrix. As discussed earlier, we just need to make sure that we don't compute the principal components fresh here:

```
val unlabeledTestData=testSplit.map(lpoint=>lpoint.features)
val testMatrix = new RowMatrix(unlabeledTestData)
val reducedTestData=testMatrix.multiply(pcomp).rows.cache()
val reducedTestSplit=testSplit.zip(reducedTestData).map{case
(labeled,reduced) => new LabeledPoint (labeled.label, reduced)}
```

Classify and evaluate the metrics

The final step is to classify and evaluate the results of the algorithm. This step is the same as the classification recipe that we saw earlier. From the output, we can see that we not only reduced the number of features from 5,000 to 100, but also managed to maintain the accuracy of the algorithm at the same levels:

```scala
val logisticWithBFGS = getAlgorithm(10, 1, 0.001)
  val logisticWithBFGSPredictsActuals = runClassification(logisticWithBF
GS, reducedTrainingSplit, reducedTestSplit)
  calculateMetrics(logisticWithBFGSPredictsActuals, "Logistic with BFGS")

  def getAlgorithm(iterations: Int, stepSize: Double, regParam: Double) =
{
    val algo = new LogisticRegressionWithLBFGS()
algo.setIntercept(true).optimizer.setNumIterations(iterations).
setRegParam(regParam)
    algo
  }


  def runClassification(algorithm: GeneralizedLinearAlgorithm[_ <:
GeneralizedLinearModel], trainingData: RDD[LabeledPoint],
    testData: RDD[LabeledPoint]): RDD[(Double, Double)] = {
    val model = algorithm.run(trainingData)
    println ("predicting")
    val predicted = model.predict(testData.map(point => point.features))
    val actuals = testData.map(point => point.label)
    val predictsAndActuals: RDD[(Double, Double)] = predicted.
zip(actuals)
    println (predictsAndActuals.collect)
    predictsAndActuals
  }


  def calculateMetrics(predictsAndActuals: RDD[(Double, Double)],
algorithm: String) {

    val accuracy = 1.0 * predictsAndActuals.filter(predActs =>
predActs._1 == predActs._2).count() / predictsAndActuals.count()
    val binMetrics = new BinaryClassificationMetrics(predictsAndActuals)
    println(s"************** Printing metrics for $algorithm
***************")
    println(s"Area under ROC ${binMetrics.areaUnderROC}")
```

```
    println(s"Accuracy $accuracy")


    val metrics = new MulticlassMetrics(predictsAndActuals)
    println(s"Precision : ${metrics.precision}")
    println(s"Confusion Matrix \n${metrics.confusionMatrix}")
    println(s"************** ending metrics for $algorithm
****************")
  }
```

This is the output:

Compared to the area under the ROC at around the same levels (95%), we have considerably reduced the time of the run by reducing the dimensions of the features ten-fold:

```
************** Printing metrics for Logistic with BFGS ***************

Area under ROC 0.9428948576675849

Accuracy 0.9829136690647482

Confusion Matrix

965.0   3.0

16.0    128.0

************** ending metrics for Logistic with BFGS ****************
```

Note that the entire code for this recipe can be found at `https://github.com/arunma/ScalaDataAnalysisCookbook/blob/master/chapter5-learning/src/main/scala/com/packt/scalada/learning/PCASpam.scala`.

Dimensionality reduction of data for unsupervised learning

Unlike reducing the dimensions of data with labels, reducing the dimensionality of data for unsupervised learning is very simple. We just apply the PCA to the entire dataset. This helps a lot in improving the performance of algorithms such as K-means, where the entire set of features has to be plotted on a higher dimension and the entire data must be visited multiple times. A lesser number of features means a lesser number of dimensions and less data to be held in the memory.

For this recipe, we use the `Iris.data` that we used for clustering earlier. The dataset already has four features, and this isn't a great candidate for dimensionality reduction as such. However, the process around reducing dimensions for unlabeled data is the same as for any other dataset.

The steps that are involved are as follows:

1. Mean-normalizing the training data.
2. Extracting the principal components.
3. Arriving at the number of components.
4. Evaluating the metrics.

 The code for this recipe can be found at `https://github.com/arunma/ScalaDataAnalysisCookbook/blob/master/chapter5-learning/src/main/scala/com/packt/scalada/learning/PCAIris.scala`.

Mean-normalizing the training data

As we saw earlier, scaling is a must before reducing dimensions:

```
val scaler = new StandardScaler(withMean = true, withStd = false).
fit(data)
val scaledData = scaler.transform(data).cache()
```

Extracting the principal components

As we saw earlier, to compute the principal components, we need to wrap our scaled training data into a `RowMatrix`. We then multiply the matrix by the principal component matrix to arrive at the reduced matrix. We can extract the feature vector from this matrix by calling the `rows()` function:

```
val pcomp: Matrix = matrix.computePrincipalComponents(3)
val reducedData = matrix.multiply(pcomp).rows
```

Arriving at the number of components

While we would like to have the least number for the components, the other goal is to retain the highest variance in the data. In this case, a run against three components was made, and we could see that holding on to just two components out of the four, we retained 90% of the variance. However, since we wanted at least 95%, 3 was chosen:

```
val svd = matrix.computeSVD(3)


val sum = svd.s.toArray.sum


svd.s.toArray.zipWithIndex.foldLeft(0.0) {
```

```
    case (cum, (curr, component)) =>

      val percent = (cum + curr) / sum

      println(s"Component and percent ${component + 1} :: $percent ::::
Singular value is : $curr")

      cum + curr

}
```

The output is as follows:

Component and percent 1 :: 0.6893434455825798 :::: Singular value is :
25.089863978899867

Component and percent 2 :: 0.8544090583609627 :::: Singular value is :
6.0078525425063365

Component and percent 3 :: 0.9483881906752903 :::: Singular value is :
3.4205353829523646

Component and percent 4 :: 1.0   :::: Singular value
is : 1.878502340103494

Evaluating the metrics

After we have reduced the dimensions of the data from four to three (! ?), for fun, we run the data against a range of one to seven clusters to see the elbow bend. When we compare the results of this with the K-means clustering without dimensionality reduction, the results looks practically the same:

```
val clusterCost = (1 to 7).map { noOfClusters =>
   val kmeans = new KMeans()
      .setK(noOfClusters)
      .setMaxIterations(5)
      .setInitializationMode(KMeans.K_MEANS_PARALLEL) //KMeans||

   val model = kmeans.run(reducedData)
   (noOfClusters, model.computeCost(reducedData))
}
```

Here is the output:

The following screenshot shows the cost across various numbers of clusters:

Cluster	Cost
1	680.824
2	152.369
3	78.941
4	57.345
5	55.821
6	42.327
7	38.466

Here is a screenshot that shows strikingly similar results for the elbow bend:

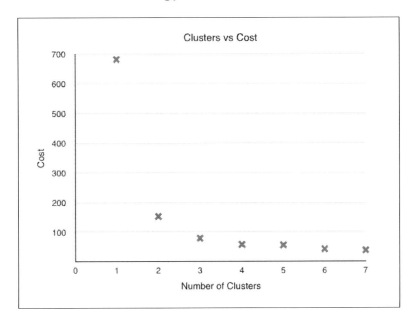

In this chapter, we first saw the difference between supervised and unsupervised learning. Then we explored a sample of machine learning algorithms in Spark: LinearRegression for predicting continuous values, LogisticRegression and SVM for classification, K-means for clustering, and finally PCA for dimensionality reduction. There are a plenty of other algorithms in Spark, and more algorithms are being added to Spark with every version, both batch and streaming.

6
Scaling Up

In this chapter, we will cover the following recipes:

- ▸ Building the Uber JAR
- ▸ Submitting jobs to the Spark cluster (local)
- ▸ Running the Spark standalone cluster on EC2
- ▸ Running the Spark job on Mesos (local)
- ▸ Running the Spark job on YARN (local)

Introduction

In this chapter, we'll be looking at how to bundle our Spark application and deploy it on various distributed environments.

As we discussed earlier in *Chapter 3*, *Loading and Preparing Data – DataFrame* the foundation of Spark is the RDD. From a programmer's perspective, the composability of RDDs such as a regular Scala collection is a huge advantage. RDD wraps three vital (and two subsidiary) pieces of information that help in reconstruction of data. This enables fault tolerance. The other major advantage is that while the processing of RDDs could be composed into hugely complex graphs using RDD operations, the entire flow of data itself is not very difficult to reason with.

Other than optional optimization attributes, such as data location, an RDD at its core wraps only three vital pieces of information:

- ▸ The dependent/parent RDD (empty if not available)
- ▸ The number of partitions
- ▸ The function that needs to be applied to each element of the RDD

Spark spawns one task per partition. So, a partition is the basic unit of parallelism in Spark.

The number of partitions could be any of these:

- ▸ Dictated by the number of blocks in the case of reading files
- ▸ A number set by the `spark.default.parallelism` parameter (set while starting the cluster)
- ▸ A number set by calling `repartition` or `coalesce` on the RDD

So far, we have just run our Spark application in the self-contained single JVM mode. While the programs work just fine, we have not yet exploited the distributed nature of the RDDs.

 As always, all the code snippets for this chapter can be downloaded from
`https://github.com/arunma/ScalaDataAnalysisCookbook/`
`tree/master/chapter6-scalingup`.

Building the Uber JAR

The first step for deploying our Spark application on a cluster is to bundle it into a single Uber JAR, also known as the `assembly` JAR. In this recipe, we'll be looking at how to use the SBT assembly plugin to generate the `assembly` JAR. We'll be using this `assembly` JAR in subsequent recipes when we run Spark in distributed mode. We could alternatively set dependent JARs using the `spark.driver.extraClassPath` property (`https://spark.apache.org/docs/1.3.1/configuration.html#runtime-environment`). However, for a large number of dependent JARs, this is inconvenient.

How to do it...

The goal of building the `assembly` JAR is to build a single, Fat JAR that contains all dependencies and our Spark application. Refer to the following screenshot, which shows the innards of an `assembly` JAR. You can see not only the application's files in the JAR, but also all the packages and files of the dependent libraries:

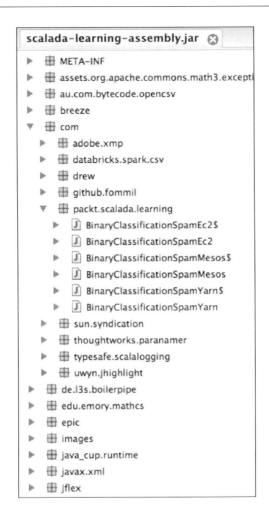

The `assembly` JAR can easily be built in SBT using the SBT assembly plugin
(`https://github.com/sbt/sbt-assembly`).

In order to install the `sbt-assembly` plugin, let's add the following line to our
`project/assembly.sbt`:

```
addSbtPlugin("com.eed3si9n" % "sbt-assembly" % "0.13.0")
```

Next, the most common issue that we face while trying to build the `assembly` JAR (or Uber JAR)
is the problem of duplicates—duplicate transitive dependency JARs, or simply duplicate files
located at the same location (such as `MANIFEST.MF`) in different bundled JARs. The easiest
way to figure out is to install the `sbt-dependency-graph` plugin (`https://github.com/jrudolph/sbt-dependency-graph`) and check which two trees bring in the conflicting JAR.

In order to add the `sbt-dependency-graph` plugin, let's add the following line to our `project/plugins.sbt`:

```
addSbtPlugin("net.virtual-void" % "sbt-dependency-graph" %
"0.7.5")
```

Let's try to build the Uber JAR using `sbt assembly`. When we issue this command from the root of the project, we get an error that tells us that we have duplicate files in our JAR.

Let's see an example of a duplicate error message that we might face:

```
deduplicate: different file contents found in the following:
```

```
/Users/Gabriel/.ivy2/cache/org.apache.xmlbeans/xmlbeans/jars/xmlbeans-
2.3.0.jar:org/w3c/dom/DOMStringList.class
```

```
/Users/Gabriel/.ivy2/cache/xml-apis/xml-apis/jars/xml-apis-1.4.01.
jar:org/w3c/dom/DOMStringList.class
```

```
deduplicate: different file contents found in the following:
```

```
/Users/Gabriel/.ivy2/cache/org.apache.xmlbeans/xmlbeans/jars/xmlbeans-
2.3.0.jar:org/w3c/dom/TypeInfo.class
```

```
/Users/Gabriel/.ivy2/cache/xml-apis/xml-apis/jars/xml-apis-1.4.01.
jar:org/w3c/dom/TypeInfo.class
```

```
deduplicate: different file contents found in the following:
```

```
/Users/Gabriel/.ivy2/cache/org.apache.xmlbeans/xmlbeans/jars/xmlbeans-
2.3.0.jar:org/w3c/dom/UserDataHandler.class
```

```
/Users/Gabriel/.ivy2/cache/xml-apis/xml-apis/jars/xml-apis-1.4.01.
jar:org/w3c/dom/UserDataHandler.class
```

This happens most commonly if:

- ▸ Two different libraries in our `sbt` dependencies depend on the same external library (or libraries that have bundled the classes with the same package)
- ▸ We have explicitly stated the transitive dependency as a separate dependency in `sbt`

Whatever the case, it is always recommended to go through the entire dependency tree to trim it down.

Transitive dependency stated explicitly in the SBT dependency

A simpler way is to export the dependency tree in an ASCII tree format and eyeball it to find the two instances where the `xmlbeans` JAR is referred to. The `sbt dependency` graph plugin lets us do that. Once we have installed the plugin as per the instructions, we can export and inspect the dependency tree:

```
sbt dependency-tree > deptree.txt
```

The graph can also be visualized using a real graph (however, this lacks the text search capabilities). The sbt dependency graph helps us analyze that too. We can export the same tree as a .dot file using this code:

```
sbt dependency-dot > depdot.dot
```

It outputs a depdot.dot file in our target directory, which can be opened using Graphviz (http://www.graphviz.org/). Refer to the following screenshot to see what the visualization of a .dot file in Graphviz looks like:

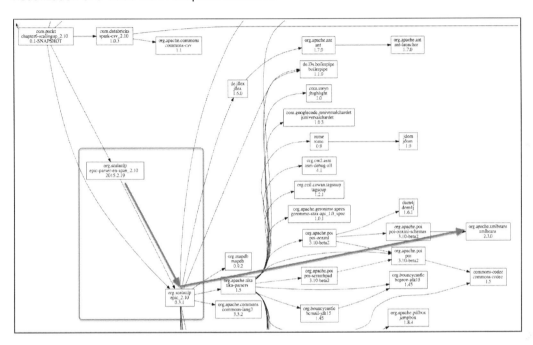

As we can see in lines 96 and 573 of the dependency tree (refer to https://github.com/arunma/ScalaDataAnalysisCookbook/blob/master/chapter6-scalingup/depgraph_xmlbeans_duplicate.txt; its screenshot is given), there are two instances of the import of xmlbeans: once in the tree that leads to org.scalanlp:epic-parser-en-span_2.10:2015.2.19, and once in the tree that leads to org.scalanlp:epic_2.10:0.3.1. If you notice the second level of the epic-parser library, you will realize that it is the epic library itself.

So, we can resolve this error by removing scalanlp:epic_2.10:0.3.1 from the list of dependencies in our build.sbt file.

Two different libraries depend on the same external library

Even after we have removed the `epic` library, we still see some issues with the `xercesImpl` and `xmlapi` JARs. When we analyze the dependency tree, we see that two dependent libraries of `epic` depend on `xerces`, the `xml` API and the `scala` library itself!

```
+—org.mapdb:mapdb:0.9.2
+—org.scala-lang:scala-library:2.10.3 (evicted by: 2.10.4)
+—org.scalanlp:breeze-config_2.10:0.9.1 [S]
| +—com.thoughtworks.paranamer:paranamer:2.2
| +—org.scala-lang:scala-library:2.10.3 (evicted by: 2.10.4)
| +—org.scala-lang:scala-reflect:2.10.3 (evicted by: 2.10.4)
| +—org.scala-lang:scala-reflect:2.10.4 [S]
|   +—org.scala-lang:scala-library:2.10.3 (evicted by: 2.10.4)
|
+—org.scalanlp:breeze_2.10:0.11-M0 [S]
| +—com.github.fommil.netlib:core:1.1.2
| | +—net.sourceforge.f2j:arpack_combined_all:0.1
| |
| +—com.github.rwl:jtransforms:2.4.0
| | +—junit:junit:4.8.2
| |
| +—net.sf.opencsv:opencsv:2.3
| +—net.sourceforge.f2j:arpack_combined_all:0.1
| +—org.apache.commons:commons-math3:3.2
| +—org.scala-lang:scala-library:2.10.3 (evicted by: 2.10.4)
| +—org.scalanlp:breeze-macros_2.10:0.11-M0 [S]
| | +—org.scala-lang:scala-library:2.10.3 (evicted by: 2.10.4)
| | +—org.scala-lang:scala-reflect:2.10.3 (evicted by: 2.10.4)
| | +—org.scala-lang:scala-reflect:2.10.4 [S]
| | | +—org.scala-lang:scala-library:2.10.3 (evicted by: 2.10.4)
| | |
| | +—org.scalamacros:quasiquotes_2.10:2.0.0 [S]
| | | +—org.scala-lang:scala-library:2.10.2 (evicted by: 2.10.4)
| | | +—org.scala-lang:scala-library:2.10.3 (evicted by: 2.10.4)
| | | +—org.scala-lang:scala-reflect:2.10.2 (evicted by: 2.10.4)
| | | +—org.scala-lang:scala-reflect:2.10.3 (evicted by: 2.10.4)
| | | +—org.scala-lang:scala-reflect:2.10.4 [S]
| | |   +—org.scala-lang:scala-library:2.10.3 (evicted by: 2.10.4)
| | |
| | +—org.scalamacros:quasiquotes_2.10:2.0.0-M8 [S] (evicted by: 2.0.0)
| |   +—org.scala-lang:scala-library:2.10.2 (evicted by: 2.10.4)
| |   +—org.scala-lang:scala-library:2.10.3 (evicted by: 2.10.4)
| |   +—org.scala-lang:scala-reflect:2.10.2 (evicted by: 2.10.4)
| |   +—org.scala-lang:scala-reflect:2.10.3 (evicted by: 2.10.4)
| |   +—org.scala-lang:scala-reflect:2.10.4 [S]
| |     +—org.scala-lang:scala-library:2.10.3 (evicted by: 2.10.4)
| |
+—org.slf4j:slf4j-api:1.7.5 (evicted by: 1.7.7)
+—org.slf4j:slf4j-api:1.7.6 (evicted by: 1.7.7)
+—org.slf4j:slf4j-api:1.7.7
+—org.spire-math:spire_2.10:0.7.4 [S]
| +—org.scala-lang:scala-library:2.10.2 (evicted by: 2.10.4)
| +—org.scala-lang:scala-library:2.10.3 (evicted by: 2.10.4)
| +—org.scala-lang:scala-reflect:2.10.2 (evicted by: 2.10.4)
| +—org.scala-lang:scala-reflect:2.10.3 (evicted by: 2.10.4)
| +—org.scala-lang:scala-reflect:2.10.4 [S]
```

We notice that the Epic library has a dependency on the Scala library, but we also know that the Scala library should already be available on the master and the worker nodes. We can exclude the Scala library altogether from getting bundled using the `assemblyOption` key:

```
assemblyOption in assembly := (assemblyOption in
assembly).value.copy(includeScala = false)
```

Next, in order to exclude the `xml-apis` library from the `epic` library, we use the `exclude` function:

```
libraryDependencies  ++= Seq(
  "org.apache.spark" %% "spark-core" % sparkVersion % "provided",
  "org.apache.spark" %% "spark-sql" % sparkVersion % "provided",
  "org.apache.spark" %% "spark-mllib" % sparkVersion % "provided",
  "com.databricks" %% "spark-csv" % "1.0.3",
  ("org.scalanlp" % "epic-parser-en-span_2.10" % "2015.2.19").
    exclude("xml-apis", "xml-apis")
)
```

As for the rest of the conflicting files, we can use the `assembly` plugin's merge strategy to resolve the conflict. Since we are merging contents of multiple JARs, there is a distinct possibility of a similarly named file being available on the same path, for example, `MANIFEST.MF`. The `sbt-assembly` plugin provides various strategies to resolve conflicts if the contents of the file in the same location don't match. The default strategy is to throw an error, but we can customize the strategy to suit our needs.

In the merge strategy, we append the contents of `application.conf` if there are multiple `conf` files in the JARs, use the first matching class/file in the order of the class path for the `org.cyberneko.html` package, and discard all the `manifest` files. For all others, we apply the default strategy:

```
assemblyMergeStrategy in assembly := {
  case "application.conf"                          =>
MergeStrategy.concat
  case PathList("org", "cyberneko", "html", xs @ _*) =>
MergeStrategy.first
  case m if m.toLowerCase.endsWith("manifest.mf")    =>
MergeStrategy.discard
  case f                                           =>
(assemblyMergeStrategy in assembly).value(f)
}
```

The entire `build.sbt` looks like this:

```
organization := "com.packt"

name := "chapter6-scalingup"

scalaVersion := "2.10.4"
val sparkVersion="1.4.1"

libraryDependencies  ++= Seq(
  "org.apache.spark" %% "spark-core" % sparkVersion % "provided",
  "org.apache.spark" %% "spark-sql" % sparkVersion % "provided",
  "org.apache.spark" %% "spark-mllib" % sparkVersion % "provided",
  "com.databricks" %% "spark-csv" % "1.0.3",
  ("org.scalanlp" % "epic-parser-en-span_2.10" % "2015.2.19").
    exclude("xml-apis", "xml-apis")
)

assemblyJarName in assembly := "scalada-learning-assembly.jar"

assemblyOption in assembly := (assemblyOption in
assembly).value.copy(includeScala = false)

assemblyMergeStrategy in assembly := {
  case "application.conf"                         =>
MergeStrategy.concat
  case PathList("org", "cyberneko", "html", xs @ _*) =>
MergeStrategy.first
  case m if m.toLowerCase.endsWith("manifest.mf")    =>
MergeStrategy.discard
  case f                                          =>
(assemblyMergeStrategy in assembly).value(f)
}
```

So finally, when we do an `sbt assembly`, `scalada-learning-assembly.jar` is created. If you would like the JAR name to be picked up from the `build.sbt` file's name and version, just delete the `assemblyJarName` key from `build.sbt`:

```
> sbt clean assembly
```

Submitting jobs to the Spark cluster (local)

There are multiple components involved in running Spark in distributed mode. In the self-contained application mode (the main program that we have run throughout this book so far), all of these components run on a single JVM. The following diagram elaborates the various components and their functions in running the Scala program in distributed mode:

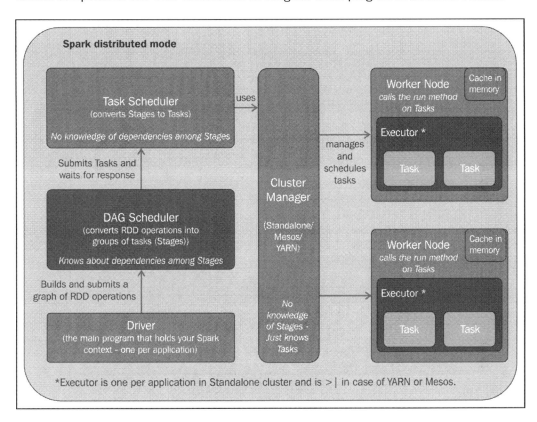

As a first step, the RDD graph that we construct using the various operations on our RDD (map, filter, join, and so on) is passed to the **Directed Acyclic Graph** (**DAG**) scheduler. The DAG scheduler optimizes the flow and converts all RDD operations into groups of tasks called stages. Generally, all tasks before a shuffle are wrapped into a stage. Consider operations in which there is a one-to-one mapping between tasks; for example, a map or filter operator yields one output for every input. If there is a map on an element on RDD followed by a filter, they are generally pipelined (the map and the filter) to form a single task that can be executed by a single worker, not to mention the benefits of data locality. Relating this to our traditional Hadoop MapReduce, where data is written to the disk at every stage, would help us really appreciate the Spark lineage graph.

These shuffle-separated stages are then passed to the task scheduler, which splits them into tasks and submits them to the cluster manager. Spark comes bundled with a simple cluster manager that can receive the tasks and run it against a set of worker nodes. However, Spark applications can also be run on popular cluster managers, such as Mesos and YARN.

With YARN/Mesos, we can run multiple executors on the same worker node. Besides, YARN and Mesos can host non-Spark jobs in their cluster along with Spark jobs.

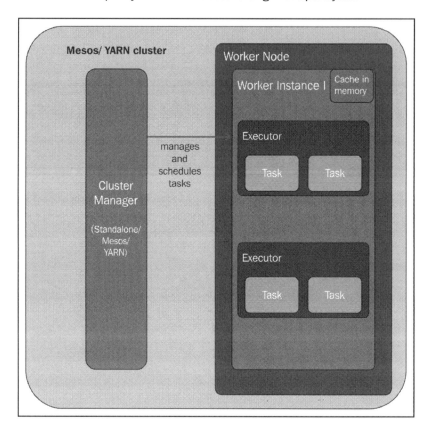

In the Spark standalone cluster, prior to Spark 1.4, the number of executors per worker node per application was limited to 1. However, we could increase the number of worker instances per worker node using the SPARK_WORKER_INSTANCES parameter. With Spark 1.4 (https://issues.apache.org/jira/browse/SPARK-1706), we are able to run multiple executors on the same node, just as in Mesos/YARN.

> If we intend to run multiple worker instances within a single machine, we must ensure that we configure the SPARK_WORKER_CORES property to limit the number of cores that can be used by each worker. The default is *all*!

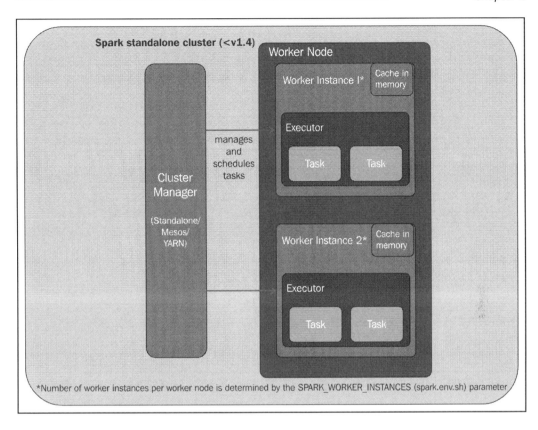

In this recipe, we will be deploying the Spark application on a standalone cluster running on a single machine. For all the recipes in this chapter, we'll be using the binary classification app that we built in the previous chapter as a deployment candidate. This recipe assumes that you have some knowledge of the concepts of HDFS and basic operations on them.

How to do it...

Submitting a Spark job to the local cluster involves the following steps:

1. Downloading Spark.
2. Running HDFS on pseudo-clustered mode.
3. Running the Spark master and slave locally.
4. Pushing data into HDFS.
5. Submitting the Spark application on the cluster.

Downloading Spark

Throughout this book, we have been using Spark version 1.4.1, as we can see in our `build.sbt`. Now, let's head over to the download page (`https://spark.apache.org/downloads.html`) and download the `spark-1.4.1-bin-hadoop2.6.tgz` bundle, as shown here:

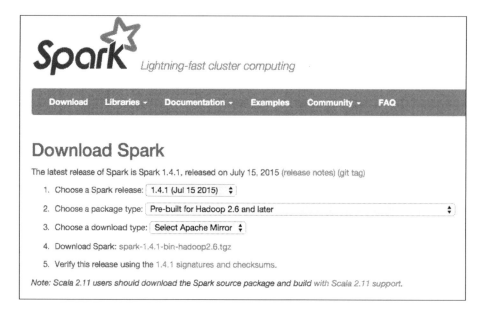

Running HDFS on Pseudo-clustered mode

Instead of loading the file from the local filesystem for our Spark application, let's have the file stored away in HDFS. In order to do this, let's have a locally running Pseudo-distributed cluster (`https://hadoop.apache.org/docs/stable/hadoop-project-dist/hadoop-common/SingleCluster.html#Pseudo-Distributed_Operation`) of Hadoop 2.6.0.

After formatting our name node using `bin/hdfs namenode -format` and bringing up our data node and name node using `sbin/start-dfs.sh`, let's confirm that all the processes that we need are running properly. We do this using `Jps`. The following screenshot shows what you are expected to see once you start the `dfs` daemon:

```
3747 DataNode
3627 NameNode
3953 SecondaryNameNode
4057 Jps
```

Running the Spark master and slave locally

In order to submit our `assembly` JAR to a Spark cluster, we have to first bring up the Spark master and worker nodes.

All that we need to do to run Spark on the local machine is go to the downloaded (and extracted) `spark` folder and run `sbin/start-all.sh` from the `spark` home directory. This will bring up the Master and a Worker node of Spark. The Master's web UI is accessible from port 8080. We use this port to check the status of the job. The default service port of the Master is 7077. We'll be using this port to submit our `assembly` JAR as a job to the Spark cluster.

```
bash-3.2$ pwd
/Users/Gabriel/Apps/spark-1.4.1-bin-hadoop2.6
bash-3.2$ sbin/start-all.sh
```

Let's confirm the running of the `Master` and the `Worker` nodes using `Jps`:

```
4144 Master
3747 DataNode
3627 NameNode
4435 Jps
4326 Worker
3953 SecondaryNameNode
```

Pushing data into HDFS

This just involves running the `mkdir` and `put` commands on HDFS:

```
bash-3.2$ hadoop fs -mkdir /scalada


bash-3.2$ hadoop fs -put /Users/Gabriel/Apps/SMSSpamCollection /scalada/


bash-3.2$ hadoop fs -ls /scalada


Found 1 items
-rw-r--r--   1 Gabriel supergroup      477907 2015-07-18 16:59 /scalada/
SMSSpamCollection
```

We can also confirm this via the HDFS web interface at 50070 and by going to **Utilities |
Browse the file system**, as shown here:

Submitting the Spark application on the cluster

Before we submit the Spark application to be run against the local cluster, let's change the
classification program (`BinaryClassificationSpam`) to point to the HDFS location:

```
val docs =
sc.textFile("hdfs://localhost:9000/scalada/SMSSpamCollection").
map(line => {
    val words = line.split("\t")
    Document(words.head.trim(), words.tail.mkString(" "))
})
```

By default, Spark 1.4.1 uses Hadoop 2.2.0. Now that we are trying to run the job on Hadoop
2.6.0, and are using the Spark binary prebuilt for Hadoop 2.6 and later, let's change `build.
sbt` to reflect that:

```
libraryDependencies   ++= Seq(
    "org.apache.spark" %% "spark-core" % sparkVersion % "provided",
    "org.apache.spark" %% "spark-sql" % sparkVersion % "provided",
    "org.apache.spark" %% "spark-mllib" % sparkVersion % "provided",
    "com.databricks" %% "spark-csv" % "1.0.3",
    "org.apache.hadoop"  % "hadoop-client" % "2.6.0",
    ("org.scalanlp" % "epic-parser-en-span_2.10" % "2015.2.19").
        exclude("xml-apis", "xml-apis")
)
```

Run `sbt clean assembly` to build the Uber JAR, like this:

```
Gabriel@Gabriels-MacBook-Pro ~/D/a/S/C/s/chapter6-scalingup> sbt clean assembly
[info] Loading global plugins from /Users/Gabriel/.sbt/0.13/plugins
[warn] Multiple resolvers having different access mechanism configured with same name 'sbt-plugin-
lver ('publishTo').
```

```
./bin/spark-submit \
  --class com.packt.scalada.learning.BinaryClassificationSpam \
  --master spark://localhost:7077 \
  --executor-memory 2G \
  --total-executor-cores 2 \
   <project root>/target/scala-2.10/scalada-learning-assembly.jar
```

Here is the output:

The following screenshot shows that we have successfully run our classification job on a Spark cluster as against the standalone app that we used in the previous chapter:

```
15/07/18 18:49:05 INFO DAGScheduler: Job 45 finished: collectAsMap at MulticlassMetrics.scala:52, took 0.061985 s
Confusion Matrix
887.0  7.0
23.0   129.0
************** ending metrics for Logistic Regression with BFGS *****************
```

Running the Spark Standalone cluster on EC2

The easiest way to create a Spark cluster and run our Spark jobs in a truly distributed mode is Amazon EC2 instances. The `ec2` folder inside the Spark installation directory wraps all the scripts and libraries that we need to create a cluster. Let's quickly go through the steps that entail the creation of our first distributed cluster.

This recipe assumes that you have a basic understanding of the Amazon EC2 ecosystem, specifically how to spawn a new EC2 instance.

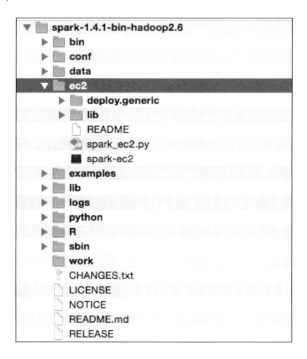

How to do it...

We'll have to ensure that we have the access key and the **Privacy Enhanced Mail** (**PEM**) files for AWS before proceeding with the steps. In fact, we are required to have these before launching any EC2 instance if we intend to log in to the machines.

Creating the AccessKey and pem file

Instructions for creating a key pair and the pem key are available at `http://docs.aws. amazon.com/AWSEC2/latest/UserGuide/ec2-key-pairs.html`. Anyway, the following are the relevant screenshots.

Select **Security Credentials** from the user menu, like this:

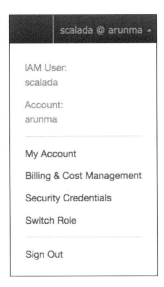

Click on the **Users** menu and create an access key, as shown in the following screenshot. Download the credentials. We'll be using this to create the EC2 instances for the Spark master and the worker nodes:

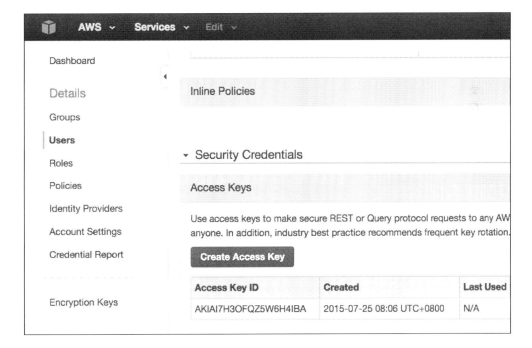

The key pair can be created from inside the EC2 instances page using the **Key Pairs** menu, as shown in the next screenshot. Your browser will automatically download the pem file once you create a pair:

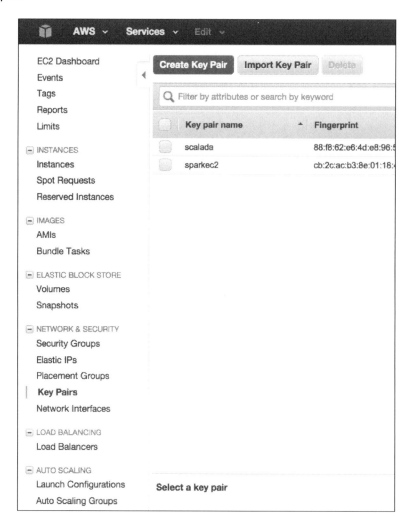

Once you have the pem file, ensure that the file permission for the pem file is 400. Otherwise, an error message stating that your pem file's permissions are too open will be shown:

```
chmod 400 spark.pem
```

Launching and running our Spark application involves the following steps:

1. Setting the environment variables.
2. Running the launch script.

3. Verifying installation.

4. Making changes to the code.

5. Transferring the data and job files.

6. Loading the dataset into HDFS.

7. Running the job.

8. Destroying the cluster.

Setting the environment variables

As the first step, let's export the access and the secret access keys as environment variables. The `ec2` script for launching our instances will use these commands:

```
export AWS_ACCESS_KEY_ID=AKIAI7H3OFQZ5W6H4IBA

export AWS_SECRET_ACCESS_KEY=[YOUR SECRET ACCESS KEY]
```

I have also copied the `pem` file to the spark installation root directory, just to make the launch command shorter (by not specifying the entire path of the `pem` file), as marked here:

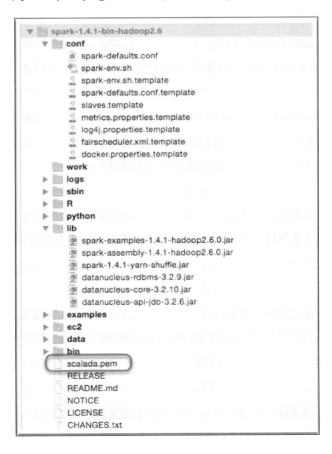

Running the launch script

Now that we have the access key (and the secret key) exported and the `pem` file in the root folder, let's spawn a new cluster:

```
cd spark-1.4.1-bin-hadoop2.6
```

```
./ec2/spark-ec2 --key-pair=scalada --identity-file=scalada.pem --slaves=2
--instance-type=m3.medium --hadoop-major-version=2 launch scalada-cluster
```

The parameters, as is clearly evident, represent the following:

 ▸ `key-pair`: This is the name of the user to whom the access key and the secret access key you exported as environment variables belong.

 ▸ `identity-file`: This is the location of the `pem` file.

 ▸ `slaves`: This is the number of worker nodes.

 ▸ `instance-type`: This is one of the AWS instance types (`http://aws.amazon.com/ec2/instance-types/`). M3 medium has one core and 3.75 GB in memory.

 ▸ `hadoop-major-version`: This is the version of Hadoop that we want Spark to be bundled with. The spark version itself is derived from our local installation (which is 1.4.1).

We can also confirm this from the EC2 console, as shown in the following screenshot:

Verifying installation

Let's log in to the Master to see the services that are running on each node:

```
ssh -i scalada.pem root@ec2-54-161-176-58.compute-1.amazonaws.com
```

Doing a `jps` on the master node shows that the Spark Master, the HDFS name node, and the Secondary name node are running on the Spark master node, as depicted in this screenshot:

```
bash-3.2$ ssh -i scalada.pem root@ec2-54-161-176-58.compute-1.amazonaws.com
Last login: Sat Aug  8 05:00:06 2015 from 132.147.72.227


     __|  __|_  )
     _|  (     /   Amazon Linux AMI
    ___|\___|___|

https://aws.amazon.com/amazon-linux-ami/2013.03-release-notes/
Amazon Linux version 2015.03 is available.
root@ip-10-150-76-158 ~]$ jps
3436 NameNode
4556 Jps
4332 TachyonMaster
4006 Master
3620 SecondaryNameNode
```

Similarly, on the worker nodes, we see that the Spark Worker and the HDFS data nodes are running, as follows:

```
bash-3.2$ ssh -i scalada.pem root@ec2-54-147-209-103.compute-1.amazonaws.com
Last login: Sat Aug  8 05:01:58 2015 from 132.147.72.227


     __|  __|_  )
     _|  (     /   Amazon Linux AMI
    ___|\___|___|

https://aws.amazon.com/amazon-linux-ami/2013.03-release-notes/
Amazon Linux version 2015.03 is available.
root@ip-10-63-156-126 ~]$ jps
3149 DataNode
3593 TachyonWorker
3373 Worker
3785 Jps
```

Making changes to the code

There is a small change that is required in our code in order to make it run on this cluster—the location of the dataset in HDFS. This, however, is not the recommended way of doing it, and the URL should be sourced from an external configuration file:

```
   val conf = new
SparkConf().setAppName("BinaryClassificationSpamEc2")
   val sc = new SparkContext(conf)
   val sqlContext = new SQLContext(sc)

   val docs = sc.textFile("hdfs://ec2-54-159-166-156.compute-1.
amazonaws.com:9000/scalada/SMSSpamCollection").map(line => {
     val words = line.split("\t")
     Document(words.head.trim(), words.tail.mkString(" "))
   })
```

Transferring the data and job files

As the next step, let's copy the dataset and the `assembly` JAR to the master node for execution from the directory where you have the `pem` file:

```
scp -i scalada.pem <REPO_DIR>/chapter5-learning/SMSSpamCollection root@
ec2-54-161-176-58.compute-1.amazonaws.com:~/.
```

```
scp -i scalada.pem  <REPO_DIR>/chapter6-scalingup/target/scala-2.10/
scalada-learning-assembly.jar root@ec2-54-161-176-58.compute-1.amazonaws.
com:~/.
```

An `ls` on the home folder of the master confirms this, as shown in the following screenshot:

```
root@ip-10-150-76-158 ~]$ ls
ephemeral-hdfs   mapreduce        scala                                SMSSpamCollection  spark-ec2
hadoop-native    persistent-hdfs  scalada-learning-assembly.jar  spark                    tachyon
```

Loading the dataset into HDFS

Now that we have uploaded our dataset to the master's local folder, let's push it to HDFS. As we saw earlier when we verified the installation, the Spark EC2 script creates and runs an HDFS cluster for us. Let's go to the `ephemeral-hdfs` folder in the root and format the filesystem. Note that the files in this HDFS, as the name indicates, will be wiped off upon restarting the cluster. Ideally, we should be installing a separate HDFS cluster on these nodes instead of depending on the ephemeral installation that was created by the Spark EC2 script.

Just as in our previous recipe, let's push the `SMSSpamCollection` dataset into the `/scalada` folder in HDFS:

```
root@ip-10-150-76-158 ephemeral-hdfs] $ ./bin/hdfs namenode -format
root@ip-10-150-76-158 ephemeral-hdfs] $ ./bin/hadoop fs -mkdir /scalada
root@ip-10-150-76-158 ephemeral-hdfs] $ ./bin/hadoop fs -put ../
SMSSpamCollection /scalada/
```

```
root@ip-10-150-76-158 ephemeral-hdfs]$ ./bin/hadoop fs -ls /scalada
Found 1 items
-rw-r--r--   3 root supergroup       477907 2015-08-08 05:24 /scalada/
SMSSpamCollection
```

Running the job

As with the previous recipe, we'll use the `spark-submit` script to submit the job to the cluster. Let's enter the spark home directory (`/root/spark`) and execute the following lines:

```
./bin/spark-submit \
  --class com.packt.scalada.learning.BinaryClassificationSpamEc2 \
  --master spark://ec2-54-161-176-58.compute-1.amazonaws.com:7077 \
  --executor-memory 2G \
  --total-executor-cores 2 \
  ../scalada-learning-assembly.jar
```

We can see that the job runs on both worker nodes of the cluster, as shown in this screenshot:

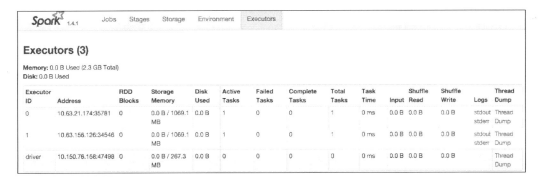

We can also see the various stages of this Job from the **Stages** tab, as shown in the following screenshot:

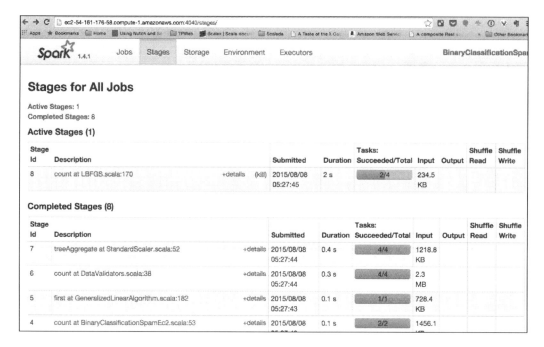

Not surprisingly, the accuracy measure is approximately the same, except that now we can use this cluster to handle much bigger data.

```
15/08/08 05:28:01 INFO BlockManagerInfo: Removed broadcast_77_piece0 on 10.63.21.174:58477 in memory (size: 1363.0 B, free: 1066.9 MB)
15/08/08 05:28:01 INFO BlockManagerInfo: Removed broadcast_77_piece0 on 10.63.156.126:58790 in memory (size: 1363.0 B, free: 1066.9 MB)
15/08/08 05:28:01 INFO ContextCleaner: Cleaned shuffle 3
Confusion Matrix
960.0  4.0
30.0   116.0
************** ending metrics for Logistic Regression with BFGS ******************
```

Destroying the cluster

Finally, if you would like to destroy the cluster, you can use the same `ec2` script with the `destroy` action. From your local Spark installation directory, execute this line:

```
./ec2/spark-ec2 destroy scalada-cluster
```

```
bash-3.2$ ./ec2/spark-ec2 destroy scalada-cluster
Searching for existing cluster scalada-cluster in region us-east-1...
Found 1 master, 2 slaves.
The following instances will be terminated:
> ec2-54-161-176-58.compute-1.amazonaws.com
> ec2-54-147-209-103.compute-1.amazonaws.com
> ec2-54-161-198-238.compute-1.amazonaws.com
ALL DATA ON ALL NODES WILL BE LOST!!
Are you sure you want to destroy the cluster scalada-cluster? (y/N) y
Terminating master...
Terminating slaves...
```

Running the Spark Job on Mesos (local)

Unlike the Spark standalone cluster manager, which can run only Spark apps, Mesos is a cluster manager that can run a wide variety of applications, including Python, Ruby, or Java EE applications. It can also run Spark jobs. In fact, it is one of the popular go-to cluster managers for Spark. In this recipe, we'll see how to deploy our Spark application on the Mesos cluster. The prerequisite for this recipe is a running HDFS cluster.

How to do it...

Running a Spark job on Mesos is very similar to running it against the standalone cluster. It involves the following steps:

1. Installing Mesos.
2. Starting the Mesos master and slave.
3. Uploading the Spark binary package and the dataset to HDFS.
4. Running the job.

Installing Mesos

Download Mesos on the local machine by following the instructions at `http://mesos.apache.org/gettingstarted/`.

After you have installed the OS-specific tools needed to build Mesos, you have to run the configure and make commands (with root privileges) to build Mesos (this will take a long time) unless you pass `-j <number of cores> V=0` to your `make` command, as shown here:

```
bash-3.2$ pwd
/Users/Gabriel/Apps/mesos-0.22.1/build
bash-3.2$ sudo make -j 2 V=0
Making all in .
make[1]: Nothing to be done for `all-am'.
Making all in 3rdparty
```

As a side note, just like Spark, the `ec2` folder inside the `mesos` installation directory provides scripts to spawn a new EC2 `mesos` cluster.

Starting the Mesos master and slave

Now that we have Mesos installed, the next step is to start the Mesos master and slave:

`bash-3.2$ pwd`

`/Users/Gabriel/Apps/mesos-0.22.1/build`

`bash-3.2$ sudo ./bin/mesos-master.sh --ip=127.0.0.1 --work_dir=/var/lib/mesos`

```
bash-3.2$ pwd
/Users/Gabriel/Apps/mesos-0.22.1/build
bash-3.2$ sudo ./bin/mesos-master.sh --ip=127.0.0.1 --work_dir=/var/lib/mesos
Password:
I0725 17:29:27.133007 2005725952 main.cpp:181] Build: 2015-07-25 17:17:47 by Gabriel
I0725 17:29:27.133209 2005725952 main.cpp:183] Version: 0.22.1
I0725 17:29:27.136255 2005725952 leveldb.cpp:176] Opened db in 2558us
I0725 17:29:27.136720 2005725952 leveldb.cpp:183] Compacted db in 440us
I0725 17:29:27.136772 2005725952 leveldb.cpp:198] Created db iterator in 23us
I0725 17:29:27.136806 2005725952 leveldb.cpp:204] Seeked to beginning of db in 11us
I0725 17:29:27.136821 2005725952 leveldb.cpp:273] Iterated through 0 keys in the db in 11us
I0725 17:29:27.136898 2005725952 replica.cpp:744] Replica recovered with log positions 0 -> 0 with 1 holes and 0 unlearned
I0725 17:29:27.138012 204685312 recover.cpp:449] Starting replica recovery
I0725 17:29:27.138303 204685312 recover.cpp:475] Replica is in EMPTY status
I0725 17:29:27.138816 2005725952 main.cpp:306] Starting Mesos master
I0725 17:29:27.139452 204148736 replica.cpp:641] Replica in EMPTY status received a broadcasted recover request
I0725 17:29:27.139735 203612160 recover.cpp:195] Received a recover response from a replica in EMPTY status
I0725 17:29:27.140017 205221888 recover.cpp:566] Updating replica status to STARTING
I0725 17:29:27.140393 206295040 master.cpp:349] Master 20150725-172927-16777343-5050-86707 (localhost) started on 127.0.0.1:5050
```

In another terminal window, let's bring up a worker node:

`Gabriel@Gabriels-MacBook-Pro ~/A/m/build> pwd`

`/Users/Gabriel/Apps/mesos-0.22.1/build`

`Gabriel@Gabriels-MacBook-Pro ~/A/m/build> ./bin/mesos-slave.sh --master=127.0.0.1:5050`

```
Gabriel@Gabriels-MacBook-Pro ~/A/m/build> pwd
/Users/Gabriel/Apps/mesos-0.22.1/build
Gabriel@Gabriels-MacBook-Pro ~/A/m/build> ./bin/mesos-slave.sh --master=127.0.0.1:5050
I0725 17:29:47.496588 2005725952 main.cpp:156] Build: 2015-07-25 17:17:47 by Gabriel
I0725 17:29:47.496911 2005725952 main.cpp:158] Version: 0.22.1
I0725 17:29:47.497195 2005725952 containerizer.cpp:110] Using isolation: posix/cpu,posix/mem
I0725 17:29:47.504981 2005725952 main.cpp:200] Starting Mesos slave
I0725 17:29:47.506161 256000000 slave.cpp:174] Slave started on 1)@192.168.2.117:5051
I0725 17:29:47.506695 256000000 slave.cpp:322] Slave resources: cpus(*):8; mem(*):15360; disk(*):470808; ports(*):[31000-32000]
I0725 17:29:47.507113 256000000 slave.cpp:351] Slave hostname: 192.168.2.117
I0725 17:29:47.507129 256000000 slave.cpp:352] Slave checkpoint: true
I0725 17:29:47.511113 255463424 state.cpp:35] Recovering state from '/tmp/mesos/meta'
I0725 17:29:47.511363 253317120 status_update_manager.cpp:197] Recovering status update manager
I0725 17:29:47.511500 255463424 containerizer.cpp:307] Recovering containerizer
I0725 17:29:47.511998 256000000 slave.cpp:3808] Finished recovery
I0725 17:29:47.512924 254926848 status_update_manager.cpp:171] Pausing sending status updates
I0725 17:29:47.512960 254390272 slave.cpp:647] New master detected at master@127.0.0.1:5050
I0725 17:29:47.513219 254390272 slave.cpp:672] No credentials provided. Attempting to register without authentication
I0725 17:29:47.513274 254390272 slave.cpp:683] Detecting new master
I0725 17:29:48.369973 253317120 slave.cpp:815] Registered with master master@127.0.0.1:5050; given slave ID 20150725-172927-16777343-5050-86707-S0
I0725 17:29:48.370090 252780544 status_update_manager.cpp:178] Resuming sending status updates
I0725 17:30:47.507956 253317120 slave.cpp:3648] Current disk usage 94.85%. Max allowed age: 0ns
```

We can now look at the Mesos status page at `http://127.0.0.1:5050`, and this is what we will see:

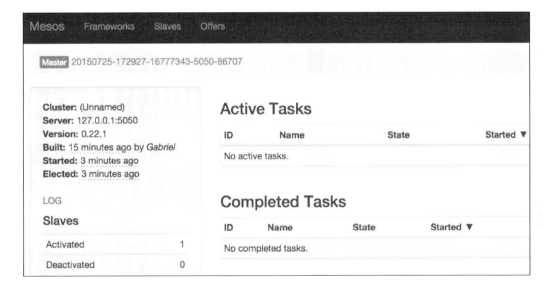

Uploading the Spark binary package and the dataset to HDFS

Mesos requires that all worker nodes have Spark installed on the machines. We can achieve this either by configuring the `spark.mesos.executor.home` property in the `spark` configuration, or by simply uploading the entire Spark `tar` bundle to HDFS and making it available to the Mesos workers:

```
./bin/hadoop fs -mkdir /scalada
```

```
./bin/hadoop fs -put /Users/Gabriel/Apps/spark-1.4.1-bin-hadoop2.6.tgz /
scalada/spark-1.4.1-bin-hadoop2.6.tgz
```

Let's set the spark binary as the executor URI

```
export SPARK_EXECUTOR_URI=hdfs://localhost:9000/scalada/spark-1.4.1-bin-hadoop2.6.tgz
```

Also, let's upload the dataset to HDFS:

```
./bin/hadoop fs -mkdir /scalada
```

```
./bin/hadoop fs -put /Users/Gabriel/Apps/SMSSpamCollection /scalada/
```

Running the job

There is one thing that we need to do before running the program itself— configure the location of the `libmesos` native library. This file can be found in the `/usr/local/lib` folder as `libmesos.so` or `libmesos.dylib`, depending on your operating system:

```
export MESOS_NATIVE_JAVA_LIBRARY=/usr/local/lib/libmesos-0.22.1.dylib
```

| Hadoop | Overview | Datanodes | Snapshot | Startup Progress | Utilities |

Browse Directory

| /scalada | | | | | | | | Go! |

Permission	Owner	Group	Size	Last Modified	Replication	Block Size	Name
-rw-r--r--	Gabriel	supergroup	466.71 KB	7/25/2015, 5:49:13 PM	1	128 MB	SMSSpamCollection
drwxr-xr-x	Gabriel	supergroup	0 B	5/21/2015, 4:20:26 AM	0	0 B	dataloading
-rw-r--r--	Gabriel	supergroup	241.41 MB	7/25/2015, 6:05:37 PM	1	128 MB	spark-1.3.1-bin-hadoop2.4.tgz

Now, let's use `cd` to enter the Spark installation directory, and then run the job:

```
cd /Users/Gabriel/Apps/spark-1.4.1-bin-hadoop2.6
```

```
export MESOS_NATIVE_JAVA_LIBRARY=/usr/local/lib/libmesos-0.22.1.dylib
```

```
./bin/spark-submit \
  --class com.packt.scalada.learning.BinaryClassificationSpamMesos \
  --master mesos://localhost:5050 \
  --executor-memory 2G \
  --total-executor-cores 2 \
  <REPO_FOLDER>/chapter6-scalingup/target/scala-2.10/scalada-learning-assembly.jar
```

As you can see in the following screenshot, the tasks run fine on this `single-worker-node` cluster:

The next screenshot shows the list of tasks that are already completed:

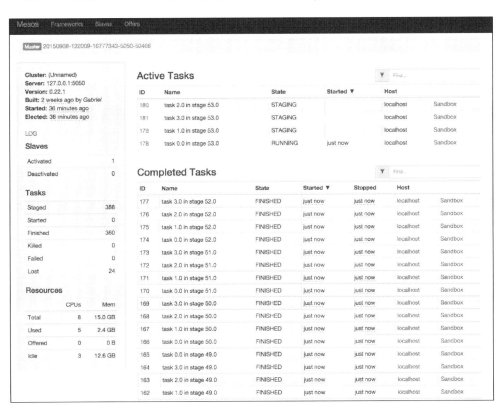

Running the Spark Job on YARN (local)

Hadoop has a long history, and in most cases, organizations have already invested in the Hadoop infrastructure before they move their MR jobs to Spark. Unlike the Spark standalone cluster manager, which can run only Spark jobs, and Mesos, which can run a variety of applications, YARN runs Hadoop jobs as first-class. At the same time, it can run Spark jobs as well. This means that when a team decides to replace some of their MR jobs with Spark jobs, they can use the same cluster manager to run Spark jobs. In this recipe, we'll see how to deploy our Spark application on the YARN cluster manager.

How to do it...

Running a Spark job on YARN is very similar to running it against a Spark standalone cluster. It involves the following steps:

1. Installing the Hadoop cluster.
2. Starting HDFS and YARN.
3. Pushing the Spark assembly and dataset to HDFS.
4. Running the Spark Job in the `yarn-client` mode.
5. Running the Spark Job in the `yarn-cluster` mode.

Installing the Hadoop cluster

While the setup of the cluster itself is beyond the scope of this recipe, for the sake of completeness, let's quickly look at the relevant site XML configurations that were made while setting up a single-node pseudo-distributed cluster on a local machine. Refer to `http://www.bogotobogo.com/Hadoop/BigData_hadoop_Install_on_ubuntu_single_node_cluster.php` for the complete details on how to set up a local YARN/HDFS cluster:

The `core-site.xml` file:

```
<configuration>
  <property>
    <name>fs.default.name</name>
    <value>hdfs://localhost:54310</value>
  </property>
</configuration>
```

The `mapred-site.xml` file:

```
<configuration>
    <property>
        <name>mapred.job.tracker</name>
        <value>localhost:54311</value>
    </property>
</configuration>
```

The `hdfs-site.xml` file:

```
<configuration>
    <property>
        <name>dfs.replication</name>
        <value>1</value>
    </property>
</configuration>
```

Starting HDFS and YARN

Once the setup of the cluster is done, let's format HDFS and start the cluster (`dfs` and `yarn`):

Format `namenode`:

`hdfs namenode -format`

Start both HDFS and YARN:

`sbin/start-all.sh`

Let's confirm that the services are running through `jps`, and this is what we should see:

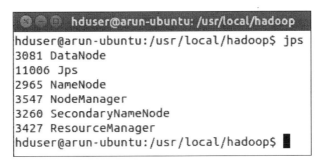

Pushing Spark assembly and dataset to HDFS

Ideally, when we do a `spark-submit`, YARN should be able to pick our `spark-assembly` JAR (or Uber JAR) and upload it to HDFS. However, this doesn't happen correctly and results in the following error:

```
Error: Could not find or load main class org.apache.spark.deploy.yarn.
ExecutorLauncher
```

In order to work around this issue, let's upload our `spark-assembly` JAR manually to HDFS and change our `conf/spark-env.sh` to reflect the location. The Hadoop config directory should also be specified in `spark-env.sh`:

Uploading the spark assembly to HDFS.

```
hadoop fs -mkdir /sparkbinary
```

```
hadoop fs -put /Users/Gabriel/Apps/spark-1.4.1-bin-hadoop2.6/lib/spark-
assembly-1.4.1-hadoop2.6.0.jar /sparkbinary/
```

```
hadoop fs -ls /sparkbinary
```

Uploading the Spam dataset to HDFS:

```
hadoop fs -mkdir /scalada
```

```
hadoop fs -put ~/SMSSpamCollection /scalada/
```

```
hadoop fs -ls /scalada
```

Entries in `spark-env.sh`:

```
HADOOP_CONF_DIR=/usr/local/hadoop/etc/hadoop
```

```
SPARK_EXECUTOR_URI=hdfs://localhost:9000/sparkbinary/spark-assembly-
1.4.1-hadoop2.6.0.jar
```

```
hduser@arun-ubuntu: ~/spark-1.4.1-bin-hadoop2.6
hduser@arun-ubuntu:~/spark-1.4.1-bin-hadoop2.6$ head conf/spark-env.sh
#!/usr/bin/env bash

# This file is sourced when running various Spark programs.
# Copy it as spark-env.sh and edit that to configure Spark for your site.

HADOOP_CONF_DIR=/usr/local/hadoop/etc/hadoop
SPARK_EXECUTOR_URI=hdfs://localhost:9000/sparkbinary/spark-assembly-1.4.1-hadoop2.6.0.jar

# Options read when launching programs locally with
# ./bin/run-example or ./bin/spark-submit
```

Before we submit our Spark job to the YARN cluster, let's confirm that our setup is fine using the Spark shell. The Spark shell is a wrapper around the Scala REPL, with Spark libraries set in the classpath. Configuring `HADOOP_CONF_DIR` to point to the Hadoop `config` directory ensures that Spark will now use YARN to run its jobs. However, there are two modes in which we can run the Spark job in YARN, namely `yarn-client` and `yarn-cluster`. Let's explore both of them in this subrecipe. But before we do that, to validate our configuration, we'll launch the Spark shell pointing the `master` to the `yarn-client`. After a rain of logs, we should be able to see a Scala prompt. This confirms that our configuration is good:

bin/spark-shell --master yarn-client

```
hduser@arun-ubuntu: ~/spark-1.4.1-bin-hadoop2.6

hduser@arun-ubuntu:~/spark-1.4.1-bin-hadoop2.6$ bin/spark-shell --master yarn-client
15/08/07 21:21:46 WARN util.NativeCodeLoader: Unable to load native-hadoop library for your platform... using builtin-
java classes where applicable
15/08/07 21:21:46 INFO spark.SecurityManager: Changing view acls to: hduser
15/08/07 21:21:46 INFO spark.SecurityManager: Changing modify acls to: hduser
15/08/07 21:21:46 INFO spark.SecurityManager: SecurityManager: authentication disabled; ui acls disabled; users with v
iew permissions: Set(hduser); users with modify permissions: Set(hduser)
15/08/07 21:21:47 INFO spark.HttpServer: Starting HTTP Server
15/08/07 21:21:47 INFO server.Server: jetty-8.y.z-SNAPSHOT
15/08/07 21:21:47 INFO server.AbstractConnector: Started SocketConnector@0.0.0.0:39472
15/08/07 21:21:47 INFO util.Utils: Successfully started service 'HTTP class server' on port 39472.
Welcome to
      ____              __
     / __/__  ___ _____/ /__
    _\ \/ _ \/ _ `/ __/  '_/
   /___/ .__/\_,_/_/ /_/\_\   version 1.4.1
      /_/

Using Scala version 2.10.4 (OpenJDK 64-Bit Server VM, Java 1.7.0_79)
Type in expressions to have them evaluated.
Type :help for more information.
```

Running a Spark job in yarn-client mode

Now that we have confirmed that the shell loads up fine against the YARN master, let's head over to deploying our Spark job on YARN.

As we discussed earlier, there are two modes in which we can run a Spark application on YARN: the `yarn-client` mode and the `yarn-cluster` mode. In the `yarn-client` mode, the driver program resides on the client side and the YARN worker nodes are used only to execute the job. All of the brain of the application resides in the client JVM that polls the application master for the status. The application master does nothing except watching out for failure of the executor nodes and reporting and requesting for resources accordingly to the resource manager. This also means that the client (our driver JVM) needs to run as long as the application executes:

```
./bin/spark-submit \
  --class com.packt.scalada.learning.BinaryClassificationSpamYarn \
  --master yarn-client \
```

```
--executor-memory 1G \

~/scalada-learning-assembly.jar
```

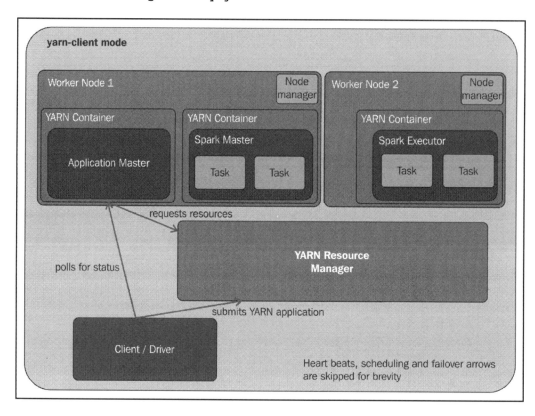

As we see from the YARN console, our job is running fine. Here is a screenshot that shows this:

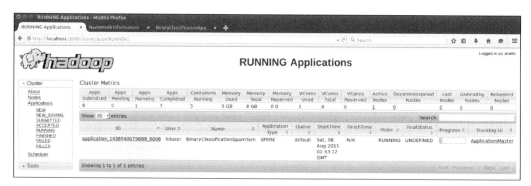

Finally, we can see the output on the client JVM (the driver) itself:

```
Confusion Matrix
913.0   7.0
35.0    127.0
************** ending metrics for Logistic Regression with BFGS *****************
```

Running Spark job in yarn-cluster mode

In the `yarn-cluster` mode, the client JVM doesn't do anything at all. In fact, it just submits and polls the Application master for status. The driver program itself runs on the Application master, which now has all the brains of the program. Unlike the `yarn-client` mode, the user logs won't be displayed on the client JVM because the driver, which consolidates the results, is executing inside the YARN cluster:

```
./bin/spark-submit \
  --class com.packt.scalada.learning.BinaryClassificationSpamYarn \
  --master yarn-cluster \
  --executor-memory 1g \
  ~/scalada-learning-assembly.jar
```

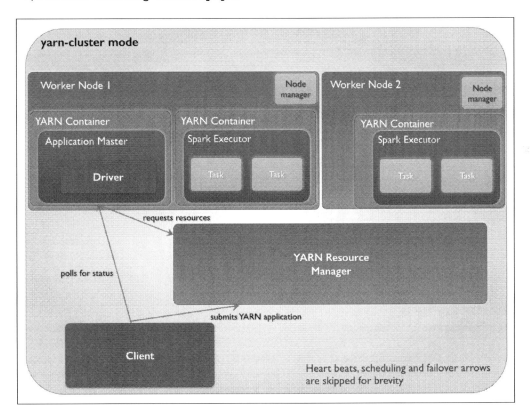

As expected, the client JVM indicates that the job has run successfully. It doesn't, however, show the user logs.

```
15/08/07 23:38:01 INFO yarn.Client: Application report for application_1438940079068_0009 (state: RUNNING)
15/08/07 23:38:02 INFO yarn.Client: Application report for application_1438940079068_0009 (state: RUNNING)
15/08/07 23:38:03 INFO yarn.Client: Application report for application_1438940079068_0009 (state: RUNNING)
15/08/07 23:38:04 INFO yarn.Client: Application report for application_1438940079068_0009 (state: FINISHED)
15/08/07 23:38:04 INFO yarn.Client:
         client token: N/A
         diagnostics: N/A
         ApplicationMaster host: 10.0.2.15
         ApplicationMaster RPC port: 0
         queue: default
         start time: 1439004971922
         final status: SUCCEEDED
         tracking URL: http://arun-ubuntu:8088/proxy/application_1438940079068_0009/A
         user: hduser
15/08/07 23:38:04 INFO util.Utils: Shutdown hook called
15/08/07 23:38:04 INFO util.Utils: Deleting directory /tmp/spark-08e26d88-e459-4c55-8813-5d00f35f6ad7
```

The following screenshot shows the final status of our client and the cluster mode runs:

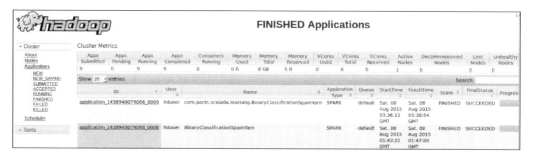

The actual output of this program is inside the Hadoop user logs. We can either go to the logs directory of Hadoop, or check it out from the Hadoop console itself, when we click on the application link and then on the logs link in the console.

As you can see in the following screenshot, the stdout file shows our embarrassing println commands:

In this chapter, we took an example Spark application and deployed it on a Spark standalone cluster manager, YARN, and Mesos. Along the way, we touched upon the internals of these cluster managers.

7
Going Further

In this chapter, we will cover the following recipes:

- ▶ Using Spark Streaming to subscribe to a Twitter stream
- ▶ Using Spark as an ETL tool (pulling data from ElasticSearch and publishing it to Kafka)
- ▶ Using StreamingLogisticRegression to classify a Twitter stream using Kafka as a training stream
- ▶ Using GraphX to analyze Twitter data
- ▶ Watching other Scala libraries of interest

Introduction

So far, the entire book has concentrated a little around Breeze and a lot around Spark, specifically DataFrames and machine learning. However, there are a whole lot of other libraries, both in Java and Scala that could be leveraged while analyzing data from Scala. This chapter goes a little more into Spark's other components, streaming and GraphX. Note that each recipe in this chapter feeds into the next recipe.

 All the code related to this chapter can be downloaded from https://github.com/arunma/ScalaDataAnalysisCookbook/tree/master/chapter7-goingfurther.

Using Spark Streaming to subscribe to a Twitter stream

Just like all the other components of Spark, Spark Streaming is also scalable and fault-tolerant, it's just that it manages a stream of data instead of a large amount of data that Spark generally does. The way that Spark Streaming approaches streaming is unique in the sense that it accumulates streams into small batches called DStreams and then processes them as mini-batches, an approach usually called **micro-batching**. The component that receives the stream of data and splits it into time-bound windows of batches is called the receiver.

Once these batches are received, Spark takes these batches up, converts them into RDDs, and processes the RDDs in the same way as static datasets. The regular framework components such as the driver and executor stay the same. However, in terms of Spark Streaming, a DStream or Discretized stream is just a continuous stream of RDDs. Also, just like `SQLContext` served as an entry point to use SQL in Spark, there's `StreamingContext` that serves as an entry point for Spark Streaming.

In this recipe, we will subscribe to a Twitter stream and index (store) the tweets into ElasticSearch (`https://www.elastic.co/`).

How to do it...

The prerequisite to run this recipe is to have a running ElasticSearch instance on your machine.

1. **Running ElasticSearch**: Running an instance of ElasticSearch is as simple as it gets. Just download the installable from `https://www.elastic.co/downloads/elasticsearch` and run `bin/elasticsearch`. This recipe uses the latest version 1.7.1.

```
bash-3.2$ pwd
/Users/Gabriel/apps/elasticsearch-1.7.1
bash-3.2$ bin/elasticsearch
[2015-08-15 13:47:33,047][INFO ][node                     ] [Harry Leland] version[1.7.1], pid[65232], build[b88f43f/2015-07-29T09:54:16Z]
[2015-08-15 13:47:33,047][INFO ][node                     ] [Harry Leland] initializing ...
[2015-08-15 13:47:33,156][INFO ][plugins                  ] [Harry Leland] loaded [], sites []
[2015-08-15 13:47:33,207][INFO ][env                      ] [Harry Leland] using [1] data paths, mounts [[/ (/dev/disk1)]], net usable_spac
e [15.3gb], net total_space [464.7gb], types [hfs]
[2015-08-15 13:47:35,860][INFO ][node                     ] [Harry Leland] initialized
[2015-08-15 13:47:35,860][INFO ][node                     ] [Harry Leland] starting ...
[2015-08-15 13:47:35,964][INFO ][transport                ] [Harry Leland] bound_address {inet[/0:0:0:0:0:0:0:0:9300]}, publish_address {in
et[/192.168.2.117:9300]}
```

2. **Creating a Twitter app**: In order to subscribe to tweets, Twitter requires us to create a Twitter app. Let's quickly set up a Twitter app in order to get the consumer key and the secret key. Visit `https://apps.twitter.com/` using your login and click **Create New App**.

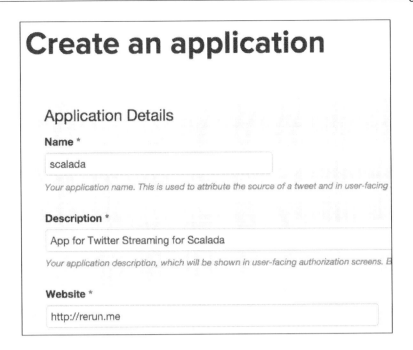

We will be using the consumer key, consumer secret key, the access token, and the access secret in our application.

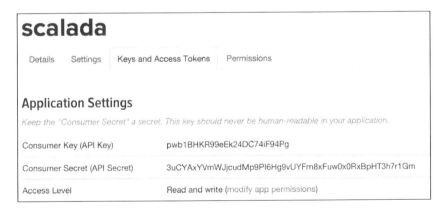

3. **Adding Spark Streaming and the Twitter dependency**: There are two dependencies that need to be added here, the `spark-streaming` and the `spark-streaming-twitter` libraries:

```
"org.apache.spark" %% "spark-streaming" % sparkVersion %
"provided",
"org.apache.spark" %% "spark-streaming-twitter" %
sparkVersion
```

4. **Creating a Twitter stream**: Creating a Twitter stream is super easy in Spark. We just need to use `TwitterUtils.createStream` for this. `TwitterUtils` wraps around the `twitter4j` library (`http://twitter4j.org/en/index.html`) to provide first-class support in Spark.

   `TwitterUtils.createStream` expects a few parameters. Let's construct them one by one.

   ❑ `StreamingContext`: `StreamingContext` could be constructed by passing in `SparkContext` and the time window of the batch:

   ```
   val streamingContext=new StreamingContext(sc, Seconds
   (5))
   ```

   ❑ OAuthorization: The access and the consumer keys that comprise the `OAuth` credentials need to be passed in order to subscribe to the Twitter stream:

   ```
   val builder = new ConfigurationBuilder()
           .setOAuthConsumerKey(consumerKey)
           .setOAuthConsumerSecret(consumerSecret)
           .setOAuthAccessToken(accessToken)
           .setOAuthAccessTokenSecret(accessTokenSecret)
           .setUseSSL(true)


   val twitterAuth = Some(new
   OAuthAuthorization(builder.build()))
   ```

   ❑ Filter criteria: You are free to skip this parameter if your intention is to subscribe to (a sample of) the universe of the tweets. For this recipe, we'll add some filter criteria to it:

   ```
   val filter=List("fashion", "tech", "startup", "spark")
   ```

   ❑ `StorageLevel`: This is where our received objects that come in batches need to be stored. The default is memory with a capability to overflow to disk. Once this is constructed, let's construct the Twitter stream itself:

   ```
   val stream=TwitterUtils.createStream(streamingContext,
   twitterAuth, filter, StorageLevel.MEMORY_AND_DISK)
   ```

5. **Saving the stream to ElasticSearch**: Writing the Tweets to ElasticSearch involves three steps:

   1. Adding the `ElasticSearch-Spark` dependency: Let's add the appropriate version of ElasticSearch Spark to our `build.sbt`:

   ```
   "org.elasticsearch" %% "elasticsearch-spark" % "2.1.0"
   ```

2. Configuring the ElasticSearch server location in the Spark configuration: ElasticSearch has a subproject called `elasticsearch-spark` that makes ElasticSeach a first-class citizen in the Spark world. The `org.elasticsearch.spark` package exposes some convenient functions that convert a case class to JSON (deriving types) and indexes to ElasticSearch. The package also provides some really cool implicits that provide functions to save RDD into ElasticSearch and load data from ElasticSearch as an RDD. We'll be looking at those functions shortly.

The ElasticSearch target node URL could be specified in the Spark configuration. By default, it points to localhost and port 9200. If required, we could customize it:

```
//Default is localhost. Point to ES node when required

val conf = new SparkConf()
    .setAppName("TwitterStreaming")
    .setMaster("local[2]")
    .set(ConfigurationOptions.ES_NODES, "localhost")
            .set(ConfigurationOptions.ES_PORT, "9200")
```

3. Converting the stream into a case class: If we are not interested in pushing the data to ElasticSearch and are interested only in printing some values in `twitter4j.Status`, `stream.foreach` will help us iterate through the `RDD[Status]`. However, in this recipe, we will be extracting some data from `twitter4j.Status` and pushing it to ElasticSearch. For this purpose, a case class `SimpleStatus` is created. The reason why we are extracting data out as a case class is that `twitter4j.Status` has way too much information that we don't want to index:

```
case class SimpleStatus(id:String, content:String,
date:Date, hashTags:Array[String]=Array[String](),

                        urls:Array[String]=Array[String](),

                        user:String, userName:String,
userFollowerCount:Long)
```

The `twitter4j.Status` is converted to `SimpleStatus` using a `convertToSimple` function that extracts only the required information:

```
def convertToSimple(status: twitter4j.Status): SimpleStatus = {
    val hashTags: Array[String] =
status.getHashtagEntities().map(eachHT => eachHT.getText())
    val urlArray = if (status.getURLEntities != null)
status.getURLEntities().foldLeft((Array[String]()))((r, c) => (r
:+ c.getExpandedURL())) else Array[String]()
    val user = status.getUser()
```

```
    val utcDate = new
Date(dateTimeZone.convertLocalToUTC(status.getCreatedAt.getTime,
false))

    SimpleStatus(id = status.getId.toString, content =
status.getText(), utcDate,
        hashTags = hashTags, urls = urlArray,
        user = user.getScreenName(), userName = user.getName,
userFollowerCount = user.getFollowersCount)
    }
```

Once we map the `twitter4j.Status` to `SimpleStatus`, we now have a `RDD[SimpleStatus]`. We can now iterate over the `RDD[SimpleStatus]` and push every RDD to ElasticSearch's `"spark"` index. `"twstatus"` is the index type. In RDBMS terms, an index is like a database schema and the index type is like a table:

```
stream.map(convertToSimple).foreachRDD { statusRdd =>
    println(statusRdd)
    statusRdd.saveToEs("spark/twstatus")
}
```

We could confirm the indexing by pointing to ElasticSearch's `spark` index using Sense, a must-have Chrome plugin for ElasticSearch, or simply by performing a `curl` request:

```
curl -XGET "http://localhost:9200/spark/_search" -d'
{
    "query": {
        "match_all": {}
    }
}'
```

 The Sense plugin for Chrome can be downloaded from the Chrome store at: `https://chrome.google.com/webstore/detail/sense-beta/lhjgkmllcaadmopgmanpapmpjgmfcfig?hl=en`.

Using Spark as an ETL tool

In the previous recipe, we subscribed to a Twitter stream and stored it in ElasticSearch. Another common source of streaming is Kafka, a distributed message broker. In fact, it's a distributed log of messages, which in simple terms means that there can be multiple brokers that has the messages partitioned among them.

In this recipe, we'll be subscribing the data that we ingested into ElasticSearch in the previous recipe and publishing the messages into Kafka. Soon after we publish the data to Kafka, we'll be subscribing to Kafka using the Spark Stream API. While this is a recipe that demonstrates treating ElasticSearch data as an RDD and publishing to Kafka using a **KryoSerializer**, the true intent of this recipe is to run a streaming classification algorithm against Twitter, which is our next recipe.

How to do it...

Let's look at the various steps involved in doing this.

1. **Setting up Kafka**: This recipe uses Kafka version 0.8.2.1 for Spark 2.10, which can be downloaded from `https://www.apache.org/dyn/closer.cgi?path=/kafka/0.8.2.1/kafka_2.10-0.8.2.1.tgz`.

Once downloaded, let's extract, start the Kafka server, and create a Kafka topic through three commands from inside our Kafka home directory:

1. **Starting Zookeeper**: Kafka uses Zookeeper (`https://zookeeper.apache.org/`) to hold coordination information between Kafka servers. It also holds the commit offset information of the data so that if a Kafka node fails, it knows where to resume from. The Zookeeper `data` directory and the client port (default `2181`) is present in `zookeeper.properties`. The `zookeeper-server-start.sh` expects this to be passed as a parameter for it to start:

   `bin/zookeeper-server-start.sh config/zookeeper.properties`

2. **Starting the Kafka server**: Again, in order to start Kafka, the configuration file to be passed to it is `server.properties`. The `server.properties`, among many things specifies the port on which the Kafka server listens (9092) and the Zookeeper port it needs to connect to (2181). This is passed to the `kafka-server-start.sh` startup script:

   `bin/kafka-server-start.sh config/server.properties`

3. **Creating a Kafka topic**: In really simple terms, a topic can be compared to a JMS topic with the difference that there could be multiple publishers as well as a single subscriber in Kafka. Since we are running the Kafka in a non-replicated and non-partitioned mode using just one Kafka server, the topic named `twtopic` (Twitter topic) is created with a replication factor of 1 and the number of partitions is 1 as well:

   `bin/kafka-topics.sh --create --zookeeper localhost:2181`
   `--replication-factor 1 --partitions 1 --topic twtopic`

2. **Pulling data from ElasticSearch**: The next step is to pull the data from ElasticSearch and treat it as a Spark DataFrame other than the optional setting in Spark configuration to point to the correct host and port. This is just a one-liner.

The configuration change (if needed) is:

```
//Default is localhost. Point to ES node when required
  val conf = new SparkConf()
    .setAppName("KafkaStreamProducerFromES")
    .setMaster("local[2]")
    .set(ConfigurationOptions.ES_NODES, "localhost")
    .set(ConfigurationOptions.ES_PORT, "9200")
```

The following line queries the `"spark/twstatus"` index (that we published to in the last recipe) for all documents and extracts the data into a DataFrame. Optionally, you can pass in a query as a second argument (for example, `"?q=fashion"`):

```
  val twStatusDf=sqlContext.esDF("spark/twstatus")
```

Let's try to sample the DataFrame using `show()`:

```
twStatusDf.show()
```

The output is:

```
+--------------+-----------------+----------------+-------------------+------------------+------------------+--------------------+
|       content|             date|        hashTags|                 id|              urls|  user|userFollowerCount|            userName|
+--------------+-----------------+----------------+-------------------+------------------+------------------+--------------------+
|HEY GUYS there's ...|2015-08-14 10:36:...|Buffer(Fashion, M...|632138605465612289|Buffer(http://www...|       lowpricesuk|     449|    LowPrices.co.uk|
|Hanbok Import Kor...|2015-08-14 10:36:...|           Buffer()|632138602667905028|Buffer(https://ww...|   happykoreamarti|     372|  Happy Korea Mart|
|Fashion brands an...|2015-08-14 10:33:...|           Buffer()|632137887492866048|Buffer(http://www...|   thehansindiaweb|    1387|     The Hans India|
|@ParkaLondonUK we...|2015-08-14 10:36:...|Buffer(menswear, ...|632138612847546368|          Buffer()|     riddlemagazine|    1477|    Riddle Magazine|
|Forget Retro. The...|2015-08-14 10:36:...|   Buffer(fashion)|632138616379211776|Buffer(http://wor...|  WordLinkFASHION|     207|WordLink #FASHION|
|RT @MarketingUK: ...|2015-08-14 10:33:...|           Buffer()|632137891435651072|Buffer(http://bit...|    GrimwoodAssoc|     320|    Jane Grimwood|
|Summer Fashion Sa...|2015-08-14 10:36:...|           Buffer()|632138611232653312|Buffer(http://bit...|  Iam_flemenkanti|     498|     Lee kuam yew|
|Summer Fashion Sa...|2015-08-14 10:36:...|           Buffer()|632138619394744320|Buffer(http://bit...|          ismelho|     543|         Still me|
|Fashion For Women...|2015-08-14 10:36:...|           Buffer()|632138612688166912|Buffer(http://fb....|          ibothman|     559|   Ibrahim Othman|
|RT @SadHappyAmazi...|2015-08-14 10:36:...|           Buffer()|632138604240850944|          Buffer()|    ItsCristalBro|     636|              Cee|
|#6: Champion Men'...|2015-08-14 10:36:...|Buffer(fashion, a...|632138634078982144|Buffer(http://amz...|  InstantTimeDeal|     854| Instant Time Deals|
|Boots by #NancySi...|2015-08-14 10:36:...|Buffer(NancySinat...|632138625275158528|Buffer(http://dlv...|         DealsMalls|     155|       Deals Malls|
|#6: Champion Men'...|2015-08-14 10:36:...|Buffer(fashion, a...|632138629662400512|Buffer(http://amz...|      RSSDealFeeds|     527|    RSS Deal Feeds|
|Summer Fashion Sa...|2015-08-14 10:36:...|           Buffer()|632138621135417344|Buffer(http://bit...|          bajulous|     132| Bajulu Olaitan|
|Summer Fashion Sa...|2015-08-14 10:36:...|           Buffer()|632138648767459328|Buffer(http://bit...|          its_3lvyz|     907|            @eLVis|
|Jam Tangan Wanita...|2015-08-14 10:36:...|           Buffer()|632138657453838336|Buffer(https://ww...|    DUNIANETdotCOM|     587|       DUNIANET.com|
|http://t.co/4ZZx8...|2015-08-14 10:36:...|Buffer(Deals, Fas...|632138659811172352|Buffer(http://ift...|         Xu_D3_004|      51|FASHION DEALS CHECK:|
|Summer Fashion Sa...|2015-08-14 10:36:...|           Buffer()|632138668690403329|Buffer(http://bit...|           HottestQ|     692|     IG:hottestq|
|#LatestNews: Summ...|2015-08-14 10:36:...|Buffer(LatestNews)|632138691637575680|          Buffer()|   diamondnewsngr|     187|    Diamond Report|
|Women's Retro fas...|2015-08-14 10:36:...|           Buffer()|632138777650176000|Buffer(http://rov...|   Daumhi__Siopki|    1356|    Daumhi Siopki|
+--------------+-----------------+----------------+-------------------+------------------+------------------+--------------------+
```

3. **Preparing data to be published to Kafka**: Before we do this step, let's go over what we aim to achieve from this step. Like we discussed at the beginning of the recipe, we will be running a classification algorithm against streaming data in the next recipe. As you know, any supervised learning algorithm requires a training dataset. Instead of us manually curating the dataset, we will be doing that in a very primitive fashion by marking all the tweets that have the word `fashion` in them as belonging to the `fashion` class and the rest of the tweets as not belonging to the `fashion` class.

We will just take the content of the tweet and convert it into a case class called `LabeledContent` (similar to `LabeledPoint` in Spark MLlib):

```
case class LabeledContent(label: Double, content:
Array[String])
```

`LabeledContent` only has two fields:

> `label`: This indicates whether the tweet is about `fashion` or not (`1.0` if the tweet is on `fashion` and `0.0` if it is not)

> `content`: This holds a space-tokenized version of the tweet itself

```
def convertToLabeledContentRdd(twStatusDf: DataFrame) = {
    //Convert the content alone to a (label, content) pair
    val labeledPointRdd = twStatusDf.map{row =>
        val content =
        row.getAs[String]("content").toLowerCase()
        val tokens = content.split(" ") //A very primitive
        space based tokenizer
```

```
              val labeledContent=if (content.contains("fashion"))
              LabeledContent(1, tokens)
              else LabeledContent(0, tokens)
              println (labeledContent.label, content)
              labeledContent
        }
        labeledPointRdd
    }
```

4. **Publishing data to Kafka using KryoSerializer**: Now that we have the publish candidate (`LabeledContent`) ready, let's publish it to the Kafka topic. This involves just three lines.

   ❑ **Constructing the connection and transport properties**: In `properties`, we configure the Kafka server port location and register the serializer that we use to serialize `LabeledContent`:

   ```
   val properties = Map[String,
   Object](ProducerConfig.BOOTSTRAP_SERVERS_CONFIG ->
   "localhost:9092").asJava
   ```

   ❑ **Constructing the Kafka producer using the connection properties and the key and value serializer**: The next step is to construct a Kafka producer using the `properties` we constructed earlier. The `producer` also needs a key and a value serializer. Since we don't have a key for our message, we fall back to Kafka's default, which fills in the hashcode by default, which we aren't interested on receipt.

   ```
   val producer = new KafkaProducer[String,
   Array[Byte]](properties, new StringSerializer, new
   ByteArraySerializer)
   ```

   ❑ **Sending data to the Kafka topic using the send method**: We then serialize `LabeledContent` using `KryoSerializer` and send it to the Kafka topic "twtopic" (the one that we created earlier) using the `producer.send` method. The only purpose of using a `KryoSerializer` here is to speed up the serialization process:

   ```
   val serializedPoint = KryoSerializer.serialize(lContent)
           producer.send(new ProducerRecord[String,
   Array[Byte]]("twtopic", serializedPoint))
   ```

For the KryoSerializer, we use Twitter's `chill` library (`https://github.com/twitter/chill`), which provides an easier abstraction over the serialization for Scala.

The actual KryoSerializer is just five lines of code:

```scala
object KryoSerializer {
  private val kryoPool = ScalaKryoInstantiator.defaultPool

  def serialize[T](anObject: T): Array[Byte] =
kryoPool.toBytesWithClass(anObject)
  def deserialize[T](bytes: Array[Byte]): T =
kryoPool.fromBytes(bytes).asInstanceOf[T]

}
```

The dependency for Twitter `chill` that needs to be added to our `build.sbt` is:

```scala
"com.twitter" %% "chill" % "0.7.0"
```

The entire publishing method looks like this:

```scala
  def publishToKafka(labeledPointRdd: RDD[LabeledContent])
{
    labeledPointRdd.foreachPartition { iterator =>

      val properties = Map[String, Object](ProducerConfig.
BOOTSTRAP_SERVERS_CONFIG ->
"localhost:9092", "serializer.class" ->
"kafka.serializer.DefaultEncoder").asJava
      val producer = new KafkaProducer[String,
Array[Byte]](properties, new StringSerializer, new
ByteArraySerializer)

      iterator.foreach { lContent =>
        val serializedPoint =
KryoSerializer.serialize(lContent)
        producer.send(new ProducerRecord[String,
Array[Byte]]("twtopic", serializedPoint))
      }
    }
  }
```

5. **Confirming receipt in Kafka**: We could confirm whether the data is in Kafka using the JMX MBeans exposed by it. We'll use JConsole UI to explore MBeans. As you can see, the count of the messages is **24849**, which matches the ElasticSearch document count (that was published in the previous recipe).

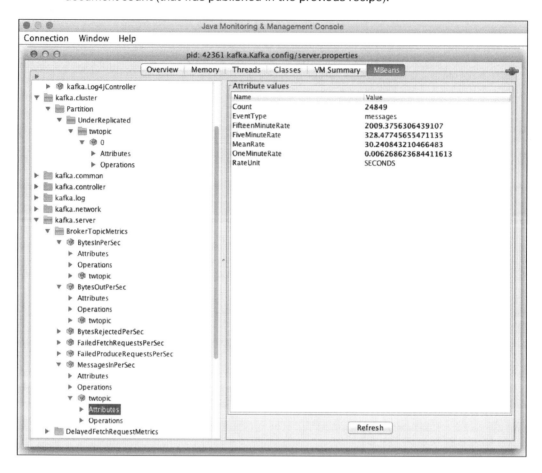

Using StreamingLogisticRegression to classify a Twitter stream using Kafka as a training stream

In the previous recipe, we published all the tweets that were stored in ElasticSearch to a Kafka topic. In this recipe, we'll subscribe to the Kafka stream and train a classification model out of it. We will later use this trained model to classify a live Twitter stream.

How to do it...

This is a really small recipe that is composed of 3 steps:

1. **Subscribing to a Kafka stream**: There are two ways to subscribe to a Kafka stream and we'll be using the `DirectStream` method, which is faster. Just like Twitter streaming, Spark has first-class support for subscribing to a Kafka stream. This is achieved by adding the `spark-streaming-kafka` dependency. Let's add it to our `build.sbt` file:

    ```
    "org.apache.spark" %% "spark-streaming-kafka" %
    sparkVersion
    ```

    The subscription process is more or less the reverse of the publishing process even in terms of the properties that we pass to Kafka:

    ```
    val topics = Set("twtopic")
    val kafkaParams = Map[String,
    String]("metadata.broker.list" -> "localhost:9092")
    ```

    Once the properties are constructed, we subscribe to `twtopic` using `KafkaUtils.createDirectStream`:

    ```
    val kafkaStream = KafkaUtils.createDirectStream[String,
    Array[Byte], StringDecoder,
    DefaultDecoder](streamingContext, kafkaParams,
    topics).repartition(2)
    ```

    With the stream at hand, let's reconstruct `LabeledContent` out of it. We can do that through KryoSerializer's `deserialize` function:

    ```
    val trainingStream = kafkaStream.map {
            case (key, value) =>
                val labeledContent =
    KryoSerializer.deserialize(value).asInstanceOf[LabeledContent]
    ```

2. **Training the classification model**: Now that we are receiving the `LabeledContent` objects from the Kafka stream, let's train our classification model out of them. We will use `StreamingLogisiticRegressionWithSGD` for this, which as the name indicates, is a streaming version of the LogisticRegressionWithSGD algorithm we saw in *Chapter 5*, *Learning from Data*. In order to train the model, we have to construct a `LabeledPoint`, which is a pair of labels (represented as a double) and a feature vector. Since this is a text, we'll use the HashingTF's `transform` function to generate the feature vector for us:

    ```
    val hashingTf = new HashingTF(5000)

    val kafkaStream = KafkaUtils.createDirectStream[String,
    Array[Byte], StringDecoder,
    DefaultDecoder](streamingContext, kafkaParams,
    topics).repartition(2)
    ```

```
val trainingStream = kafkaStream.map {
        case (key, value) =>
            val labeledContent =
KryoSerializer.deserialize(value).asInstanceOf[LabeledContent]
            val vector =
hashingTf.transform(labeledContent.content)
            LabeledPoint(labeledContent.label, vector)
}
```

trainingStream now is a stream of LabeledPoint, which we will be using to train our model:

```
val model = new StreamingLogisticRegressionWithSGD()
        .setInitialWeights(Vectors.zeros(5000))
        .setNumIterations(25).setStepSize(0.1).setRegParam(0.001)


model.trainOn(trainingStream)
```

Since we specified the maximum number of features in our HashingTF to be 5000, we set the initial weights to be 0 for all 5,000 features. The rest of the parameters are the same as the regular LogisticRegressionWithSGD algorithm that trains on a static dataset.

3. **Classifying a live Twitter stream**: Now that we have the model in hand, let's use it to predict whether the incoming stream of tweets is about fashion or not. The Twitter setup in this section is the same as the first recipe where we subscribed to a Twitter stream:

```
val filter = List("fashion", "tech", "startup", "spark")
    val twitterStream =
TwitterUtils.createStream(streamingContext, twitterAuth,
filter, StorageLevel.MEMORY_AND_DISK)
```

The crucial part is the invocation of model.predictOnValues, which gives us the predicted label. Once the prediction is made, we save them as text files in our local directory. It's not the best way to do it and we will probably want to push this data to some *appendable* data source instead.

```
val contentAndFeatureVector=twitterStream.map { status =>
        val tokens=status.getText().toLowerCase().split(" ")
        val vector=hashingTf.transform(tokens)
        (status.getText(), vector)
    }
```

```
val contentAndPrediction=model.predictOnValues(contentAndFeatu
reVector)


//Not the best way to store the results. Creates a whole
lot of files
    contentAndPrediction.saveAsTextFiles("predictions",
"txt")
```

In order to consolidate the predictions that are spread over multiple files, a really simple aggregation command was used:

```
find predictions* -name "part*" |xargs cat >> output.txt
```

```
Gabriel@Gabriels-MacBook-Pro ~/D/a/S/C/s/chapter7-goingfurther> pwd
/Users/Gabriel/Dropbox/arun/ScalaDataAnalysis/Code/scaladataanalysisCB-tower/chapter7-goingfurther
Gabriel@Gabriels-MacBook-Pro ~/D/a/S/C/s/chapter7-goingfurther>
find predictions-1439587* -name "part*" |xargs cat >> output.txt
```

Here is a sample of the prediction. The results are fairly okay considering the training dataset itself was not classified in a very scientific way. Also, the tokenization is just space-based, the data isn't scaled nor was the IDF used.

```
(RT vee_vetrano: its always the ppl that talk about fashion all the time that actually have no idea what it is theyre talking about. #stfu,1.0)
(RT @fieldsofvintage: Etsy #voguet #vintage #jewelry #fashion #silverware #homedecor #accessories http://t.co/mqrCC9xCnC #etsyretwt #etsy ht…,1.0)
(New York City is getting a fleet of eco-friendly food carts http://t.co/ZB1Ydryxqk #tech,0.0)
(RT ZubizuBags: RT lefrenchgem: Summer Fashion Earrings, Sun Earrings, Long Dangle Earrings, Summer Jewlery for the .. …,1.0)
(Which are the communal benefits in relation with stream of fashion lanyards: pUD,1.0)
(RT @darylelockhart: Red Planet Fashion: Mars Colony Project Inspires Sportswear Line http://t.co/BETl2JekbB,0.0)
(Tianjin explosion destroys over 8,000 new cars in China http://t.co/TVffK6CIA6 #tech | https://t.co/xWW1G9JpwM http://t.co/NatoZevHuU,0.0)
(Read The Best Fashion,Travel, and Cuisine Coverage, at http://t.co/72e8y16AKr https://t.co/OtpVbYqRe2,0.0)
(RT eclippings: Fashion Womens Envelope Clutch Purse Lady Handbag Tote Shoulder Evening on http://t.co/DbEEr5ei4p http://t.co/QFSloVw5un,1.0)
(1961 Schlitz Beer Ski Theme Blonde Man Sweater Skiing Vintage 60's Fashion Ad http://t.co/0cg2VLGK7o #Deals_US http://t.co/XMqUQHtDZL,1.0)
(Free Shipping !10PCS  Original monster high dolls fashion clothing accessories b90 - Only … http://t.co/iy7l71CaNV http://t.co/z7IatL27my,1.0)
(Free Shipping !10PCS  Original monster high dolls fashion clothing accessories b90 - Only … http://t.co/Kx9juvZVYp http://t.co/SGO48dGqJI,1.0)
(RT GetHiggyWit_it: Now this is fashion  https://t.co/o1ZNnDnpCf,1.0)
(#KCA #VoteJKT48ID BusEconYMO_HGS: Documents confirm #Apple is building #self-driving #CARvsBUF  #automotive #tech #business #economics,0.0)
(RT FlasherNight: #fashion "arbib cek Villarreal telah mencapai kesepakatan untuk merekrut penyerang Totten... http://t.co/4caquAhH8J Foll…,1.0)
(The ticket read "broke adapter while trying to move computer" via /r/techsupportgore http://t.co/hEolAV550G #tech… http://t.co/nwhdgjF6SW,0.0)
(RT Nina_LaChapelle: From bananas to phones: How cheaper #yuan could reverberate http://t.co/ee9GNm84fA
#china #finance #fashion #lifestyl…,1.0)
(RT @BBCMedia: Fashion meets function in Montblanc's e-strap @montblanc_world http://t.co/L9ZaN8ylzc http://t.co/sR6HCDWzMH,1.0)
(RT FlasherNight: #fashion "arbib cek Bayern Muenchen mengalahkan Hamburg dengan skor telak 5-0 pada laga p... http://t.co/UCfBGUZT8T Foll…,1.0)
(Gostei de um video @YouTube de @davyjonesrj http://t.co/ArYISJTaLn GTA V - QUEM É MAIS RIDÍCULO? PIRATAS FASHION WEEK,1.0)
(Dow tumbles on weak United Tech, IBM earnings,0.0)
(@Got_Six @TourneySport That one is over https://t.co/MRptEchcG2,0.0)
(RT @BlingThings2011: A Mermaid's Tale by Lilli Carter http://t.co/oq3a2kQcXY via @GrowthhackRt  #growthhacking #entrepreneurship #startup,0.0)
```

Using GraphX to analyze Twitter data

GraphX is Spark's approach to graphs and computation against graphs. In this recipe, we will see a preview of what is possible with the GraphX component in Spark.

How to do it...

Now that we have the Twitter data stored in the ElasticSearch index, we will perform the following tasks on this data using a graph:

1. Convert the ElasticSearch data into a Spark Graph.

2. Sample vertices, edges, and triplets in the graph.

3. Find the top group of connected hashtags (connected component).

4. List all the hashtags in that component.

1. **Converting the ElasticSearch data into a graph**: This involves two steps:

    1. **Converting ElasticSearch data into a DataFrame**: This step, like we saw in an earlier recipe, is just a one-liner:

    ```
    def convertElasticSearchDataToDataFrame(sqlContext:
    SQLContext) = {
        val twStatusDf = sqlContext.esDF("spark/twstatus")
        twStatusDf
    }
    ```

    2. **Converting DataFrame to a graph**: Spark Graph construction requires an RDD for a vertex and an RDD of edges. Let's construct them one by one.

    Vertex RDD requires an RDD of a tuple representing a `vertexId` and a `vertex` property. In our case, we'll just do a primitive hash code on the `hashTag` as the vertex ID and `hashTag` itself as the property:

    ```
    val verticesRdd:RDD[(Long,String)] = df.flatMap { tweet =>
        val hashTags =
        tweet.getAs[Buffer[String]]("hashTags")
        hashTags.map { tag =>
          val lowercaseTag = tag.toLowerCase()
          val tagHashCode=lowercaseTag.hashCode().toLong
          (tagHashCode, lowercaseTag)
        }
    }
    ```

For the edges, we construct an RDD[Edge] , which wraps a pair of vertex IDs and a property. In our case, we use the first URL (if present) as a property to the edge (we aren't using it for this recipe so an empty string should also be fine). Since there is a possibility of multiple hashtags for a tweet, we use the combinations function to choose pairs and then connect them together as an edge:

```
val edgesRdd:RDD[Edge[String]] =df.flatMap { row =>
        val hashTags = row.getAs[Buffer[String]]("hashTags")

        val urls = row.getAs[Buffer[String]]("urls")
        val topUrl=if (urls.length>0) urls(0) else ""

        val combinations=hashTags.combinations(2)

        combinations.map{ combs=>
          val firstHash=combs(0).toLowerCase().hashCode.toLong
          val
secondHash=combs(1).toLowerCase().hashCode.toLong
          Edge(firstHash, secondHash, topUrl)
        }
}
```

Finally, we construct the graph using both RDDs:

```
val graph=Graph(verticesRdd, edgesRdd)
```

2. **Sampling vertices, edges, and triplets in the graph**: Now that we have our graph constructed, let's sample and see what the vertices, edges, and triplets of the Graph look like. A triple is a representation of an edge and two vertices connected by that edge:

```
graph.vertices.take(20).foreach(println)
```

The output is:

```
(-980086641,rtくれたeighterさんて気になった人お迎え)
(114820,thx)
(1280862560,statementneckpiece)
(789040,恋愛)
(-706379056,shoppershour)
(165548515,silversurfers)
(-1221262756,health)
(3155,bu)
(110132375,taste)
(231197415,ridnola15)
(109801725,supra)
(106006350,order)
(-121429366,shoebykidsnaaldwijk)
(3046020,cams)
(1444965940,sneakpreview)
(47780855,2488y)
(100270,edm)
(98371450,gizmo)
(249051115,blogmonetization)
(-1638853121,citycenterdc)
```

```
graph.edges.take(20).foreach(println)
```

The output is:

```
Edge(-2137707097,-1266394726,https://instagram.com/p/6aGvaIqDv3/)
Edge(-2132286556,-1109908296,https://instagram.com/p/6XNiG2rrhy/)
Edge(-2132286556,-1077469768,https://instagram.com/p/6XNiG2rrhy/)
Edge(-2132286556,108486107,https://instagram.com/p/6XNiG2rrhy/)
Edge(-2132286556,109201981,https://instagram.com/p/6XNiG2rrhy/)
Edge(-2132286556,109780401,https://instagram.com/p/6XNiG2rrhy/)
Edge(-2132286556,1728911401,https://instagram.com/p/6XNiG2rrhy/)
Edge(-2128842253,-2128633716,)
Edge(-2128842253,844562933,)
Edge(-2128633716,844562933,)
Edge(-2128468089,1316818326,http://bit.ly/1OUEvIz)
Edge(-2121085849,-1077469768,http://ldig.it/1LyY3nH)
Edge(-2121085849,729501500,http://ldig.it/1LyY3nH)
Edge(-2120890375,3267670,http://neuvoo.com/job.php?id=dstcj5hvsb&source=twitter&lang
Edge(-2120890375,1075463261,http://neuvoo.com/job.php?id=dstcj5hvsb&source=twitter&l
Edge(-2120156555,3555990,http://trkt.co/1LbQlNR)
Edge(-2118473344,109270,http://ift.tt/1UHhQ6h)
Edge(-2118473344,3555990,http://ift.tt/1UHhQ6h)
Edge(-2116411129,-1392531550,https://instagram.com/p/6N-c0zFVNt/)
Edge(-2116411129,-1077469768,https://instagram.com/p/6N-c0zFVNt/)
```

```
graph.triplets.take(20).foreach(println)
```

The output is:

```
((-2137707097,traditional),(-1266394726,french),https://instagram.com/p/6aGvaIqDv3/)
((-2132286556,instamakeup),(-1109908296,lashes),https://instagram.com/p/6XNiG2rrhy/)
((-2132286556,instamakeup),(-1077469768,fashion),https://instagram.com/p/6XNiG2rrhy/)
((-2132286556,instamakeup),(108486107,glamour),https://instagram.com/p/6XNiG2rrhy/)
((-2132286556,instamakeup),(109201981,salon),https://instagram.com/p/6XNiG2rrhy/)
((-2132286556,instamakeup),(109780401,style),https://instagram.com/p/6XNiG2rrhy/)
((-2132286556,instamakeup),(1728911401,natural),https://instagram.com/p/6XNiG2rrhy/)
((-2128842253,startcoin),(-2128633716,startjoin),)
((-2128842253,startcoin),(844562933,maxcoin),)
((-2128633716,startjoin),(844562933,maxcoin),)
((-2128468089,startpath),(1316818326,startups),http://bit.ly/1OUEvIz)
((-2121085849,earthtweet),(-1077469768,fashion),http://ldig.it/1LyY3nH)
((-2121085849,earthtweet),(729501500,ecofriendly),http://ldig.it/1LyY3nH)
((-2120890375,cardiovascular),(3267670,jobs),http://neuvoo.com/job.php?id=dstcj5hvsb&source=twitter&
((-2120890375,cardiovascular),(1075463261,technologist),http://neuvoo.com/job.php?id=dstcj5hvsb&sour
((-2120156555,mobilenews),(3555990,tech),http://trkt.co/1LbQlNR)
((-2118473344,happening),(109270,now),http://ift.tt/1UHhQ6h)
((-2118473344,happening),(3555990,tech),http://ift.tt/1UHhQ6h)
((-2116411129,ecofashion),(-1392531550,berlin),https://instagram.com/p/6N-c0zFVNt/)
((-2116411129,ecofashion),(-1077469768,fashion),https://instagram.com/p/6N-c0zFVNt/)
```

3. **Finding the top group of connected hashtags (connected component)**: As you know, a graph is made of vertices and edges. A connected component of a graph is just a part of the graph (a subgraph) whose vertices are connected to each other by some edge. If there is a vertex that is not connected to another vertex directly or indirectly through another vertex, then they are not connected and therefore don't belong to the same connected component.

   GraphX's `graph.connectedComponents` provides a graph of all the vertices along with their component IDs:

   ```
   val connectedComponents=graph.connectedComponents.cache()
   ```

   Let's take the component ID with the maximum number of vertices and then extract the vertices (and eventually the hashtags) that belong to that component:

   ```
   val ccCounts:Map[VertexId,
   Long]=connectedComponents.vertices.map{case (_, vertexId)
   => vertexId}.countByValue


       //Get the top component Id and count
       val topComponent:(VertexId,
   Long)=ccCounts.toSeq.sortBy{case (componentId, count) =>
   count}.reverse.head
   ```

Since `topComponent` just has the component ID, in order to fetch the `hashTags` of the top component, we need to have a representation that maps `hashTag` to a component ID. This is achieved by joining the graph's vertices to the `connectedComponent` vertices:

```
//RDD of HashTag-Component Id pair. Joins using vertexId
    val
hashtagComponentRdd:VertexRDD[(String,VertexId)]=graph.vertices.
innerJoin(connectedComponents.vertices){ case
(vertexId, hashTag, componentId)=>
      (hashTag, componentId)
    }
```

Now that we have `componentId` and `hashTag`, let's filter only the `hashTags` for the top component ID:

```
val topComponentHashTags=hashtagComponentRdd
            .filter{ case (vertexId, (hashTag,
componentId)) => (componentId==topComponent._1)}
            .map{case (vertexId, (hashTag,componentId)) =>
hashTag
    }

    topComponentHashTags
```

The entire method looks like this:

```
def getHashTagsOfTopConnectedComponent(graph:Graph[String,String])
:RDD[String]={
    //Get all the connected components
    val connectedComponents=graph.connectedComponents.cache()

    import scala.collection._

    val ccCounts:Map[VertexId,
Long]=connectedComponents.vertices.map{case (_, vertexId) =>
vertexId}.countByValue

    //Get the top component Id and count
    val topComponent:(VertexId,
Long)=ccCounts.toSeq.sortBy{case (componentId, count) =>
count}.reverse.head
```

```
    //RDD of HashTag-Component Id pair. Joins using
vertexId
    val
hashtagComponentRdd:VertexRDD[(String,VertexId)]=graph.vertices.
innerJoin(connectedComponents.vertices){ case
(vertexId, hashTag, componentId)=>
      (hashTag, componentId)
    }

    //Filter the vertices that belong to the top component alone
    val topComponentHashTags=hashtagComponentRdd
          .filter{ case (vertexId, (hashTag,
componentId)) => (componentId==topComponent._1)}
          .map{case (vertexId, (hashTag,componentId)) =>
hashTag
    }

    topComponentHashTags

  }
```

4. **List all the hashtags in that component**: Saving the `hashTags` to a file is as simple as calling `saveAsTextFile`. The `repartition(1)` is done just so that we have a single output file. Alternatively, you could use `collect()` to bring all the data to the driver and inspect it:

```
def saveTopTags(topTags:RDD[String]){
    topTags.repartition(1).saveAsTextFile("topTags.txt")
}
```

The number of hashtags in the top connected component for our run was 7,320. This shows that in our sample stream there are about 7,320 tags related to fashion that are interrelated. They could be synonyms, closely related, or remotely related to fashion. A snapshot of the file looks like this:

```
plussize
empowerment
la
tagstagram
fredericksburg
macaraibo
fez
topnotchscholars
芸能
paca
tshirt
homes
investment
indiegamelover
pregnancy
florence
mayoristas
가지마
uae
nba
search
forver
fifthfashionue
traceitchi
flagship
shrewsbury
garden
bloggerstyle
olshopmedan
property
americasnexttopmodel
newyork
j2tlaunchparty
winter
frrole
lookoftheday
pittsburgh
snow
```

In this chapter, we briefly touched upon Spark streaming, Streaming ML, and GraphX. Please note that this is by no means an exhaustive recipe list for both topics and aims to just provide a taste of what Streaming and GraphX in Spark could do.

Index

transitive dependency stated explicitly,
    in SBT dependency 172, 173
unsupervised learning 127, 128

V

vector concatenation
  about 11
  basic statistics, computing 12
  mean, calculating 12
  variance, calculating 12
  vector of Int, converting to vector
      of Double 12
vectors
  appending 11
  arithmetic 9
  Breeze vector, creating from Scala vector 8
  concatenating 11
  constructing, from values 6, 7
  converting from one type to another 11
  creating 6
  creating, by adding two vectors 10
  creating, out of function 7
  dot product of two vectors, creating 9, 10
  entire vector with single value, creating 8
  largest value, finding 12
  log, finding 13
  Log function 13
  scalar operations 9
  sqrt function 13
  square root, finding 13
  standard deviation 12
  sub-vector, slicing from bigger vector 8
  sum, finding 13
  vector of linearly spaced values, creating 7
  vector with values, creating in specific
      range 8
  with normally distributed random values,
      creating 26
  with randomly distributed values 25, 26
  with random values with Poisson distribution,
      creating 27
  with uniformly distributed random values,
      creating 26
  working with 5, 6
  zero vector, creating 7

W

Worker nodes 37

Y

YARN
  Spark job, running 198

Z

Zeppelin
  custom functions, running 106
  data, visualizing on HDFS 103-106
  external dependencies, adding 108-110
  external Spark cluster, pointing to 110, 111
  inputs, parameterizing 103-106
  installing 100, 101
  server, customizing 102
  URL 100
  used, for visualizing 100
  websocket port, customizing 102
Zookeeper
  starting 214
  URL 214

Thank you for buying
Scala Data Analysis Cookbook

About Packt Publishing

Packt, pronounced 'packed', published its first book, *Mastering phpMyAdmin for Effective MySQL Management*, in April 2004, and subsequently continued to specialize in publishing highly focused books on specific technologies and solutions.

Our books and publications share the experiences of your fellow IT professionals in adapting and customizing today's systems, applications, and frameworks. Our solution-based books give you the knowledge and power to customize the software and technologies you're using to get the job done. Packt books are more specific and less general than the IT books you have seen in the past. Our unique business model allows us to bring you more focused information, giving you more of what you need to know, and less of what you don't.

Packt is a modern yet unique publishing company that focuses on producing quality, cutting-edge books for communities of developers, administrators, and newbies alike. For more information, please visit our website at www.packtpub.com.

About Packt Open Source

In 2010, Packt launched two new brands, Packt Open Source and Packt Enterprise, in order to continue its focus on specialization. This book is part of the Packt open source brand, home to books published on software built around open source licenses, and offering information to anybody from advanced developers to budding web designers. The Open Source brand also runs Packt's open source Royalty Scheme, by which Packt gives a royalty to each open source project about whose software a book is sold.

Writing for Packt

We welcome all inquiries from people who are interested in authoring. Book proposals should be sent to author@packtpub.com. If your book idea is still at an early stage and you would like to discuss it first before writing a formal book proposal, then please contact us; one of our commissioning editors will get in touch with you.

We're not just looking for published authors; if you have strong technical skills but no writing experience, our experienced editors can help you develop a writing career, or simply get some additional reward for your expertise.

Scala for Machine Learning

ISBN: 978-1-78355-874-2   Paperback: 520 pages

Leverage Scala and Machine Learning to construct and study systems that can learn from data

1. Explore a broad variety of data processing, machine learning, and genetic algorithms through diagrams, mathematical formulation, and source code.

2. Leverage your expertise in Scala programming to create and customize AI applications with your own scalable machine learning algorithms.

3. Experiment with different techniques, and evaluate their benefits and limitations using real-world financial applications, in a tutorial style.

Scala for Java Developers

ISBN: 978-1-78328-363-7   Paperback: 282 pages

Build reactive, scalable applications and integrate Java code with the power of Scala

1. Learn the syntax interactively to smoothly transition to Scala by reusing your Java code.

2. Leverage the full power of modern web programming by building scalable and reactive applications.

3. Easy to follow instructions and real world examples to help you integrate java code and tackle big data challenges.

Please check **www.PacktPub.com** for information on our titles

R for Data Science

ISBN: 978-1-78439-086-0   Paperback: 364 pages

Learn and explore the fundamentals of data science with R

1. Familiarize yourself with R programming packages and learn how to utilize them effectively.

2. Learn how to detect different types of data mining sequences.

3. A step-by-step guide to understanding R scripts and the ramifications of your changes.

Practical Data Science Cookbook

ISBN: 978-1-78398-024-6   Paperback: 396 pages

89 hands-on recipes to help you complete real-world data science projects in R and Python

1. Learn about the data science pipeline and use it to acquire, clean, analyze, and visualize data.

2. Understand critical concepts in data science in the context of multiple projects.

3. Expand your numerical programming skills through step-by-step code examples and learn more about the robust features of R and Python.

Please check **www.PacktPub.com** for information on our titles

Printed in Great Britain
by Amazon